Nietzschean Narratives

Studies in Phenomenology and Existential Philosophy

GENERAL EDITOR
JAMES M. EDIE

Gary Shapiro

Nietzschean Narratives

INDIANA UNIVERSITY PRESS

Bloomington & Indianapolis

Manufactured in the United States of America

Library of Congress Cataloging-in-Publication Data

Shapiro, Gary
    Nietzschean narratives.

    (Studies in phenomenology and existential philosophy)
    Bibliography: p.
    Includes index.
    1. Nietzsche, Friedrich Wilhelm, 1844-1900. I. Title.
II. Series.
B3317.S55   1989   193   88-45451
ISBN 0-253-34063-2
ISBN 0-253-20523-9 (pbk.)

1 2 3 4 5 93 92 91 90 89

For my mother

CONTENTS

Acknowledgments

As Nietzsche suggests, the roots of any intellectual project are likely to be complex, entangled, and not easily accessible to that person whom we call the author. Yet such obscurities do not lessen the sense of indebtedness that the latter feels toward the people and institutions that support or provoke his work. My own debts with regard to Nietzsche go back some way and could, without excessive punning, be called genealogical. I recall with gratitude my discovery, around the age of fifteen, of *The Genealogy of Morals* and *Beyond Good and Evil* in the small but significant library that my grandfather, Leon Gleckman, had passed on to my mother, Florence Shapiro. Although I never knew that grandfather, it has been instructive to speculate on what Nietzsche might have thought about the seeds of his "wild wisdom" sprouting in a soil so different from that of "old Europe" and in a picaresque life far from the academy.

The University of Kansas supported my work with several research grants, including a sabbatical leave in 1985. The Wesleyan University Center for the Humanities invited me to spend that leave as a senior research fellow and I'm indebted to Richard Vann, the Center's director, to the other fellows of the Center, and to others at Wesleyan for a semester of significant discussion and for responses to a draft of chapter 1. I owe much of what I've learned about contemporary literary and cultural theory to the stimulus of a much earlier year (1976–77) spent as a fellow of the School of Criticism and Theory at the University of California at Irvine. Murray Krieger and Hazard Adams were excellent hosts, Hayden White alerted me to the resources of rhetorical and tropological analysis, and Ralph Freedman offered valuable suggestions on my first attempt at a commentary on the language and action of *Thus Spoke Zarathustra*. Since then many colleagues and students have responded to various stages of my thought and writing on Nietzsche; I'm particularly grateful to Benjamin C. Sax and Ronna Burger for critical readings. Harold Alderman read the manuscript for Indiana University Press and made thoughtful suggestions about matters of style and substance. The text has benefited from the editorial suggestions of Mary Jane Gormley at Indiana University Press.

Cindi Hodges, Janice Criss, Pam Le Row, and Beth Ridenour transformed scrawls into clean typed copy with patience and good humor at the University of Kansas; I'm also indebted to the genial work of Pat Camden and Shirley Lawrence at Wesleyan in providing the same invaluable service. My thanks to Ted Vaggalis for timely help with the index.

My wife, Lynne Margolies Shapiro, and my children Marya, David, and Rachel have been as tolerant and supportive a family as anyone who chooses to write on such topics as this could possibly expect or desire.

Earlier versions of some of this book have appeared in article form:

> "The Rhetoric of Nietzsche's *Zarathustra*," in *Philosophical Style*, edited by Berel Lang (Chicago: Nelson-Hall, 1980), and in *boundary 2*, Winter 1980.
> "Zarathustra's Hermeneutics Lesson," in *Mosaic*, 1981.
> "Nietzsche on Envy" in *International Studies in Philosophy*, 1983.
> "Festival, Carnival and Parody in *Zarathustra IV*" in *The Great Year of Zarathustra*, edited by David Goicochea (Lanham MD: University Press of America, 1983).
> "The Psychology of Eternal Recurrence," in *Southwest Philosophical Studies*, 1983.

Chapter 5 is substantially the same as "Nietzsche's Graffito: A Reading of the *Antichrist*," in *boundary 2*, Spring/Fall 1981 and in *Why Nietzsche Now?*, Daniel O'Hara, editor (Bloomington IN: Indiana University Press, 1984).

I'm grateful to those journals and publishers for permission to use the materials here.

References

References to Nietzsche's writings are generally given in two parts, e.g., (BT, 1; 1, 25). The second citation always indicates the volume and page number of *Kritische Studienausgabe*. The first reference is to the numbered sections that Nietzsche gave to his writings, except that *Thus Spoke Zarathustra, Untimely Meditations*, and *Ecce Homo* are cited in their first reference by the page number of the English translation listed below. I have generally relied on the translations indicated, but have introduced occasional variations. References consisting of only two numbers, e.g., (*14*, 293), are to sections of the *Kritische Studienausgabe* that are not as a rule available in English.

GERMAN EDITION

Friedrich Nietzsche, *Sämtliche Werke: Kritische Studienausgabe*, edited by Giorgio Colli and Mazzino Montinari (Munich: Deutscher Taschenbuch Verlag; Berlin: Walter de Gruyter, 1980).

ABBREVIATIONS AND TRANSLATIONS:

A   *The Antichrist*, translated by R. J. Hollingdale (London: Penguin Books, 1968)
BGE   *Beyond Good and Evil*, translated by Walter Kaufmann (New York: Random House, 1966)
BT   *The Birth of Tragedy*, translated by Walter Kaufmann (New York: Random House, 1967)
D   *Daybreak*, translated by R. J. Hollingdale (Cambridge: Cambridge University Press, 1982)
EH   *Ecce Homo*, translated by Walter Kaufmann (New York: Random House, 1968)
GM   *On the Genealogy of Morals*, translated by Walter Kaufmann (New York: Random House, 1968)
GS   *The Gay Science*, translated by Walter Kaufmann (New York: Random House, 1974)
HAH   *Human, All Too Human*, translated by R. J. Hollingdale (Cambridge: Cambridge University Press, 1986)
T   *Twilight of the Idols*, translated by R. J. Hollingdale (London: Penguin Books, 1968)
UM   *Untimely Meditations*, translated by R. J. Hollingdale (Cambridge: Cambridge University Press, 1983)
WP   *The Will to Power*, translated by Walter Kaufmann and R. J. Hollingdale (New York: Random House, 1967)
Z   *Thus Spoke Zarathustra*, translated by R. J. Hollingdale (London: Penguin Books, 1961)

LETTERS

Citations of Nietzsche's letters are from Friedrich Nietzsche, *Briefwechsel: Kritische Gesamtausgabe*, edited by Giorgio Colli and Mazzino Montinari (Berlin and New York: Walter de Gruyter, 1975–   ), 6 volumes to date. I have used some translations from *Selected Letters of Friedrich Nietzsche*, edited and translated by Christopher Middleton (Chicago: The University of Chicago Press, 1969).

Nietzschean Narratives

Introduction: The Philologist's Stories in the Postal Age

Friedrich Nietzsche is usually portrayed as having lived an intensely solitary and painful life; much of the pain is said to be that of loneliness itself. Indeed, Nietzsche tells us as much himself, in writings such as *Ecce Homo* or in the operatic cries of despair that appear so frequently in his letters. Even in *Thus Spoke Zarathustra*, however, a distinction is made between solitude and loneliness in which the former is not necessarily a deficiency but may be lived as a rich opportunity in the adventure of coming to terms with one's very own thoughts, as Zarathustra's solitude is the condition for his struggle with the thought of eternal recurrence. Whether Nietzsche himself could always distinguish his own solitary pursuits (including Zarathustra's confrontation with that "most abysmal thought") from a more mundane loneliness may be doubted. We expect, and Nietzsche documents it for us in all the usual ways, that living apart from family and friends, having no settled formal occupation, and having no fixed dwelling must produce an acute sense of loss and disconnection (if that mode of life is not simply the acting out of such a sense). Perhaps Nietzsche was the first truly homeless philosopher, imposing an exile on himself that we might contrast with Socrates' refusal (in the *Crito*) to save his life by leaving Athens.

Yet in another perspective Nietzsche's life of constant travel and writing may appear a little less strange and more in keeping with the culture of which he had become an emblem. Nietzsche was never in hiding; his solitude was never as absolute as that of Zarathustra or of the hermit he meets who lives so far from men that he has yet to hear that God is dead. Nietzsche was always hooked in to the universal systems of transportation and communication that provided what we might think of as the material foundations for being a "good European" and for posing the question "who will be the lords of the earth?" Always on the move, Nietzsche was a close student of railway timetables, seeking the most efficient routes, connections, and opportunities for occasional meetings with friends and colleagues who travelled the same circuit. His correspondence was prolific and diverse; its sheer quantity, together with the fact of its distribution to its recipients, suggests a writer energetically disseminating his work on all fronts. Much of the correspondence itself is concerned with travel (where to go, whom to see, how to get there), and with publishers (how many copies, what kind of paper, when will it appear, and will there finally be any royalties).

It would be possible to develop a portrait of Nietzsche then as the philosopher of the postal age, that is, of the era in which the universality of communication and transportation are taken for granted. In this picture we would be reminded that the mountains Nietzsche climbed were never very far from his hotel or *pension*, which was itself convenient to the railway and serviced by the postal system. Such a story might begin to bring out some of the similarities between Nietzsche and many modern academics. Both are indefatigable note-takers and writers; having little time for face-to-face contact with friends, they rely instead on letters, memos, and messages that maintain their circulation in the loop of signs.

Nietzsche sometimes seems to have asked himself what sort of writing was appropriate to the age of travel; in a long draft of a preface for *Daybreak* he explains how such writings are appropriate for busy modern men whose journeys might provide a break in their routines. The reader ought to read just a few sections at a time; the very fragmentation and discontinuity of the experience will serve as an antidote to the order enforced by the routines of career and daily life. In such Nietzschean aphoristic strategies some readers see the marks of a much larger project of radical pluralization, a praxis of writing directed toward shaking and decentering the traditional fixed points—notably God, substance, and soul—of the philosophical and religious tradition. This postal or post-modern Nietzsche would also be exhibiting the fact that the postal system and the railway system themselves are not completely closed and efficient, so that every letter and every train may fail to arrive at its destination. Multiple interpretations of all signs and messages are always available, and this is notoriously true of Nietzsche's aphorisms which can be read as junctions in an indefinitely ramified network. Not only can varying sense be ascribed to a single aphorism but the "same" aphorism will vary depending upon whether it is a point of departure, way station, or terminus with regard to others.

In many ways Nietzsche's thought is the product of an intersection that one could hardly have anticipated between the work of philology and the nascent global network just described. That Nietzsche began his intellectual life as a *Wissenschaftler*, specifically as a scientific philologist, is often overlooked; and philology is not just an accidental point of departure for Nietzsche but a touchstone to which he often recurs, explicitly or implicitly reminding his readers that he is an "old philologist" who demands the greatest attention and perspicacity in the reading of texts. Such care is laced with suspicion, the sort of suspicion that led to the Homeric problem and to the Biblical scholarship of the young David Friedrich Strauss and to Julius Wellhausen's reading the Hebrew scriptures as a palimpsest of revisions, amalgamations of disparate texts, and forgeries. Philology was doing to the literary and cultural tradition what the postal system was doing to the presumed stable identities of work, residence, character, and the customary shared understandings of daily life. Nietzsche's philological suspicions extended from the *loci classici* (Homer, the Bible) to those narrative "texts" of philosophy, religion, and folk wisdom by which we attribute meaningful trajectories to the arts and sciences, to nations, to the development of culture itself, and on which each one of us tends to model an ideal story of the life he or she is living.

As a philologist Nietzsche is always suspicious of the claims to originality, authenticity, and exclusivity accompanying the grand stories or metanarratives that would provide a final accounting of first and last things. The task of the studies that follow is to show, however, that such suspicion does not exclude narrative strategies, styles, or views of the world from Nietzsche's work. The alternative to the traditional stories, from the Bible to Hegel, is not simply an intensive immediacy of the moment; that move would simply reconfirm the metaphysics of presence, shifting its burden back from the fully achieved and transparent ends of teleological narrative to the phenomenological deliverance of the given. From a Nietzschean perspective the metanarratives of Hegel and the turn to immediate experience in the philosophy of the early twentieth century (including, for example, Edmund Husserl and Bertrand Russell) represent different variations on a common quest for absolute certainty. Nietzsche proposes a way around and out of this oscillation by describing and exemplifying a battery of narrative forms and styles. To see that such styles are included among the many that Nietzsche claimed to deploy, we should recall his praise for the Greek attention and dedication to *surfaces*. After many years of commentary and criticism that vilify or celebrate the Nietzschean fragment or aphorism, there is a need to assert the value of a certain *superficial* reading which will recall such things as these: *The Birth of Tragedy* offers a continuous picture of Western history from earliest Greece to the cultural politics of 1870; *Thus Spoke Zarathustra* tells us the story of a central figure, struggling with the great gift and terrible burden of an uncanny teaching; *The Antichrist* undertakes a rethinking of *the* exemplary Western narrative and *a fortiori* of narrativity as we know it; and *Ecce Homo* offers an account of the "life and work" of the transvaluator of all values. This is but a partial catalogue of the narratives that appear on a superficial reading of Nietzsche. One might begin to expand it by mentioning *Toward a Genealogy of Morals*, which Michel Foucault has credited with founding a new approach to what has been called history; or *On the Future of Our Cultural Institutions*, Nietzsche's most conventional exercise in storytelling despite the fact that it lacks a conclusion. The superficial identification of these stories *as* stories should not preclude our reading them as well with the care and suspicion of the old philologist, with an eye to the laws and structures which they both assume and transgress.

The readings I will be suggesting of these texts are not innocent, and I have attempted to acknowledge at least some of my debts to Nietzsche's other readers within various traditions. The activity of reading is complicated here by the fact that Nietzsche is, we might say, always already narrativized. His texts consistently offer the reader the temptation to relate them to the enigmatic "Mr. Nietzsche," and few have avoided that seductive ploy. But even when Nietzsche's person is apparently put into the background, as in Heidegger's monumental work, the entire thematics of reading are determined by two stories. One is the magisterial account of the career of onto-theology from Plato's earliest formulation of the metaphysics of presence to its tragic denouement in what Heidegger takes to be Nietzsche's doctrine of the will to power. This larger story both is empowered by and requires a smaller scale story about Nietzsche, according to which his published works were simply a foreground to the system towards which he was working. When Heidegger was excluded from the Nietzsche Archive during the time in which Germany's coming defeat in the second world war came to seem probable, he showed much more concern for the first, because from his point of view he was being told that he could not finish his work on the track of the biggest story of all. Heidegger's anxiety indicates an uneasy conjunction of the desire to make some coherent order (often an explicitly narrative one) out of Nietzsche's writing and thought with the strategy of presenting the form of his writings as fragmentary and chaotic. The only way to render Nietzsche relatively consistent, we are implicitly told, is to go beyond the alleged accidents of the verbal text. The pursuit of a certain kind of order *requires* that there be a disorderly situation to be straightened out. In this way the philosophical interpretation of Nietzsche invokes those very ancient hermeneutical categories of form and matter which, we might recall, are put into question by the thinker himself.

We may not yet be in a position to say what the consequences of a more superficial reading of Nietzsche will be. *If* in his case there is indeed an operative principle requiring that the consistency and integrity of thought be inversely proportional to the orderliness of his writings, then we could anticipate that a high degree of the latter would lead us to view the thought as amorphous and incoherent. In formulating such an interpretation we must take care not to confuse the thought of fragmentation or incoherence with a fragmentary or incoherent thought; if Nietzsche sees the unitary self or soul as a fiction, he may do so quite cogently. But on a still deeper interpretive level questions ought to be raised about the principle that sees philosophical thought and style as having to compete in Nietzsche's case (or in others) for the same limited amount of scarce goods, whether conceived as order, coherence, richness of implication, or significance within (or against) a tradition. It is also likely that in the wake of Nietzsche and the radical questioning of philosophical modernity by thinkers like Heidegger, Foucault, and Derrida, we are not yet in a position to say what a genuinely persistent or coherent thinking is or in what forms we ought to expect it to manifest itself.

In these readings of a few of Nietzsche's narratives, I would like to indicate some of the ways in which Nietzsche's path of thinking and writing maintains a constant vigilance with regard to the possibility and limits of narrative. The old philologist's encounter with the postal age issues in a suspicion of some traditional narratives and their implicit teleological metaphysics; but the encounter itself generates other forms of narrative, stories that begin to make a break with those patterns. Zarathustra, for example, seems to believe that he has a message to deliver, but he soon discovers that there may be no proper recipient for his teaching (the hermit and the men of the marketplace can't understand him, and the disciples that he begins to attract seem little more than sycophants). When he finally faces the thought of eternal recurrence he discovers that he had never really understood the gift or letter that he had to deliver and that his search for an external recipient should really have been conducted within the network of partial selves or souls that constitute himself. The reversal and inversion of an expected narrative framework requires an appropriate reading, one that neither dismisses *Zarathustra* as fragmentary rhapsody nor places it prematurely within the boundaries of a literary genre that it may be challenging. In an analogous way, I will be suggesting that *The Antichrist* can be read as a rigorous exploration of the narrative function in the constitution of value and truth, and that *Ecce Homo* exhibits the ways in which telling the story of one's own life requires a motivated interplay of knowledge and ignorance of oneself. For Nietzsche, narratives are among the hinges or junctures by which thought circulates from classical ontological formulations to engaging with the abyss, the chaotic, and the sheerly perspectival. In *Beyond Good and Evil*, Nietzsche called for the appearance of "philosophers of the perilous perhaps," thinkers who would think on the edges or peripheries of thought. In his revaluation of the narrative mode, with all of its ancient traditions and baggage, Nietzsche himself takes a step into those perilous margins.

ONE

How Philosophical Truth Finally Became a Fable

Philosophers have a practice of working out their thoughts in struggle with or commentary on their great predecessors. At the high tide of medieval scholasticism, Aristotle was "the philosopher," the constant reference point of all thought. Descartes has sometimes played a similar role, especially for the French, and Hume has been the historical focus of the controversies concerning meaning, causality, and the connection between the "is" and the "ought" that have until recently occupied the almost exclusive attention of Angloanalytic philosophers in this century. It may be that Nietzsche is coming to play such a role in American and European philosophical discourse. Despite Jürgen Habermas's announcement in 1968 that "Nietzsche is no longer infectious,"[1] it is fairly clear that the malady, if that is what it is, has become the subject of diagnosis among philosophical physicians from a number of different traditions. Those in the systematic wing of the German school sometimes refer to "the French disease," in speaking of the fear of closure characterizing the poststructuralist thinkers for whom Nietzsche's texts are exemplary: as with all epidemics, the attempt to place the responsibility for the disease elsewhere, on the one who is perceived as the *other*, is operative here. The French, on the other hand, tend to see the phenomenon not as a disease but as part of that great good health that Nietzsche, who described the philosopher as a physician of his culture, hoped to inaugurate. Anglophone philosophy has not been able to remain completely aloof from the problem; its senior physicians have been called in to diagnose the patient and have recommended either a healthy regime of Aristotelian virtue or a strict diet of semantic analysis, purged of aesthetic sweets.

Health and illness, to continue with a metaphor never absent from a Nietzschean text, are never simple matters in those texts. In *Ecce Homo*, for example, Nietzsche provides a complex self-diagnosis of himself as both sick and decadent, convalescent and healthy, portraying himself as a point of intersection of the contradictory tendencies of culture and life. The contemporary diagnosis of Nietzsche has achieved some areas of apparent consensus, even if the diagnoses differ widely, with some suggesting that the virus might be profitably disseminated as widely as possible while others engage in a serious search for an effective antibody or at least a quarantine of those who carry the infection. One of these apparent agreements, to which I want to devote some critical attention, has to do with Nietzsche's supposed rejection of narrative thought and discourse. Let me begin, then, by citing two prominent diagnosticians, Jacques Derrida and Jürgen Habermas, who, despite their other differences, seem to agree on this much. Habermas has recently mounted a critique of postmodernism in philosophy and art; in this critique Nietzsche emerges as a "dark author" of the bourgeoisie, responsible not only for much of the current "French disease" but also for the deviations from rationality of some of Habermas's own models of critical theory. In an article on Adorno and Horkheimer's *Dialectic of Enlightenment*, Habermas sees his predecessors as occupying a tenuous position between Hegelian historical rationalism and what he takes to be a Nietzschean historical aestheticism. In his *Genealogy of Morals*, said to have exercised a bad influence on Horkheimer and Adorno, Habermas claims that Nietzsche "explained the assimilation of reason to power with a theory of power which, instead of truth claims, retains only the rhetorical claim of the aesthetic fragment."[2] Habermas characterizes Nietzsche's position as the first elaboration of aesthetic modernity, and central to that characterization is the idea of a revolt against temporality and history:

> The heightened appreciation of the transitory, the celebration of dynamism, and the glorification of this spontaneity of the moment and the new—these are all expressions of an aesthetically motivated sense of time and the longing for an immaculate, suspended presence. The anarchical intention of the Surrealists to explode the continuum of history is already effective in Nietzsche.[3]

Since Habermas regards Nietzsche as having foreclosed the possibility of giving a rational account of why some values are better than others, he sees him as being forced to appeal to a principle of archaicism: "That which is *more originary* is considered more venerable, respectable, natural and pure. *Ancestry* and *origin* serve simultaneously as the criteria of rank in the social as well as in the logical sense."[4] I will be examining Habermas's claims (and similar interpretations) at some length. At this point, however, it is worthwhile noting that the book which Habermas cites as a document of antitemporal, antihistorical aesthetic modernity—*The Genealogy of Morals*—is actually a narrative text, one that purports to trace a sequence of events in the rise, transformation, and dissolution of a set of complexly interrelated moral, religious, and philosophical values. Habermas perceives clearly that Nietzsche does not provide a foundationalist critique of these values by an appeal to rational principles. But is the only possible alternative to such foundationalist critique the method of aesthetic fragmentation that seeks a pure, atemporal presence? Habermas in fact qualifies that view by attributing to Nietzsche a fetishism of origins and beginnings, an approach that Nietzsche himself was to delineate in his account of "monumental history" in his second *Untimely Meditation*. And how are we to relate this oscillation as to whether Nietzsche's text is primarily aesthetic or narrative to Habermas's description of Nietzsche as wanting to "explode the continuum of history?" Perhaps Habermas means that Nietzsche himself oscillates, or speaks a double language. While Nietzsche does express, in both *Ecce Homo* and his last letters, the expectation that his work will "split the history of mankind into two parts," it is not immediately clear that such a split is to be understood as the abolition of all narrative thought and discourse. On the contrary, to see the split as a split requires some form of narrative representation.

Yet it might be suggested that Habermas's construction of an aestheticist Nietzsche whose text dissolves into fragments is confirmed by the parallel picture of a "new Nietzsche" that emerges in such French thinkers as Jacques Derrida and Gilles Deleuze.[5] It may also be, however, that Habermas's critique is simply an acceptance of the reading that such thinkers perform on Nietzsche, accompanied by a reversal of their valorization of the discontinuous, fragmentary, and irrational. This reading is paralleled in Anglo-American philosophy by Alasdair Macintyre's view of Nietzsche as opposed to both virtue and narrative; this supposed double opposition makes him the anti-Aristotle. But if there are grounds to question Habermas's characterization of Nietzsche's texts as non-narrative, then there will be similar grounds to question some aspects of the French "new Nietzsche" construction. Consider Derrida's analysis of Nietzsche in *Spurs*. The most general aim of Derrida's reading there is to suggest the indeterminacy and undecidability of Nietzsche's texts. Perhaps the most general strategy for accomplishing this goal consists in the interrogation of two narratives of vastly different scope: Heidegger's reading of Nietzsche, on the one hand, which is in effect a tragic story of the whole of Western philosophy; and, on the other, the brief, unexplained and perhaps inexplicable entry in one of Nietzsche's notebooks, " 'I have forgotten my umbrella.' "

By selecting his texts from the extremes of narrative practice Derrida seems to have loaded the dice. Even the most intrepid hermeneut, he suggests, will hesitate to offer an interpretation of " 'I have forgotten my umbrella' "; although on the surface its form suggests that it is a narrative statement, and its placement in quotation marks might even lead to our attributing it to a narrative voice, text and context are far too underdetermined to allow any coherent interpretation, even the minimal narrativist reading just sketched. At the other extreme, Derrida seeks to show that Heidegger's metahistory or metanarrative of philosophy, from the Platonic quest for the presence of the ideas to Nietzsche's ultimate working out of Western destiny in the doctrine of the will to power (Plato to NATO), supposes a more univocal and systematic reading of Nietzsche's text and of philosophy's history than can possibly be sustained. There is much to sympathize with in Derrida's critique of Heidegger, including the suspicion he directs toward teleological, Hegelian views of history as the actualization of the potential, his demonstration that there is a plurality in Nietzsche's text which escapes Heidegger's reconstructive efforts, and his attempt to suggest how we might rethink and rewrite the traditional philosophemes of history, gender, and writing that have been developed in terms of identity and the proper by inscribing them in differential, non-totalistic terms. However, the plausibility of Derrida's suggestion that Nietzsche's text is radically plural and indeterminate rests on his juxtaposition or grammatological collage of the two furthest possible extremes that can be discovered in or evoked from that text: the underdetermined fragment and the tendentious, world-historical interpretation that sees Nietzsche's career as a thinker as the emblem and realization of the West's confusion of Being with beings. If one were, instead, to focus on what might be called the middle range of the Nietzschean text, that is, to read those books which he published under his signature, the appearance of radical indeterminacy would be more difficult to establish.

Although Nietzsche's books take many forms, I want to suggest that a significant number of them are narratives. And by this I mean, first, to make the very general point that their overall structure and texture present features in many ways typical of narrative forms known and discussed by literary critics and other anatomists of the text; but I also want to propose that the narrative forms of these works (and I use the plural advisedly) have much to do with Nietzsche's articulation of history, his presentation of the thoughts of will to power, eternal recurrence, and the *Übermensch* ("man beyond"), and with his representation of his own life. The very titles of *The Birth of Tragedy* and *The Genealogy of Morals* indicate that these texts offer something like a sequential, historical account of their subjects; *Thus Spoke Zarathustra* is a philosophical tale; *The Antichrist* is a critical study of the narrative foundations of Christianity combined with a proposal for rewriting the Christian story, and if one take seriously Nietzsche's late identification of this book as the whole of his planned *summa, The Transvaluation of Values*, then that project could be said to be an essentially narrative one; *Ecce Homo* purports to tell "how one becomes what one is" and has obvious (if parodic) associations with the traditions of European autobiography.

Of course such classifications are initial and crude; perhaps they follow a "law of genre" which a close reading of the texts involved would subvert. Perhaps, for example, as Paul de Man claims in his reading of *The Birth of Tragedy*, the apparent dependence of that book on narrative notions of birth, growth, and death cannot be sustained once it is seen that the very statements in which such notions are deployed must be interrogated in the light of the book's "conclusions" which would render suspect both these notions and the narrative voice that seems to invoke them.

Clearly Nietzsche must be read with such possibilities in mind. But before proceeding to such readings, let me suggest another approach that would begin by distinguishing the fact that Nietzsche does have what might be called a critical narratology from the view that he must be an anti-narrative thinker. Nietzsche is, of course, notoriously skeptical of the truth claims of a number of religious, philosophical, and mundane narratives. *The Antichrist* argues that both the Hebrew Bible and the Christian tradition are enormous historical falsifications; in *Twilight of the Idols* philosophy is portrayed as inconsistent: on the one hand it is opposed to the idea of process or becoming, and yet it relies on a narrative that tells how human life has fallen from its purer origins (in a Platonic world, for example). Then too, beginning with works like *Human, All Too Human*, Nietzsche elaborates a critical narratology that dissects or deconstructs the fabulous, dream-like quality of our everyday narrative consciousness. Just as the dream constructs a sequence of events to explain bodily sensations or unconscious desires during sleep, so the stories that we tell about ourselves and others are said to be the flimsiest *ad hoc* constructions, generated by the pressures of the moment.

Such criticism is consistent with the view that we neither can nor ought to escape altogether from a narrative perspective. Nietzsche's second *Untimely Meditation, On the Advantage and Disadvantage of History for Life*, is sometimes taken to be a general indictment of historical consciousness. While it is true that Nietzsche calls there for a *balance* between the historical and the unhistorical in human life (surprisingly reminding us of the Aristotelian mean) he does not suggest that the quantity or intensity of either side of the balance is subject to any other limit than an individual's power or strength. Although Nietzsche has not yet formulated his conception of the will to power, he comes close to articulating something like that notion in an attempt to demonstrate the power required by the historical sense:

> The stronger [*stärkere*] the innermost roots of a man's nature, the more readily will he be able to assimilate and appropriate the things of the past; and the most powerful [*mächtigste*] and tremendous nature would be characterized by the fact that it would know no boundary at all at which the historical sense began to overwhelm it. (*UM*, 62–63; *1*, 251)

In the same text Nietzsche tries to imagine what it would be like to have a completely affirmative and self-conscious monumental approach to history. That is, he asks how we might rejoice in the possibility of greatness that we see in some magnificent events of the past, without having to hide from ourselves a twofold realization: that those events depended on a specific context or concatenation of past circumstances and that there are vast stretches of history that do not by themselves strengthen the expectation that such possibilities are realizable. The only form of consciousness which could embrace the monumental without losing the sense of its historical limitations (and without lapsing into a form of *ressentiment* in which the monumental is used as a weapon against the present) would be that which saw events as eternally recurrent. But in the *Untimely Meditations* Nietzsche seems to believe that such a view is impossible. It would, he supposes, have to be based on a speculative astronomy like that of the Pythagoreans, and such a view will become available "only when the astronomers will have again become astrologers" (*UM*, 70; *1*, 261). Once the thought of recurrence has become his own, however, Nietzsche presents it precisely as a way of redeeming the past, not as a result of arcane astronomy. Here Nietzsche offers the hypothesis that the person who wills eternal recurrence has the power to will all the narratives of history:

> Only if, when the fifth act of the earth's drama ended, the whole play every time began again from the beginning, if it was certain that the same complex of motives, the same *deus ex machina*, the same catastrophe were repeated at definite intervals, could the man of power [*der Mächtige*] venture to desire monumental history in full icon-like *veracity*,

that is to say with every individual peculiarity depicted in precise detail. (*UM*, 70; *1*, 261)

The greater a person's or culture's power, the more history can be comprehended; and the greatest comprehension of history is made possible by the conception of eternal recurrence. Neither the will to power nor eternal recurrence, then, should be hastily supposed to be an antihistorical or antinarrative thought.

Yet it might be said that Nietzsche is a postmodern thinker *avant la lettre* and that postmodernism is clearly an anti-narrativist form of thought and practice. Of course one might contest the identification of Nietzsche as a postmodernist or question whether, in fact, any clear conception of postmodernism is available to us. But I think that it is worth considering the conjunction of Nietzsche and postmodernism in order to clarify his relation to narrativity. If there is a postmodern philosophy, then, as the term suggests, we can understand it as what is both different from and later than another philosophical movement, modernism. And modernism also defines itself, in part, as later than and other than its predecessor. Similarly, that and other predecessor movements might be understood (either by us or by themselves) as different and later than their own predecessors. In looking at the career of Western philosophy in the largest sense, it is usual to identify three major phases or types: classical, medieval, and modern. To these we are now encouraged to add a postmodernist era or mode. If postmodernism is to be understood in its relation to narrativity, and if Nietzsche is seen as an exemplary postmodernist, then there may be a point in seeing how narrative thought enters into the larger array of philosophical movements, since each later movement is presumable internally related to its predecessors. Let me, then, give a brief narrative sketch that may help to situate Nietzsche in relation to a postmodern conception of narrativity.

Classical philosophy, as typified by Plato and Aristotle, is generally committed to a cyclical view of time that is expressed gnomically in Heraclitus and is eventually literalized in such views as the one that we have just seen Nietzsche attributing to the Pythagoreans. On the classical view the *mythoi* of the poets and the stories narrated by historians such as Thucydides or Polybius are exemplary patterns that will, in their formal aspect, be repeated indefinitely. Even the highest human achievements, political and philosophical, are destined to be destroyed in their present form, but will be restored and renewed as part of the cyclical "great year" of becoming that embraces all changeable things. Lying behind the "great year," however, is an eternal stratum: the gods, the stars, and the objects of Platonic and Aristotelian *nous*. The philosophical significance of narrative, on this view, is that it can make us aware of the eternal and exemplary; but to the extent that narratives blind us to that level of reality by focussing on the particular and the changeable for their own sake, they ought, as Plato notoriously suggested, to be subjected to the strictest philosophical censorship.

A radical transvaluation of the significance of narrative appears in the traditions of Western religion, which contain a polemical moment directed against the cyclical views held by the Greeks, Romans, and various polytheistic religions of the Near

East. Jews, Christians, and Muslims regard their bibles as sacred narratives that tell of first and last things and whatever there is of significance that might occur in the interval. While there are important senses in which the most important things are held to be eternal, there are also tendencies in all of these traditions to historicize or at least temporalize the divine, in so far as it acts in history. Wisdom becomes tied to the sacred stories as commentary and interpretation; because truth itself is conceived as narrative in form, the question of getting it right, of reading the privileged narrative in the way that it is meant to be read, becomes crucial. The sacred text is to be read not simply as a collection of loosely related stories (as it was for the Greeks and Romans) but as a single, all-embracing narrative. It is such comprehensive stories that Jean-François Lyotard has called metanarratives, in his attempt to define postmodernism as the rejection of metanarrative.

While modern philosophy, usually said to begin with Bacon or Descartes, has traditionally been conceived as a radical break with the medieval and religious traditions, it is possible to investigate that alleged break in a more analytical fashion. The critique of biblical or religious authority can be separated from the question of the legitimacy of the narrative or historical mode of consciousness and discourse. Modern philosophy is a return to the ancients in so far as it refuses to recognize any uniquely valid *traditional* story or set of stories; but in so far as it is tied to a vision of progressive scientific discovery and social enlightenment it introduces new forms of metanarrative. In *The Postmodern Condition* Lyotard suggests that these metanarratives, which are to be found in crucial thinkers of the modern period from Descartes through Hegel to Marx to Habermas, serve as legitimations for various forms of political projects and for the educational and scientific practices and institutions that are bound up with them. There may be some implicit or explicit tension between a legitimating metanarrative that focusses primarily on the achievement of knowledge and one that emphasizes social and political emancipation; that is, the story may vary "depending on whether it represents the subject of the narrative as cognitive or practical, as a hero of knowledge or a hero of liberty."[6] Hegel, of course, is responsible for the most ambitious and influential attempt to show that the two stories and the two heroes were ultimately identical. That is why Nietzsche, Heidegger, Foucault, and Derrida direct their critiques of modernism at Hegel's attempt to produce a *summa* of the modernist metanarrative.[7]

One way of understanding the elusive, if not fundamentally ambiguous, conception of postmodernism, or at least the somewhat more determinate notion of a postmodern philosophy, would be to follow Lyotard in seeing it as a systematic and principled rejection of metanarrative. That is, postmodern philosophy could be understood as the project of attempting to understand knowledge, history, art, politics, and so on by extirpating that tendency toward metanarrative that would see each of these endeavors as having a meaningful, teleological history and also see those histories reinforcing one another in order to contribute a single larger story. Such skepticism about the possibility of metanarrative and the accompanying suspicion of the ways in which we might be led into fundamental errors by such a story might be thought to be a reversion to the classical point of view, for both are apparently able to be satisfied with a plurality of narratives; if Nietzsche is taken as a paradigm of the postmodern, then it may seem that there is also a recurrence of the thought of recurrence itself. So far as Nietzsche is concerned, however, such an identification will not work. Even a first, tentative understanding of his thought of eternal recurrence suggests that for him the cycle of events and experiences would never be described in Platonic terms as the "spume / That plays upon a ghostly paradigm of things" (Yeats). That is, there is nothing behind, under, above, or outside the moments that eternally recur. More generally, for the thinkers whom I am calling postmodernists, it could be said that just because they do not acknowledge any level of timeless or ahistorical reality, individual narratives become of greater consequence in their individuality; there is no tendency of the sort that surfaces in Neoplatonism or late classicism generally which would read the many myths allegorically or symbolically as ways of pointing toward the eternal. To put it somewhat schematically, it can be said that if philosophy always exists in some kind of relationship or tension with narrative, then postmodern philosophy aspires to a fully pluralistic narrativity, rejecting both metanarrative and the transhistorical; in some respects it repeats and is indebted to the medieval concern with commentary and interpretation, although those practices must now be reconceived and reconstituted in the absence of a sacred text. Perhaps it is necessary to add that pluralistic narrativity is not the same as the project, often attributed to both Nietzsche and the postmoderns, of seeing or constructing all texts as totally indeterminate in meaning. I am suggesting that Nietzsche believes that our awareness of history, ourselves, and the world is always mediated by narratives (or texts) and that no unique narrative (or text) takes precedence over or embraces all the others; this does not entail, however, that all narratives (or texts) are equally valuable or that there are no practices or principles at work in the production of narrative that would limit their variety or number.

Nietzsche's postmodern narratives can be articulated in term of his rather explicit critique of Hegelian thought, including his autocritique of his own Hegelian tendencies. The current generation of French writing about Nietzsche, notably Gilles Deleuze's *Nietzsche and Philosophy*, has highlighted the decisive break with Hegel that characterizes his thought. Where Hegel sees contradictions that are dialectically resoluble and patterns of development that culminate in increasingly comprehensive visions of their earlier stages, Nietzsche sees differences as differences, as a multiplicity of rather loosely related genealogies. Deleuze's powerful reading of Nietzsche proceeds by elaborating the contrast between the accounts given by Hegel and Nietzsche of the relation between master and slave. For Hegel, the driving force of that relation is the desire to be a free, self-conscious being; and the road to freedom and self-consciousness turns out to coincide with a process of mutual recognition. Hegel sees the master-slave relationship as inherently unstable, and so yielding something like a typical pattern of development through conflict to higher and higher forms of recognition. It is the schematic narratology of domination, struggle, and the recognition of the other as one's own other that has haunted French philosophy for almost fifty years. It is elaborated paradigmatically in the lectures of Alexander Kojéve; Sartre gives his own ahistorical version of it, without the happy ending, in *Being and Nothingness*, and a more historical and less unhappy (because open-ended) account in the *Critique of Dialectical Reason*. There are indeed some serious questions concerning the validity and limits of Kojéve's reading, which makes the chapter on lordship and bondage central to Hegel's *Phenomenology* and then makes that work alone the real expression of Hegel's thought. But aside from such questions, it is fairly clear that Hegel does propose a kind of absolute narratology, a "master plot," that will embrace all human stories, both real and fictional.

As Deleuze and others suggest, it is instructive to understand Nietzsche in terms of his own later critique of what he came to call the "offensively Hegelian" smell of his first book, *The Birth of Tragedy*. Part of what Nietzsche meant by accusing himself of Hegelian tendencies in this earlier work is fairly clear. *The Birth of Tragedy* employs a polar opposition between an original or primitive unity and the principle of individuation; these are expressed in the activities of intoxication (*Rausch*) in which we are at one with the world and in the dream in which we experience well-defined, visual forms. In art the two tendencies are the well known pair of the Dionysian and the Apollinian. The question of *The Birth of Tragedy* is how to reconcile these pairs of contrasting terms in a culturally viable form that will justify life and redeem suffering. How can we see the world both as a living unity and as an array of individuated forms? How can we be ecstatically orgiastic while enjoying dream visions of perfected images separate from ourselves? How can we surrender to a powerful Dionysiac music while contemplating the luminous figures of an Apollinian painting or sculpture? The all-too-pat Hegelian answer is given in Nietzsche's construal of tragedy as the identity in difference of the contradictory modes. That account is of great interest and it surely contains much in addition to the invocation of an abstract Hegelian schema of contradiction and resolution. If we look carefully at Nietzsche's later account of this book in *Ecce Homo* we will see that it is not only Hegelian metaphysics and logic that are at stake but also Hegelian history. In the first of his sketches "Why I Write Such Good Books," Nietzsche writes:

> It smells offensively Hegelian, and the cadaverous perfume of Schopenhauer sticks only to a few formulas. An "idea" [*Idee*]—the antithesis of the Dionysian and the Apollinian—translated into the realm of metaphysics; history itself as the development of this "idea"; in tragedy this antithesis is sublimated into a unity; and in this perspective things that had never before faced each other are suddenly juxtaposed, used to illuminate each other, and comprehended [*begriffen*]—opera, for example, and the revolution. (*EH*: *BT*, 1; 6, 310)

Part of what "smells offensively Hegelian" in *The Birth of Tragedy*, then, is that it sees "history itself as the development of this 'idea' ''. As a Hegelian narrative, Nietzsche's text exhibits a familiar structure: a conflict or contradiction is identified, an initial resolution is described, that resolution is then unravelled, and a new resolution at a higher level is analyzed or projected. The original contradiction of unity and individuation is resolved for a while by Greek tragedy; Euripidean and Socratic rationalism initiate that long downward spiral that we call Western culture; and Wagnerian music drama promises to renew the earlier achievement. That renewal will be more than a simple repetition since the myths and materials of Wagner's operas incorporate a kind of encyclopedia of the exemplary cultural motifs that have emerged since the Greeks: romantic love, the destructive quest for wealth, and the institutionalization of art. As Nietzsche points out, the form of this work is reminiscent of a time fifty years before its publication; one assumes that he means the time of Hegel and his followers.

Following an earlier suggestion, it is not difficult to see this late self-criticism as emblematic of Nietzsche's general attack on metanarratives of any sort. We know, in relation to this particular story, that Nietzsche soon lost his veneration for Wagner and his extravagant expectations for a German cultural renaissance with its capital at Bayreuth. The duality of the Apollinian and Dionysian, with its susceptibility to dialectical thought, disappears in order to be replaced by a more nuanced genealogical analysis. In fact, the whole nineteenth-century "religion of art," of which *The Birth of Tragedy* is one of the finest expressions, is subjected to a merciless critique in Nietzsche's first aphoristic (and so very anti-Hegelian) book, *Human, All Too Human*. The individual work of art, or even the *oeuvre* of the great artist, are no longer seen as possible instantiations of a Hegelian absolute knowledge. One might quibble about whether *The Birth of Tragedy* stands under the influence of Schiller rather than Hegel; Schiller is cited more frequently than any other modern theorist of the arts (excepting Wagner) and the structural foundation of Nietzsche's argument—there are antithetical drives that can, in the best circumstances, find a fruitful harmony—is reminiscent of the kind of argument that Schiller makes in his *Letters on Aesthetic Education* where the two drives are formal and material with a possible reconciliation in play. Yet here Schiller is, we might say, at his most Hegelian, so that the question of Nietzsche's specific use of these sources ought not to detract from the general validity of his later diagnosis of the text's aroma.[8]

Following Nietzsche's self-critique I want to suggest that there is something like an "epistemological break" in his thought and writing that marks the interval between *The Birth of Tragedy* and his next published works, *The Untimely Meditations* and the aphoristic books that follow them. The break has to do, among other things, with the theory and practice of narrative. It would be a mistake, I think, to see Nietzsche's later writings as poetic productions that carry out the aesthetic program of *The Birth of Tragedy*; this is a line of interpretation that has frequently been suggested by Nietzsche's critics. Interpretations of Nietzsche's project as essentially aesthetic often rely on a supposed periodization of his work, according to which early glorification of art (as in *The Birth of Tragedy*) is followed by a scientific reaction which is followed in turn by a return to the aesthetic or the mythical. Such a periodization displays an unconscious irony, since it invokes the very pattern of Hegelian history against which Nietzsche so often polemicizes.[9]

The tendency to use "aesthetic" or "artistic" in an undifferentiated way is bound to be misleading here because there is no universal sense of these terms in Nietzsche's writings, and in many ways he could be said to be an enemy of the aesthetic and artistic. When Nietzsche says of the "voice" of his first book, "It should have *sung*, this 'new soul'—and not spoken!" (*BT*, A 3; *1*, 15), he may seem to endorse such an aestheticizing view. Nietzsche did write songs, and poems, but he also wrote stories that have more in common with the genres of history, the novel, and autobiography than they do with that of the lyric. What may have obscured this realization is that Nietzsche is well known for deploying a critical narratology, which seems to direct a radical hermeneutics of suspicion at a wide range of narrative forms and practices. But it is possible to deploy such a critical narratology while continuing to produce narrative texts; and this need not be understood as the basis of some quasi-Derridian model, according to which we continue to work with a philosopheme that has been thrown into question only because of our inability to imagine how things might be done otherwise. It may very well be that narrative is an inevitable feature of thought and discourse, and it may also be possible to combine some narratives with a critical narratology without falling into simple self-referential contradiction. In order to see the specific configuration that these possibilities assume in the Nietzschean text, it is necessary to situate Nietzsche's epistemological break regarding narrative in relation to what could be called a pedagogical break having to do with the modalities of writing and speaking; that is, with what Derrida has called the question of logocentrism. And from the beginning Nietzsche's pedagogical break with logocentrism touches on the nature of narrativity.

Here let me invoke the name of one of Nietzsche's most significant others, the paradigmatically logocentric historian Jacob Burckhardt. It was Burckhardt whom the young Nietzsche revered more than any of his other colleagues at the University of Basel, and it was Burckhardt's lectures, *Welthistorische Betrachtungen*, that Nietzsche heard with the conviction that he was the only member of the audience who understood them. It was also Burckhardt to whom Nietzsche wrote shortly after his "collapse" in Turin, in 1889:

Dear Professor:

Actually I would much rather be a Basel professor than God; but I have not ventured to carry my private egoism so far as to omit creating the world on this account. You see, one must make sacrifices, however and wherever one may be living. . . .

Burckhardt's receipt of this letter sent him to Nietzsche's friend Franz Overbeck; Overbeck left soon to bring Nietzsche back by train and so delivered him into the care of various psychiatric clinics, whence he entered the even more regressive, infantilized condition of being in the custody of his mother and his sister.

I do not mean to psychologize the Nietzschean texts that I am about to discuss, nor to suggest that Burckhardt is a more significant other than the other Others—

living, historical, or imaginary, not to mention his own "shadows" or internal *Doppelgängers*—with whom Nietzsche engages in a constant play of identification and distantiation. But it is Burckhardt, the lecturer and historian to whom Nietzsche wrote toward the end of the letter already quoted, "What is disagreeable and offends my modesty is that at bottom I am every name in history."[10] Burckhardt came to Basel after publishing *The Civilization of the Renaissance in Italy*, *The Age of Constantine the Great*, and his art-historical guidebook, *Cicerone*. But once he was installed in the Basel *Lehrstuhl*, he wrote no more for publication but devoted himself exclusively to lecturing. As Werner Kaegi documents in his massive biography of Burckhardt, he saw his vocation as a professor or teacher of history for the people of Basel, not as a scholar writing books that might be read by people at other times or places.[11] Also afflicted with a certain hypochondria not unusual among German professors, Burckhardt came to believe that writing for publication was bad for his health.

The background for Burckhardt's commitment to teaching and his abstinence from writing seem to be twofold, based both on a cultural analysis and on a general philosophy of education. His pessimism and cultural conservatism led him to suppose that any possibility of keeping alive some sparks of the great European tradition depended on a direct communication between a wise judge and connoisseur of that tradition and an audience; the danger of historical scholarship was that of degeneration into the minutiae of the professional monograph, which was itself a symptom of the cultural crisis that he diagnosed. Moreover, he seems to have seen the requirements of the moment coinciding with a general principle of all education. As his reservations about the healthfulness of writing suggest, he shared the suspicions of the Platonic Socrates who warns us in the *Phaedrus* that writing is a dangerous drug, distracting both writer and reader from the enterprise of thinking. Burckhardt, then, is a fine example of logocentrism; he is the brilliant lecturer, firing up his students with a passion for the subject and by his living presence always guiding them away from inappropriate interpretations or judgments. "You had to hear him to get the point," we say about such teachers. This historian tells a single great narrative history, one that is made living again in each lecture by his personal presence through the tone, gesture, and anecdote that make each performance both an immediate communication in the context of the day and a part of a "worldhistorical reflection." And the young Nietzsche was impressed, as were many of the solid burghers of Basel. In 1870 Nietzsche wrote to a friend, Erwin Rohde, of his three great joys; one of them is that "Jacob Burckhardt is giving a weekly lecture on the study of history—in the spirit of Schopenhauer—a lovely but rare refrain. I am attending the lectures." Nietzsche's description of the lectures as both Schopenhauerian and musical suggests Schopenhauer's own melocentrism; Burckhardt would then be the lyric voice expressing the endurance and survival of the will that struggles to sing while beset by the great inertial mass of what has been and the knowledge that things are getting worse.

Yet although Burckhardt too was a disciple of Schopenhauer, Nietzsche's praise may be read as inconsistent with Burckhardt's own philosophy of education. For if what is sung is "a lovely but rare refrain," that suggests that the spoken word may not—at least in these circumstances, in this context, and in connection with the great *topoi* of history—attain its end of communication. Burckhardt sought to speak but sang despite himself; we remember here Nietzsche's later introduction to *The Birth of Tragedy*: "it should have *sung*, this 'new soul'—and not spoken!" The problem Nietzsche implicitly raises here is that of whether one should try to speak to everyone or sing a rare refrain for "the happy few." That Burckhardt had not fully addressed this question, or at least that Nietzsche understood him as not having addressed it, can be inferred from the latter's report of the lecture series *Worldhistorical Reflections*; Nietzsche writes that he believed himself to be "the only one among his sixty listeners [*Zuhörer*] [who understood] the deep movements of his thought with its strange breaks and bends, just where the subject is most delicate [*wo die Sache an das Bedenkliche streift*]" (*BW* 2:I, 155). Nietzsche's *Thus Spoke Zarathustra* claims to address the problem by describing itself as "a book for all and none." If we accept Charles Jencks's characterization of postmodern art as double-coded, simultaneously and in different ways addressing both an audience of specialists and a more general public, then we might have some grounds for describing Nietzsche's writing as postmodern.

I want to explore the possibility that Nietzsche's practice of writing, including in particular the writing of narratives, can be construed as a response to another way of doing things that Burckardt exemplifies. I do not mean to suggest that Nietzsche was obsessed with Burckhardt but rather that the teaching and writing connected with these names exhibit a significant set of relationships that revolve around questions of meaning, interpretation, history, speech, and writing. One place where we might begin to trace out some of these themes is in Nietzsche's own writing and teaching concerning the two apparently diverse themes of rhetoric and the nature of the university in the period 1872–73, and it is here that I would locate the "epistemological break" that follows the appearance of *The Birth of Tragedy*. In his lectures on rhetoric, which were probably heavily indebted to the oral teachings of his own mentor, Ritschl, Nietzsche's most extravagant language is reserved for his account of the transition from an oral to a written style in the ancient world:

> One can imagine the image of the Greek reader at the time of Socrates: he is a slow reader who sips sentence by sentence, with lingering eye and ear, and takes in a text like a costly wine, empathizing with all the art of the author; it is a delight to write for one who doesn't have to be intoxicated or carried along but has the natural mood [*Stimmung*] of a *reader*: the acting or passionate or suffering man is not a reader.[12]

This paean to the pleasure of the text is paralleled by Nietzsche's denunciation of logocentric education in his series of lectures *On the Future of Our Educational Institutions*. Jacques Derrida has recently drawn attention to these remarkable lectures in which Nietzsche attacks the lecture method itself. In the essay "Otobiography" included in the book *The Ear of the Other*, Derrida asks us to listen to (or read) what "Nietzsche's fictitious philosopher" of the fifth lecture has to say about the independence of mind said to be the goal of the German university system:

> Permit me however to measure this autonomy [or independence *Selbständigkeit*] of yours by the standard of this culture [*Bildung*], and to consider your university solely as a cultural establishment. If a foreigner desires to know something of our university system, he first of all asks emphatically: "How is the student connected with [*hängt zusammen*] the university?" We answer: "By the ear, as a listener [*Hörer*.]" "Only by the ear?" he asks once more. "Only by the ear," we reply once more. The student listens. When he speaks, when he sees, when he walks, when he socializes, when he practices some art: in brief, when he lives he is autonomous, that is, independent of the cultural institution. Very often the student writes at the same time that he listens; and it is only at these moments that he hangs by the umbilical cord of the university. (*I*, 739)

Elaborating on Nietzsche's text Derrida shows that this image contains the kernel of a far-reaching critique of acroamatic or phonocentric teaching, the institution to which it is the key, and the political state that stands in the background. The old philosopher continues:

> As for the teacher, he speaks to these listening students. Whatever else he may think or do is cut off from the students' perception by an immense gap. The professor often reads when he is speaking. . . . One speaking mouth, with many ears, and half as many writing hands—there you have, to all appearances, the external academic apparatus; there you have the university culture machine in action. Otherwise the proprietor of the one mouth is separated from and independent of the owners of the many ears; and this double autonomy is enthusiastically called "academic freedom." (*I*, 739–40)

The status of this Nietzschean text is, of course, problematic. There is an inversion of the paradox of Plato's *Phaedrus*: there a written philosophical text is the instrument for the condemnation of writing, while Nietzsche's lectures are directed against the lecture method itself. Although delivered as a set of lectures and never published by its author the text was provided with a brief *Vorrede*. This *Vorrede*, he says, is to be read *before* the lectures "although it really has nothing to do with them." In this anomalous text Nietzsche imagines a careful, slow, patient reader closely resembling the ideal reader described in his lectures on rhetoric. In the lectures themselves, which depict the merely listening student (*Hörer*) as hanging on the umbilical cord of the university, Nietzsche constantly reminds his audience of their own status, addressing them even in the midst of the lecture as *meine verehrte Zuhörer* ("my distinguished listeners"). Perhaps the appropriate listener's response would be to leave the lecture at such a point, thus breaking the umbilical cord. But the text is perhaps complex enough to preclude that as the only responsible option. In the introduction (which *was* read to his audience), Nietzsche says that the lectures were *not* composed with any thought of Basel University where both he and his auditors are; he does not wish to draw any inferences concerning Basel nor does he wish to be responsible for any such inferences that might be drawn.

The structure of displacement is further intensified by the nature of the narrative or fiction that Nietzsche constructs about the German (not the Swiss) university (German institutions are both ours and not ours, Nietzsche seems to be saying). Because the story is unfinished its genre is uncertain. The last lecture, although announced, was not delivered and was apparently never written. But the lectures might be seen as an incomplete comedy. The story concerns two students, one of them said to be Nietzsche (so the lecturing professor appears before students as a student), who are part of a cultural club or association. They encounter a venerable but gruff old philosopher and his companion in the mountains. A ludicrous struggle over turf ensues, for both parties claim the same site for a prearranged meeting. After an accommodation is reached the students become eavesdroppers (*Zuhörer*), listening while the old philosopher details his critique of the *Gymnasium* and university system. Toward the end of the extant lecture course there is some indication that the rest of the students' companions have joined with the philosopher's friend(s) in the valley below where there is singing and torchlight. The comedic expectation then is that students and professors have reached some community of understanding about their cultural institution, despite the emeritus philosopher's abhorrence of students in groups. One is tempted to read the break in the story in the light of another of the lecturer's introductory remarks:

> Thus, while I disclaim all desire of being taken for an uninvited adviser on questions relating to the schools and the University of Basel I repudiate even more emphatically still the role of a prophet standing on the horizon of civilization and pretending to predict the future of education and scholastic organization. (*1*, 694)

In other words, Nietzsche eludes the comic resolution by giving us an incomplete narrative that leaves us, teachers and students, in a somewhat indeterminate situation, like the characters in his fiction. As with some Nietzschean aphorisms we are left to fill in the space that the text opens out by ourselves. The renunciation of prophecy contrasts sharply with both the tone and the structure of *The Birth of Tragedy* which is concerned at the end with plotting the course of *Zukunftsmusik*, Wagner's music of the future. The lack of closure in the lectures *On the Future of Our Educational Institutions* can be construed as a break with Hegelian narrative. Despite Hegel's renunciation of prophecy, as in his saying that "the owl of Minerva takes flight only when the shades of night are falling," it is only a minor alteration in the program of Hegelian history to place the comedic resolution which he saw in the present (that is, his own present) in a future that is already dawning. Nietzsche rejects Hegelian absolute narrative and its master plot; but to leave the narrative open, as he does in these lectures, is not to avoid narrative altogether. In Derrida's two discussions of Nietzsche the question of narrative is hardly touched. *Spurs* proceeds by taking what might be a micronarrative ("I forgot my umbrella") and arguing that it is too indeterminate for any interpretation, narrative or otherwise. In his essay on "Otobiography" Derrida calls our attention to Nietzsche's figure of the ear in its many modalities and relations, but omits pointing out either the conventional narrative structure of the text or the effect produced by its breaking off.

If we take "Burckhardt" to be the name of the historian, the professional historian who speaks rather than writing, then we can see that Nietzsche's narrative production is rigorously *other* than Burckhardt in two ways. If Nietzsche lectures he will call into question the lecturing institution itself as well as the larger institution, the state, which lies in the background. And if Nietzsche tells stories, they will not be the kind that invite us to be listeners only, but stories that might provoke us to reflect on the narrative activity itself. Above all, he will tell a variety of stories, not just in the way that "Burckhardt" might lecture now on Greece, now on the Renaissance, and now on Dutch art of the seventeenth century. The pluralization of narrative ranges from the comic book history of logocentrism entitled "How the True World Finally Became a Fable," to *Thus Spoke Zarathustra* which might serve as a libretto for a truly philosophical opera (perhaps the only one), to the displaced and striated history of *The Genealogy of Morals*.

As Derrida argues, there is a dangerous temptation in the logocentric tradition to suppose that only the spoken word (spoken by the wise man, the teacher) can be a really determinate form of discourse. In the *Phaedrus* Socrates develops that claim by portraying writing or the text as a fatherless child without a parent to come to its defense, at the mercy of any and all readers. It is not a living word, as Socrates and the logocentric tradition would have it, but an artifact or machine. The wise teacher (Socrates) knowingly plants seeds of wisdom in the souls of his students; the machine of the text, so it seems, produces indeterminate effects through a law or economy overseen by no conscious mind. But Nietzsche's fictional professor uses the figure of the machine to suggest that speech is no better off than writing:

> One speaking mouth, with many ears, and half as many writing hands—there you have, to all appearances, the external academic apparatus [*aüsserliche akademische Apparat*]; there you have the university culture machine in action [*das ist die in Thätigkeit gesetzte Bildungsmaschine der Universität*]. (1, 740)

Let us not suppose the contrary view which can be associated with the American New Critics, namely the notion that there are at least some texts—poems, or successful ones—which are so perfectly structured, so organic, so living that they have no machine-like characteristics. But let us be aware of how often the denial of the machine-like characteristics of a practice in which we are engaged means that we will exhibit such characteristics in uncontrollable ways. Hubert Dreyfus and Paul Rabinow report Michel Foucault saying "People know what they do; they frequently know why they do what they do; but what they don't know is what what they do does."[13]

Writing notoriously leaves itself open to interpretation and Nietzsche's writings are one of the best examples of this openness. In *The Ear of the Other* Derrida acknowledges that there is no way in which Nietzsche's text could be said to exclude categorically the use that the Nazis made of it.[14] For the old professor in Nietzsche's narrative also says

> All culture begins with the very opposite of that which is now so highly esteemed as "academic freedom": with obedience, with subordination, with discipline, with subjection. And as leaders must have followers, so also must the followers have a leader [*Führer*]. . . . The eternal hierarchy to which all things naturally tend is always threatened by that pseudo-culture which now sits on the throne of the present. (*1, 750*)

We cannot simply seek the "true" Nietzsche who did not mean to say what the Nazis had him say. For undoubtedly part of that "true" Nietzsche would be the thinker who affirms that language is not the instrument of non-linguistic intentions and that "facts is precisely what there is not, only interpretations." If I will be proposing a reading of some Nietzschean narratives it will be not so much to solve the hermeneutic mystery of who the "true" Mr. Nietzsche is or even what his texts are finally saying; the point of such a reading is rather to articulate one production of the text machine that converges with our apparently inevitable interest in hearing and telling stories. In any case Nietzsche's "other," Burckhardt, can be seen to have had an effective history that is also diverse, if not as spectacular as that of the writer who abandoned the university cultural machine. Burckhardt's students are not known for revitalizing European culture; the most famous, such as Heinrich Wölfflin, achieved a kind of academic success by regularizing and thereby narrowing branches of study (the history of art, in Wölfflin's case) that Burckhardt thought should remain part of a common culture.

In this context, framed by the logocentric practices of the German university and Burckhardt's vision of history, we might imagine the question of philosophical communication appearing to Nietzsche in something like the following way: How can meaningful stories be told that escape the encroachments of the "university culture machine" and that offer a significant alternative to the debilitating forms of historical consciousness that the same culture machine was celebrating as the highest manifestations of the Western tradition? One step, taken in the essay *On the Advantage and Disadvantage of History for Life*, is to tell an alternative story about the rise of historical consciousness itself. That story will at least raise suspicions about the claims which that historical consciousness and the formal enterprise of historical scholarship make about the inevitability of their attempt to establish history as a "pure sovereign science" that "would be for mankind a sort of conclusion of life and a settling of accounts with it" (*UM*, 67; *1, 257*). Another step is to explain how other ways of narrating—the monumental antiquarian, and critical modes of history—may be deployed "in the service of life," that is, they may tell stories that are an ongoing part of cultural life rather than serving either as Hegelian legitimization for the state or Burckhardtian elegy for the decline of Europe into a world of factories and democracy. But Nietzsche's most dramatic alternative to these forms of historical consciousness is to reconstitute his own activity as a writer of narratives. He will be a writer, rather than a lecturer, because he is aware of the illusions of immediacy and community that are fostered by the university and its enabling philosophy of logocentrism. The written text is avowedly material rather than ideal. It does not create the illusion that language is a diaphanous medium between a knowing mind and an intelligible object. Nietzsche's texts, especially his aphoristic ones, often seem designed to frustrate such logocentric prejudices and expectations. The numbered aphorism, physically distinct from others in a sequence and depending on such material features of language as punning and multiple meaning, defeats the idea that in reading we are identifying with a single continuous thought process.[15] Of these very material Nietzschean texts, I want to direct attention to those that are also narratives. As written narratives they participate in Nietzsche's general critique of idealism, and as narratives they offer alternatives to idealistic history.

But did Nietzsche really write narrative discourses? The view of Nietzsche as an exclusively anti-narrative thinker may seem to gain support from the fact that he deploys a critical narratology in a number of texts. Nietzsche, that is, has a narratology in so far as he attempts to identify some of the typical classes of narratives and some of the typical devices or patterns of narrative construction. Yet it is a *critical* narratology because it addresses not only the obviously fictional narratives of literature and the dream, but also those narratives that are commonly supposed to possess the possibility of being true. In Nietzsche's analysis this important class of narratives ranges from the accounts we give of our daily life to the historian's account of the meaning of longer or shorter *durées*, to the attempts of religion and philosophy to offer accounts of ends and origins. A little reflection quickly suggests that a critical narratology addressed specifically to those problematic narratives claiming a questionable truthfulness is not incompatible with a very large degree of acceptance of narratives not making such claims, or even of narratives of the questionable sort if they can be read independently of those misleading claims.

The anti-narrativist reading may find another support in the stylistic context of Nietzsche's critical narratology. For most of Nietzsche's remarks on this subject are in his aphoristic works, in particular in *Human, All Too Human*, *Daybreak*, and *The Gay Science*. Such books are series of horizons ("aphorism" is related to the Greek *horismos*, boundary or horizon) rather than continuous narratives or conventional philosophical arguments. If we should make a mistake in this respect and sit down to read one of Nietzsche's aphoristic books from beginning to end, we are likely to be brought up short by a passage such as this one, about three-quarters of the way though *Daybreak* (454):

> *Digression*—A book such as this is not for reading straight through or reading aloud but for dipping into, especially when out walking or on a journey; you must be able to stick your head into it and out of it again and again and discover nothing familiar around you.

Now while the aphoristic books are not large-scale narratives, and while they do contain a critical narratology, it would be a mistake to suppose that all of Nietzsche's works are aphoristic, or that individual aphorisms themselves cannot have a narrative form. The first assumption will lead to a drastically reduced reading as I hope the following essays on some Nietzschean texts will demonstrate. The second assumption is more easily challenged by pointing out a few of the many aphorisms or sketches that do have an explicit narrative form; we might begin a partial list of the latter with some of the many aphorisms in which Nietzsche aims to narrate the "natural history" of a custom, religion, moral code, passion or belief (e.g., *Daybreak* 29, 31, 42, 49, 68, 71, 102, 112). It could be and has been argued that the narrative form of such works is only apparent, that they deconstruct the narrative form by reason of a number of gaps, inconsistencies, and double codings. This is no doubt true to some extent; and to the extent that it is true the texts in question might be described as self-critical, open, or indeterminate narratives. Certainly something of this sort could be said even of Nietzsche's longer and more complex texts such as *Zarathustra*; but recent modes of reading have suggested that some of the same things could with equal justice be said about reputedly classical texts of literature and history. Whether there is still some value in considering any given text as a narrative will depend on the reading of the text that the approach enables. So the suggestion that none of Nietzsche's texts are really narratives might have to rely on an argument that would deny the narrative status of any writing whatsoever.

When we begin to examine the critical narratology embedded in Nietzsche's aphoristic texts we may immediately note that it is often associated with a call for the introduction of a historical approach into philosophy. The first part of *Human, All Too Human* bears the ironic title "Of First and Last Things," suggesting a critical relation to all conceptions of an absolute origin or end. But opposition to eschatology does not entail opposition to narrative. And in the first entry of that section Nietzsche decries the fact that philosophy as practiced at the time that he is writing tells the same old stories, formally speaking, that it has told for two thousand years. It asks such questions as:

> How can something arise from its opposite—for example, reason from unreason, sensation from the lifeless, logic from the illogical, disinterested contemplation from covetous desire, altruism from egoism, truth from error?

The questions then begin from the experienced nature of change, process, or transformation. That is, they assume something like a mundane narrative standpoint in which a development or event is noted and some kind of account is sought for it. Metaphysics, however, responds to this request for a story by offering a reductionistic account, a story in which it is demonstrated that there are no real events:

> Until now, metaphysical philosophy has overcome this difficulty by denying the origin of the one from the other, and by assuming for the more highly valued things some miraculous origin, directly from out of the heart and essence of the "thing in itself."

Philosophy's story, we might say, is no story at all, for it tells us that nothing has really happened and that all change is merely a surface phenomenon. The alternative to such metaphysical philosophy is "historical philosophy":

Historical philosophy, on the other hand, the very youngest of all philosophical methods, which can no longer be even conceived of as separate from the natural sciences, has determined in isolated cases (and will probably conclude in all of them) that they are not opposites, only exaggerated to be so by the popular or metaphysical views, and that this opposition is based on an error of reason. (*HAH*, 1; 2, 22)

"Historical philosophizing," a recurring term in *Human, All Too Human*, can be understood as *historia,* or inquiry into particulars, as *natural* history which examines things in the light of their coming to be, and as *narrative* history which traces the course of a thing's rise and transformations through all variations of its career. All of these senses of history are present in Nietzsche's suggestion of an historical antidote to the (traditional) philosopher's view that man has an eternal nature: "Everything the philosopher asserts about man is basically no more than a statement about man within a very *limited* time span. A lack of historical sense is the congenital defect of all philosophers" (*HAH*, 2; 2, 24). The scope of Nietzschean narrative will include, then, what historians of the Annales school call the *longue durée* as well as the moments of existence (*Augenblicke*) celebrated in *Zarathustra.*

Does Nietzsche have a single narrative paradigm or a favored model either for the understanding of narrative discourse in general or for the construction of his own narratives? Alexander Nehamas seems to suggest that in both cases Nietzsche's model is the unified literary work as it might be construed by Aristotle, or Hegel, or an American New Critic.[16] And Nehamas points out that Nietzsche advertises his own multiplicity of styles: "I have many stylistic possibilities—the most mul-tifarious art of style that has ever been at the disposal of one man" (*EH*, "Books" 4; 6, 304). Nietzsche *does* have many styles of his own and a good number of them are variations of narrative, although not necessarily of the well-formed novel of the nineteenth century. The bulk of this book will be concerned with exploring some of those narrative forms.

As a narratologist and particularly as a critical narratologist, Nietzsche has some suspicions concerning the narratives that we construct through or use to characterize our dreams. Dream narratives are typical, for Nietzsche, of the stories that people tell both about themselves and the world. Moreover, to the extent that dreams can be seen as a model for understanding narrative practice, we ought to be able to indicate how some of Nietzsche's own story-telling can be construed in terms of the logic of the dream (I will explore this particularly in reading *Ecce Homo*, but the perspective could be brought to bear on any of Nietzsche's writings).

What dreams share with many other narratives is that they seek and offer ex-planations for experiences and sensations that are not understood. Nietzsche men-tions such things as processes of digestion, movements, and changes in temperature or position as phenomena that impinge on the dreamer.

There are a hundred occasions for the mind to be amazed, and to seek *reasons* for this stimulation. It is the dream which *seeks and imagines the causes* for those stimulated feelings—that is, the alleged causes. . . . Everyone knows from experience how fast the dreamer can incorporate into his dream a loud sound he hears, bells ringing, for example, or cannon fire, how he can explain it *after the fact* from his dream, so that he *believes* he is experiencing first the occasioning factors and then that sound. (*HAH*, 13; 2, 32–3)

The general form of reasoning that lies behind the construction of dream-narratives is what Charles Peirce called abduction: a surprising fact is noted and an inquiry is launched to find a likely cause of the fact to be explained. The facts or experiences to be explained are such things as "I am waking up to a noise" or "my feet feel constricted" and the dream-explanations are "the church bells are ringing" or "there are snakes wrapped around my feet." As a critical narratologist Nietzsche points out the obvious: such confused and arbitrary forms of reasoning depend upon the weakening of memory consequent upon sleep. What is not so obvious is the extrapolation from the confusions of dream-narrative to the typical thought processes of early humans. He suggests that "man still draws conclusions in his dreams as mankind once did, *in a waking state*, through many thousands of years"; in each case the principle is simply to explain the unexpected by "the first *cause* which occurred to the mind."

Nietzsche's account both of the dream and of "primitive" thought in these texts is extremely schematic and simple, falling short of his rich appreciation of the texture of the dream in the analyses of *The Birth of Tragedy* or the dream narratives of *Zarathustra*. What I mean to highlight here is both the abductive pattern Nietzsche sees as the essential constructive principle of certain narratives and the extrapolation of that pattern to domains beyond the dream proper; he concludes the aphorism from which I have been quoting by suggesting that the poet and the artist proceed in the same fashion to attribute moods and states "to causes that are in no way the true ones."

So far one might take Nietzsche's analysis of dreams to be a variety of a standard form of enlightenment criticism and might associate it with the scientism that is sometimes held to characterize the so-called "middle period" of his thought. The analogy between dreaming and primitive thought processes certainly seems to exemplify an enlightenment metanarrative that would read human history as a progressive emancipation from confusion and superstition, while noting both the residues of earlier states in the present and the similarities between savage thought and exceptional states. The enlightenment view depends, however, on having a clear comprehension of causes and effects, such that all properly constructed narratives would attribute events only to true causes. Nietzsche, of course, cannot be identified with such an enlightenment perspective. It is clear that he sees the dream as much more than a residue of an earlier state or as a tolerable interruption of a more rational life; and he also suggests that it is not only the mundane narratives of savage life that are analogous to the dream but also those waking narratives that we relate about ourselves as well as the culturally central narratives of history, religion, and philosophy. So Nietzsche can write:

Waking life does not have this *freedom* of interpretation possessed by the life of dreams, it is less inventive and unbridled—but do I have to add that when we are awake our

drives likewise do nothing but interpret nervous stimuli and, according to their requirements, posit their "causes"? that there is no *essential* difference between waking and
dreaming? . . . that all our so-called consciousness is a more or less fantastic commentary
on an unknown, perhaps unknowable, but felt text? (*D*, 119; 3, 113)

Given this view, there is no possibility that the narrative logic of the dream can be
altogether expunged from waking life. We are always already in the position of
producing a narrative commentary on the unknown text, or, we might say, we are
always already narrative beings.

Descartes thought that at a certain stage of reflection we should take seriously
the suggestion that all of our thought is a kind of dreaming, or at least that we
might be dreaming right now, at the moment of reflecting on the question. In the
process of reflection, however, we do (so he claims) discover good grounds for
distinguishing our dreaming and our waking experiences. Descartes was indeed
aware of the strange form of narrative productivity in dreams, in which a vaguely
perceived condition is vaguely inferred to have an outlandish cause; we produce
stories, for example, in which we are made of glass. If it is the dream-like logic
that philosophy wishes to free us from, then Nietzsche's claim is that no such
procedure of emancipation is possible. The construction of the rational self or
reflecting ego, Nietzsche suggests, is a kind of dream-like inference: we discover
some kind of continuity or coherence in thought and so suppose that there is a soul
or psychic atom that is responsible for that unity. The original edition of *Human,
All Too Human* begins with a quotation from Descartes's *Discourse on Method*, in
which Descartes announces that he has systematically reviewed human occupations
and has determined that the regular cultivation of reason is the best. Given his very
anti-Cartesian sentiments concerning the ego, waking and dreaming, and many other
issues (for example, mind-body dualism), what is it that Nietzsche wishes to retain
of this Cartesian program? In part, he seem to have been citing Descartes's great
satisfaction in having achieved a method whose employment is accompanied by
the greatest pleasure and which can be turned to a new area every day to yield
useful and interesting discoveries. Such a method is at work in Nietzsche's aphoristic
texts, a method that yields pleasure and is constantly transferable to fresh fields of
inquiry. Like Descartes, with his criticism of history and poetry, Nietzsche has
adopted a critical narratology, but he had decoupled that method both from a Cartesian conception of analysis and from an ontology.

Nietzsche's very unCartesian idea that we are, in principle, always dreaming
may help us to understand how a critical narratology can be combined with a
narrative practice that supposes the inevitability of the process of producing and
commenting on stories. Nietzsche's texts are full of extravagant praise for the dream
or the dreamer and of frequent attempts to justify dreaming (in the narrower sense)
as a vital component of our psychic economy. Surely part of the point of such praise
and analysis is to suggest how foolish would be the project of eliminating the dream
or minimizing its role. Accordingly there is a kind of paradigmatic first-person
speech act that Nietzsche performs or cites repeatedly, although it is an utterance

that would be nonsensical either for Cartesian rationalism or for contemporary speech act theory: "It is a dream—I will dream on!" The utterance is unintelligible if we presuppose that we are seeking certainty and that there is no certainty in dreams; or if we suppose that it is impossible for a sleeper or dreamer to make any intelligible utterance whatsoever (even if he should manage to produce some sounds that normally have an intelligible meaning). What Nietzsche dramatizes or narrates again and again, however, is the experience that we have of making just such an utterance. One might proceed some way in reading *The Birth of Tragedy* as a parody or reversal of Descartes's *Meditations*, for it begins with just such an affirmation. Whereas Descartes says "I too have been deceived many times in sleep" Nietzsche proclaims:

> And perhaps many will, like myself, recall how amid the dangers and terrors of dreams they have occasionally said to themselves in self-encouragement, and not without success: "It is a dream! I will dream on!" I have likewise heard of people who were able to continue one and the same dream for three and even more successive nights—facts which indicate clearly how our innermost being, our common ground, experiences dreams with profound delight and a joyous necessity. (*BT*, 1; *1*, 27)

Here the explicit purpose is to explain the delightfulness and necessity of dreaming alongside the other great psychic possibility of intoxication. Elsewhere, Nietzsche suggests that the entire enterprise of knowledge and the individuation of the knower as a singular being are means to "*preserve* the universality of dreaming and the mutual comprehension of all dreamers and thus also *the continuation of the dream*" (*GS*, 54; *3*, 417). In *Thus Spoke Zarathustra*, a book replete with the relation and interpretation of dreams, Nietzsche's hero dreams that he is struggling abjectly and dejectedly to climb a mountain path under the weight of a dwarf, the spirit of gravity. He recalls "I was like one sick whom his wicked torture makes weary, and who as he falls asleep is awakened by a still more wicked dream." It is Zarathustra's courage which allows him to confront the dwarf and which adumbrates the thought of eternal recurrence through affirming what, in this context, is the continuation and repetition of the dream; it is courage which says " 'Was *that* life? Well then! Once more!' "

It should be clear from all this that for Nietzsche no absolute distinction is to be made between dream narratives and other sorts of stories. Nietzsche's most explicit examples of the extension of the principle of dream narratives to others come in his accounts of the way in which we compose mundane, short-term stories about our own lives and in the way a culture produces a stock of narrative adages, or parables, that postulate a cause-effect relationship between human actions and their consequences. Perhaps the most consecutive statement of Nietzsche's critical narratology is in the section of *Twilight of the Idols* called "The Four Great Errors." All of the errors are recognizable as specifications of the sort of thinking that Nietzsche attributes to the dream, and he sometimes illustrates them by reference to the dream. The first is "*the error of confusing cause and effect*"; it consists in noting a correlation of some kind between events but reversing their causal priority. In Nietzsche's example, a famous diet of his time is said to be the cause of long life. But the diet, Nietzsche argues, is not good for everyone, but only for someone with a certain kind of metabolism; so one might say that the type of metabolism is the cause or perhaps the cause when reinforced by the appropriate diet. When religion and morality speak in hypothetical imperatives, promising happiness for the performance of certain actions and unhappiness or worse for others, then they typically engage in the same kind of error. The other typical errors consist of: "*false causality*," in which our inner self, or will, is taken as model for all causality, when in fact there is no inner realm of will; "*imaginary causes*," in which, as in typical dream examples, a narrative is provoked by that which comes at the end (a dream is composed almost instantly to account for a far-off cannon shot); and the "*error of free will*," in which individuals are held to be responsible agents when in fact "the fatality of a person's essence is not to be disentangled from the fatality of all that has been and will be." We must defer for a bit the question of whether a world characterized by such fatality would lend itself to any kind of narrative presentation whatsoever, that is, whether Nietzsche's views allow for a truly awake, non-dreamlike awareness of the world.

In considering Nietzsche's account of these four errors we might begin by noticing an apparent discrepancy between his sense of the fatality of all events in their interconnection and his critique (at least in the case of the first error of reversing cause and effect) of certain causal attributions. Clearly, if there is no unique cause of any event then the mere reversal of any supposed causal sequence, where the terms are less than the whole of what there is, cannot yield a correct causal account. The first step in saving Nietzsche's critique would be to suggest that even if it is a very complex concatenation of events and states which is the causal condition of long life (where metabolism is of special interest because of its being a property of the individual concerned), still that set is the cause of another complex state that includes long life. The picture becomes even more complex, however, if we add the idea of eternal recurrence (one of whose versions Nietzsche seems to be invoking here). For on one interpretation of that thought the entire state of affairs at *any* moment of the world is both the cause and effect of all that will follow it and of all that preceded it; it is the latter because the specific nature of all that there is now is such as to bring about, eventually, the recurrence of everything that has been. Still it is possible to distinguish various sorts of causal accounts in so far as they approximate or deviate from this vision of the fatality of the whole.

Looked at systematically, Nietzsche's four errors form a kind of *catalogue raisonné* of the forms of narrative discourse. They can perhaps be mapped on to some older rhetorical and linguistic categories that have become prominent again in some recent theories of discourse.[17] The production of imaginary causes can be seen as the invention of a narrative *metaphor* for a "felt but unknown text." The notion that narratives can be understood as causal sequences that are sometimes constructed by altering an original sequence points to the *metonymic* character of narrative in which events are connected only sequentially or by conjunction and not by internal bonds of similarity in meaning. When it is supposed that the will is the model of all causality, then a *synecdochic* mode of narrative construction is being employed in which one type of causality (here a "false" or nonexistent one) is seen as the principle of all narratives. The analysis of those narrative accounts that operate by means of free will suggests that the point of such stories lies in singling out one specific kind of agency that is to be contrasted with the regularity and inertia of everything else that might provide material for a story; this setting aside of an individual as a putative sole cause is structurally similar to the figure of *irony*, whose literary origins go back to the false claims of agency and importance made by a single pretentious figure. The errors, then, can also be regarded as principles of composition, especially if Nietzsche has no non-narrativist form of discourse or consciousness available to substitute for those that are familiar to us. What I am suggesting is that Nietzsche offers us no directly non-narrative discourse but rather a strategy of pluralistic narration and critical narratology that will provide an alternative to a fixation on any of those religious or metaphysical versions of the dream that tend to institutionalize the errors just discussed. Dreams, Nietzsche suggests, when interpreted in a certain way, lead the dreamer to suppose that his or her visions are sent from another, higher world (*HAH*, 5; 2, 27). But dreams need not be interpreted this way; an alternative philology of *Traumdeutung* (of the interpretation of dreams) is possible. And the nature of dreams (both in the narrow and in the extended sense) may vary.

Such principles may be applied to Nietzsche's discussion of the various modalities of history in *On the Advantage and Disadvantage of History for Life*. Dreams, Nietzsche suggests, are often nocturnal compensations for something that has been lacking during the day, or as Freud would put it, they are imaginative wish-fulfillments. Monumental history, by valorizing that which is great and noble in a traditional past, may serve as a compensatory and wish-fulfilling device in response to an unheroic present. If the present is heavy with threats of the disruption or fragmentation of a prized continuity, then the historian may resort to the antiquarian mode, in which all signs of continuity with the past, no matter how trivial, are highlighted. Critical history consists in "breaking up and dissolving the past"; Nietzsche suggests that it is a dangerous attempt to free oneself from one's past by the mechanisms of denial and rewriting:

> It is an attempt to give oneself, as it were *a posteriori*, a past in which one would like to originate in opposition to that in which one did originate. (*UM*, 76; 1, 270)

The thought of eternal recurrence can be seen as contributing to such a critical history because it allows us to think of the present (or the future, for that matter) as that which gives rise to all other moments of existence and therefore to our past as well.

It would be possible to produce a typology of other Nietzschean narratives that can only be briefly indicated here. One might begin by noting that myth is only one of these forms, reaching its fullest expression in *Zarathustra*. Contrary to the early rhapsodic and often proto-Nazi reception of Nietzsche in Germany typified by Ernst Bertram, and to such a Marxist reappropriation of that reading as we find in Georg Lukacs, there are other significant forms of narrative in Nietzsche's work.[18] Michel Foucault has found genealogy to be the most enabling and empowering of these and it would indeed be possible to work out a detailed account of the role that *The Genealogy of Morals* plays in the construction of such a Foucauldian narrative as *Discipline and Punish*. There is also a form of deconstructive analysis of narrative that can trace its credentials to Nietzsche if it wishes. *The Antichrist*, for example, is a sustained attempt to show that the central narratives of Christianity, including both biblical and later traditions, can be decentered by removing their false center, demonstrating Jesus to be merely a signifier or a blank page that has been overinscribed with interpretations. *Ecce Homo* is Nietzsche's autobiography, we might say, but it is both more and less than that. For it challenges the integrity of the self, or of "autobios," one's own life, in order to suggest that Nietzsche is a *Doppelgänger*, a double constituted by a play of oppositions; since there is no external point from which that play can be controlled it tells the story of how one becomes what one is not just as much as it tells the story promised by its subtitle "how one becomes what one is."

Having suggested the essential plurality of Nietzschean narrative I want to look more closely at two examples of story-telling, *Thus Spoke Zarathustra* and a rather brief but pregnant sketch in *The Twilight of the Idols* called "How the 'True World' Finally Became a Fable: History of an Error." This last purports to distil the entire history of philosophy into six theses on a single page; at first it appears to be almost a comic-strip reduction of its theme. Yet Martin Heidegger and subsequently Jacques Derrida have devoted extensive efforts of interpretation to it. Beginning with Plato's conception of the wise man as living in the truth, it concludes with Nietzsche's announcement that the entire opposition between the true and apparent worlds has been overcome.

Should we read this text as a metanarrative that purports to tell us of first and last things? Certainly it is something of a parody of Hegel's metahistory of philosophy, although Heidegger has appropriated it with an inspired seriousness for his own account of our forgetting of Being (as Derrida points out). It is not the story of progressive realization of truth, but the history of an error. And the final position that would be occupied in the biblical metanarrative tradition by apocalyptic revelation or in the philosophical one by a Hegelian or Marxist transformation of that into the realization of freedom and knowledge is here filled by the inscription "INCIPIT ZARATHUSTRA." That is, just where we might expect a conclusion of the story that would comprehend and make clear all its earlier stages, we get a reference to another story and (to anticipate just a bit) that story will not complete a metanarrative. Nietzsche's story about philosophy follows quickly upon his account of the philosophers' idiosyncrasies. These consist in their Egyptianism, their belief in an unchanging world and *also* in their production of stories that purport to show that once we lived in an eternal world from which we have somehow fallen into the world of appearance. At this point the idiosyncrasies of philosophers display what Freud called "kettle logic." On the one hand, if the true world is eternal there should be no need for narrative, and any narrative must distort the truth of that eternal world; but, on the other, philosophers *must* tell narratives in order to account for our fallen status. In Freud's anecdote the man to whom we have lent the kettle replies to our request for its return "(a) you never lent me a kettle; (b) I already returned it to you; (c) the kettle was worthless and full of holes." The philosopher says: "the world is timeless and I will tell you a story about how it becomes other than that." But perhaps not all philosophers do this, Nietzsche seems to say in the "True World"'sketch. Consider the first stage of this history:

> 1. The true world—attainable for the sage, the pious, the virtuous man; he lives in it, *he is it*. (The oldest form of the idea, relatively sensible, simple and persuasive. A transcription or reinscription [*Umschreibung*] of the sentence "I, Plato *am* the truth.")

To take Nietzsche's understanding of Plato seriously involves seeing the latter as freed from the Platonism that is introduced only with the second stage in which the idea "*becomes woman*, Christian."

The "history of an error" proceeds on two levels, which are marked in Nietzsche's text by a division between "straight" statements of the position in question and the parenthetical stage directions or narrative contextualization that follows these. For *this* Plato, who *is* the truth, no stories are yet necessary to explain the fall from the truth; this way of looking at Plato suggests the need for a radically revised reading of the narrative form of his dialogues, and especially of those myths that become the mainstay of Platonism and Christianity. As Derrida notes, it is only with the second stage, in which the true world is "unattainable for now, but promised for the sage, the virtuous man ('for the sinner who repents')" that narratives become an essential defensive mechanism of philosophy: "At this moment history begins. Now the stories start."[19] It is these narratives that are in Nietzsche's view the Heideggerean "unthought" of subsequent philosophy, and the rest of the sketch consists in juxtaposing the shifting tenses and modalities of these philosophical stories with the story that Nietzsche tells, taking us through the cycle of the day. The idea's becoming "more subtle, insidious, incomprehensible" is its darkening, followed by the sun's appearing dimly through Kantian fog, then beginning a new day with positivism's demotion of the unknown "true world" from its place of honor, and concluding—at least for the time being—with the bright day of its abolition. Let us look more closely at the double stories constituting this history of error. When Nietzsche writes that the view of truth as accessible now to the wise man is an *Umschreibung* (transcription) of "I, Plato, *am* the truth" we might ask who it is who utters that sentence. Nietzsche does not say that Plato explicitly makes this claim; in fact the sentence would seem to be much too solipsistic and egoistic to be identified simply as equivalent to the more impersonal version that allows the truth to be accessible to wise men generally. And looking at the parallel with the other parenthetical comments or stage directions in the sketch, it becomes clear that the latter are not the ways in which the various philosophical positions think of themselves. The parenthetical remarks could be described as the dreams that are then translated or reinscribed in the more sober language of philosophy. The dream "I, Plato, *am* the truth" is the expression of a fully imaginary stance (in Lacan's sense of the imaginary), representing the subject as simply and presently identical with the highest object. The reinscription of the dream is the more symbolic, linguistic version of this fantastic conception of the self. The Platonic dialogues, we might say, show that we can be in the truth just to the extent that we actively practice dialectics and so in their own narrative form they give a richly symbolic version of being in the truth which is socially acceptable just because that position is open to all (to Socrates, to his younger auditors as they mature, to those anonymous place-holders like the "Athenian stranger," and then finally to the reader who reproduces the dialectical movement of the dialogues).

Each successive stage in Nietzsche's sequence is constituted by a new dream and its corresponding reinscription in the symbolic mode. But as Derrida notes the tenses of both dream and reinscription alter, as the truth is displaced to a mythical past, deferred to the future, or placed behind a veil or barrier of some sort. The second state in which truth *"becomes woman,* becomes Christian" is also a kind of collective dream, an imaginative vision that challenged (in some ways) the patriarchy of the Greek and Roman world. This dream of truth as a woman renders possible the narrativization of philosophy in the succeeding stages, although philosophy finds it difficult to acknowledge either the dream or its own turn to narrative. Similarly, the subsequent dreams or stages of a great collective cultural cycle of dreams are expressed in terms of a mood, a setting, an atmosphere that are then reinscribed as symbolic narratives offering explanations of the circumstances of truth's deferral. The Kantian stage exhibits such a linkage of dream and reinscribed narrative:

3. The true world—unattainable, indemonstrable, unpromisable; but the very thought of it—a consolation, an obligation, an imperative. (At bottom, the old sun, but seen through mist and skepticism. The idea has become elusive, pale, Nordic, Königsbergian.)

The dream of truth as an elusive Nordic woman sometimes appearing through or behind a veil of mist inspired Kant's play with the dualities of present imperative and (possible) future fulfillment, between our limited understanding and the categorical imperative of morality on the one hand and the demand of reason for a fuller, systematic cognitive and moral totality on the other.

It is not only the absence of Hegel's name and of his particular way of reinscribing a dream as symbolic narrative that renders Nietzsche's history of an error so very unHegelian. It is rather the doubled structure of the narrative, the absence of a comfortable collective narrator (a "we" with whom the reader can identify), and the fact that this story is not a history of truth but the history of an error that leads to the production of a text that would offer an alternative to philosophical metanarrative. Here Nietzsche is deploying the sun of our "White Mythology" in a way that reverses the classical mode of philosophical narrative. Unlike the Hegelian story that ends with the setting of the sun and the flight of Minerva's owl, Nietzsche's account suggests there is life at the end of *this* story. After all, it is just an error and there is always a new day. Or we might say, with Derrida, that as the philosophical idea becomes woman it learns the art of story-telling and perfects the art to such a point that it no longer needs the support of a "true world." It learns to tell stories without taking revenge against these stories; that is, it produces narratives without having to reduce them to a single metanarrative. For such reduction, in which for example the metanarrative tells the unique Christian or Hegelian story, is generated by a *ressentiment* against the pluralistic tendencies of story-telling as monotheism is generated by the jealousy of one god toward all the other gods. As Nietzsche never tires of pointing out, a god who would be unique must be a very jealous god indeed; there is perhaps a common principle then in polytheism and in pluralistic narrativity. The "true world" here is demoted to the level of just a fable, a story that no longer has any special force, one which can perhaps be included in the set available to our culture but without its earlier pretensions.

The sixth and last stage of Nietzsche's sketch, then, makes no claims to finality:

6. The true world—we have abolished. What world has remained? The apparent one perhaps? But no! *With the true world we have also abolished the apparent one.*

(Noon, moment of the briefest shadow; end of the longest error; high point of humanity; INCIPIT ZARATHUSTRA).

What emerges at the end of this sequence is not an apparent world that would occupy the place once held by the "true world." Such an apparent world might be construed, for example, on empirical lines as a set of relatively discrete sensory experiences or, in a phenomenological perspective, as consisting of a rich network of intentions and contents. But the point of Nietzsche's story is to show that since such conceptions of the apparent world are constructed only as the "others," alternatives to the true world, they will consequently lose their claims to plausibility once their contrast-terms have been eliminated. The apparent world as conceived by the positivists, for example, is one in which changing appearances are governed by unchanging natural laws; but aren't these eternal laws a ghostly residue of the "true world" and mustn't their status become questionable once the "true world" is eliminated? So there is no philosophical telos at the end of this story. In contrast to the story Hegel tells we have not the ultimate identity-in-difference of the apparent and true worlds, where we would be both object and knower, but the disappearance of both. Perhaps this is like waking from a dream as in a Shakespearean scene and finding that a conflict we had taken very seriously has simply vanished with the disappearance or transformation of both sides. On one level this discovery of the mutual implication and mutual vanishing of apparent and true can be articulated by the deconstructive or genealogical philosopher who explores the tangled affiliations of these concepts. On the dream level Nietzsche's narrative says that the stories are not over yet (they never will be). If the dream side of deconstruction and genealogy is the high noon dream of *Zarathustra*, then the "true world" has not only turned into a (mere) fable but has been displaced by a tale. In other words (of Nietzsche's) we might say that deconstruction and genealogy are the reinscription of "It is a dream! I will dream on!" In thus being led from one fictive story or dream to another we should beware of the hermeneutic fallacy of supposing that somewhere at the end of the sequence, in the heart of the labyrinth, is a story that will finally yield up the "true world" of the Nietzschean text. The elimination of the true world and its double, the apparent world, should, then, be a governing principle of the reading and interpretation of texts as well as of the book of the world.

Heidegger takes Nietzsche's last parenthetical comments as having a finalistic or teleological reference within the development of Nietzsche's own philosophy; he reads the parenthesis as "Thus the onset of the final stage of his own philosophy."[20] For Heidegger, who still reads Nietzsche logocentrically, that final stage is understood as based on the doctrine of the will to power, where will to power is conceived as the last, doomed expression of Western philosophy's hubristic fixation on the metaphysics of presence. "INCIPIT ZARATHUSTRA" is not for Heidegger a way of leading us from one narrative to another, but a signal that helps us sort Nietzsche's philosophy out into stages. What this means is that Heidegger will not see Nietzsche as a story-teller, or at least that he will rank a final stage of Nietzsche's thought as more important than a narrative or aphoristic form in which it happens to be cast. Although Heidegger praises Nietzsche for his deeply informed wrestling with history, he will not acknowledge that Nietzsche is almost always constructing histories or narratives; he must be the one to tell the last story of philosophy in which Nietzsche is the tragic hero.

It is symptomatic of Heidegger's stance that he wants to read all of Nietzsche's published texts as a mere foreground philosophy and that he sees the notebooks, especially those of the last few years, as pointing to that genuine expression of his thought that Nietzsche never quite completed. Derrida radicalizes that approach by asking us to see the value in the notes as notes with all of their gaps, crudeness, and ambiguities. But suppose, differing from both, that we read Nietzsche's notebooks as we do those of a novelist. Then we could read Nietzsche's narratives for the stories that they tell without either reconstructing a secret unwritten philosophy (a true Nietzsche behind the apparent one) or committing ourselves to an infinite process of deconstructing whatever there was in his writings that seemed to constitute a meaningful expression. Such a narrativist reading might also be helpful in looking at Nietzsche's published remarks about his own writing. In *Ecce Homo*, for example, Nietzsche begins his discussion of *Zarathustra* with a passage that is often cited by philosophers attempting to elucidate the idea of eternal recurrence:

Now I shall relate the history [*Geschichte*] of *Zarathustra*. The basic conception [*Grundconception*] of this work, the thought [*Gedanke*] of eternal recurrence, this highest formula of affirmation that is at all attainable, belongs in August 1881: it was penned on a sheet with the notation underneath, "6000 feet beyond man and time." (*EH*, *Z* I; 6, 335)

Here, in a very writerly fashion, Nietzsche refers to eternal recurrence as the *Grundconception* of his literary masterpiece. The German *Concept* is more like a sketch, outline, or draft (a notebook can be called a *Konzeptbuch*). So Nietzsche can be read here as saying something about the genesis of his philosophical tale by indicating how he came across what a novelist like Henry James would call "the germ of a story." We might then be better prepared to read *Zarathustra* as a narrative.

What might Nietzsche be about, then in announcing *Zarathustra* as the dream-narrative that follows those of the Platonic tradition? *Thus Spoke Zarathustra* could easily tempt us toward a hermeneutic reading of its presumed secret or it could educate us to avoid that temptation. Derrida expresses the concern that a hermeneutic approach, believing that "Nietzsche's mastery is infinite," might "use parody or the simulacrum" as a weapon in the service of truth or castration "and this would be in fact to reconstitute religion, as a Nietzsche cult for example, in the interest of a priesthood of parody interpreters."[21] Keeping this warning in mind, it may still be possible to make a few suggestions about the kind of narrativity that is at work in *Zarathustra*. Marxists and critical theorists from Georg Lukacs to Jürgen Habermas have read *Zarathustra* as an exercise in archaicizing myth to serve the interests of imperialism and irrationalism. But I want to suggest instead that it can be seen as an exemplary postmodern philosophical tale in which are inscribed an encyclopedic variety of the narrative functions of the West. It is highly textual: as written it largely effaces the *speaking* attributed to its chief agent. Nietzsche's later testimony to its inspired composition may be taken as his acknowledgment that it is in many ways a dream-narrative written in response to causes at best dimly understood. Its rhetorical structure involves a strategic decentering that can function as a critique of the many efforts such as Heidegger's to discover the true *Rangordnung* (order of rank) of Nietzsche's thought. Without desiring (and certainly without the power) to foreclose other readings of Nietzsche's polyvalent text, let me suggest that *Thus Spoke Zarathustra* exhibits something like a reversal and reinscription of the "four great errors" that Nietzsche finds to be generative of most narratives. These reinscriptions tend to be identified with what are usually taken to be the chief philosophical ideas of the text; and although the operations traverse all of *Zarathustra* they can, to some extent, be localized as dominant strategies of its four marked parts.

If it is an error of thought to seek an imaginary cause for a felt or experienced condition, that is, to create an unconscious metaphor of that condition, then it becomes clear why Zarathustra calls on his listeners in part one (and Nietzsche on his readers) to create a fiction, to dream beyond themselves of the *Übermensch* (or "man beyond") rather than indulging in retroactive visions fueled by envy or *ressentiment*. The error of reversing the causal sequence, an operation that empowers metonymic narrative, is highlighted in *Zarathustra* II by the announcement that the will to power is always operative; such will is at the beginning of any sequence and so conventional sequences—Zarathustra reviews those of poets, metaphysicians, priests, and historians—can be rewritten. But the great problem for the will to power then becomes the very fact of sequentiality itself, rather than the specific narratives that are constructed by the error of reversal. The second reinscriptive strategy comes perilously close to the "great error" that consists in identifying the will as the sole cause of everything; but this error is averted in *Zarathustra* by the impasse that arises when the will discovers that "it cannot will backwards." How then can the will be prevented from backtracking and producing resentful, nostalgic narratives of religious creation or of an eternal world from which we are fallen? To the error that consists in making the will the cause of everything, Nietzsche juxtaposes an ambitious reinscription of such a synecdochic program with his "most abysmal thought" of eternal recurrence. Both are totalistic programs, but eternal recurrence requires our recognizing ourselves as "not to be disentangled from the fatality of all that has been and will be." But this thought, which is the hinge of part three of *Zarathustra*, is also a call to will that our experiences recur eternally since they will do so in any case. It is the paradox of willing our fate which replaces the error of voluntarism and, in doing so, points the way to a more pluralized narrativity. An allied error discussed by Nietzsche in *Twilight of the Idols* consists in hypostatizing the individual consciousness as center of activity. This error is opposed in *Thus Spoke Zarathustra*, and especially in its fourth part, by a thoroughgoing carnivalization and ironic pluralization of agents and voices. The higher men who come to Zarathustra's cave are themselves often doubles (two kings, Zarathustra's Shadow, the Enchanter who parodies both himself and Wagner). Zarathustra not only has a Shadow, but announces himself to be in principle his own double, declaring himself to be the *Hanswurst* or buffoon of his carnival. These doubling, reversing, pluralizing strategies, which have been so acutely described by Mikhail Bakhtin, render the identity of the individual self radically indeterminate and, along with the reinscriptions of the other errors, they counteract the philosophical obsession with establishing an order and hierarchy of concepts. In their public transformation of philosophers and their *topoi* they reduce these concepts to an economy of philosophemes.

It would be a mistake, I think, to assume that Nietzsche is always in conscious control of the narrative of *Zarathustra*, or even that we really know what we mean when we talk about a unitary author or self who could serve as a directing consciousness for texts that bear his name. This is the case not simply because Nietzsche was an odd person or mad or deliberately seeking to create a fascinating literary surface rather than undertaking what Hegel called the labor of the concept. Because of his crucial place at the fault-lines of a number of significant intellectual and cultural conjunctions we are able to see the various uses and abuses to which Nietzsche's narratives and his other texts have been subjected. But the general situation of the philosophical text *as* a text, a piece of writing that can have no uniquely privileged meaning, if it is truly general, would have to have consequences for the reading and interpretation of the works of many writers and many traditions.

This has been the burden of Derrida's reading of texts from Plato to Heidegger and it could, I think, be extended to the classics of the British empiricist tradition which not only seem to resist such analysis, but to empower an apparently quite different conception of philosophy.

Nietzsche then cannot be represented as a founding father of postmodern philosophy (or even as its matriarch, as some Derrideans might suggest), if founding supposes self-knowledge. There is no equivalent in Nietzsche's thought of the kind of inaugural act that Kant and Husserl, for example, attribute to originary thinkers in science and philosophy; such an act would open up a tradition and would have to be rethought by anyone who wanted to reactivate that tradition. There are, however, two possible candidates that might serve as the enabling foundation of a Nietzschean tradition and that might be the foundation of a Nietzschean metanarrative. The first would be the thought of eternal recurrence, a thought that never seems to be absent from any Nietzschean text. I want to discuss eternal recurrence within the narrative context of *Zarathustra*. But in a preliminary way it might be asked (this is in effect the question of the French Nietzscheans): why should we suppose that there is a *single* idea of eternal recurrence? To assume that we are dealing here with a unitary thought which is to be assimilated to other supposed unitary great thoughts of the philosophical tradition would beg almost all of the questions that Nietzsche raises. Even if we emphasize that what is important is *thinking* the eternal recurrence through for oneself, it is still not clear that such thinking could have an inaugural or foundational role. For the consequences of the thought are precisely to decenter the self who thinks it; unlike other great ideas, its own terms require us to value our ignorance of the idea as well as our knowledge of it, our forgetting it as well as remembering it. Yet if the thought of eternal recurrence could not inaugurate a tradition in this way, Nietzsche does at times contemplate a historical watershed, a new definitive marking of time that would be associated with this thought and his textualizations of it. This would be a second candidate for an inaugural role. So in his last year of writing and thinking Nietzsche comes to concentrate his attention increasingly on his project of the *Transvaluation of All Values*, a project which is sometimes described as the completion of a text with that title and sometimes as the world-historical epoch that the text was to usher in. The indications from Nietzsche's notes and plans for the text are that it was to be a kind of metanarrative beginning with a critical deconstruction of Christianity (eventually published as *The Antichrist*), including a history of European nihilism, and ending with the philosophy of Dionysus or eternal recurrence. Yet, notoriously, Nietzsche did not complete this work, although in his last working months before his breakdown he called the one short book *The Antichrist* the whole of the *Transvaluation*; its text by the way includes a final page, only recently restored by the valiant editors Colli and Montinari, of a "Decree against Christianity," suitable for reproduction as a wall-poster of the sort that might be used by an army of occupation. Signed "The Antichrist" and dated from "the first day of the year one (September 30, 1888 of the false system of reckoning time)," it displays that intention to "break the history of mankind into two" which forms the subject of

Nietzsche's last writings (6, 254). Nietzsche sometimes speaks with fervent anticipation of a great noon when humanity will finally reflect on itself and its purposes, a noon that will either coincide with or follow upon the transvaluation. These apocalyptic hints and promises are not the weakest of the seductive attractions that Nietzsche has exercised upon his readers. In the readings that I will be suggesting of Nietzsche's narratives I do not want to deny the possibility of such apocalyptic themes, but I do want to put these themes in their place. That is, I want to guard against giving them the dominant status that they assume in Nietzsche's own temptation to indulge in metanarrative in which so many readers have followed him.

TWO

■■■■■

Metaphorical Overcoming/ Metonymical Strife

(*Zarathustra* I and II)

I

Thus Spoke Zarathustra: *A Book for Everyone and No One*. The duplicity of Nietzsche's subtitle is obvious but its sense is uncertain. If *Zarathustra* is read thematically, the suggestion is that it contains a teaching with significant and shattering implications for everybody—the doctrine of the eternal recurrence, for example—which hardly anyone will grasp. Interpreted intentionally, the motto draws attention to Nietzsche's isolation and loneliness, seeming to express simultaneously both a desperate wish for a universal audience and a defensive move in which he assures himself that a degenerate nineteenth-century audience could hardly appreciate his prescient work. Both views, which may be complementary, can find some support in letters or other Nietzschean texts; he refers to the "most abysmal" thought, eternal return, as the "basic conception" of the work in *Ecce Homo*, and his later writings on art constantly contrast the strength of the artist who writes for himself with the weakness of one who needs an audience ("Wagner needs Wagnerians"). There is a place for such thematic and intentional considerations. More directly, however, we are told that *Zarathustra* is a *book* for all and none. Contrary to much Anglo-American opinion, Nietzsche is generally a meticulously careful writer. It is not the doctrine or the author's personality which is said to be duplicitous here but the text itself. There is something uncanny in the textuality of *Zarathustra* (as there may be in its doctrines—if it has them—or its author). This preliminary ambiguity is heightened when we juxtapose the subtitle with the title. Zarathustra spoke, but what we have in our hands is a book. The great sages of religion and philosophy (Socrates, Jesus, Zoroaster) did not write: they were fully present to those contemporary with them. The writings which seek to preserve their sayings testify to an absence, as the gospels mark the need to compensate for Jesus' failure to reappear in such a way as to put an end to the constant loss which is time and history. As the history of religious texts suggests, there is a constant threat of the ostensibly secondary book replacing the primary sayings and a further danger of the text being displaced by its interpreters who are in turn displaced by the next generation of interpreters. These reverberations on Nietzsche's title-page suggest dualities of speech and writing, authorial meaning and reader's interpretation.

By centering attention on its own facticity as a book, *Zarathustra* leads us to question the importance of its thematics or the personality of its author. Yet we would arrive at the questionability of the text by starting from either thematic or authorial premises. The "doctrine" of the eternal recurrence is absurd when taken literally. How can we make sense of the idea that *precisely* the same events happen in *precisely* the same order in infinite succession? The question is not about the truth of the notion—for which no arguments are given in *Zarathustra*—but about its meaning, given some rather prosaic criteria of meaning. How does an infinitely repeated cycle vary from one which occurs five or seven times—or only once? There is no principle of individuation which would allow us to count repetitions of the cycle nor can there be any experiential difference for anyone in these various circumstances, for experience in all cycles is precisely the same. So we quickly come back to Nietzsche's strategy in placing such a view in his book. The problematics of origin and authorship again return us to questions of textual strategy. *Zarathustra*, on one level, purports to be a privileged book, a bible containing "Old and New Law-Tables," plus records of teaching to disciples about the state, scholarship, marriage, and education. Yet the authority of such teachings is put in question by one of them: "God is dead." Alternative sources of authority—reason, society, nature—are all undercut within the text. Perhaps the eternal return is to be grasped in a formal sense as the circle of self-referential questions which the book raises about itself.

Philosophers can be tempted to avoid the embarrassments of this circle by doggedly insisting on thematic or authorial approaches. Some of them may find it a relief to classify the text as having the self-containment or opacity of a poem, for it can then be excluded from philosophy's charmed circle. In the ancient quarrel between philosophy and poetry, however, *Zarathustra* is not simply an object to be classified, captured, or surrendered to the enemy but is itself one of the more self-conscious reconsiderations of the struggle itself. (I say "self-conscious" in the sense of *Selbstbewusst*, which does not carry the associations of uneasiness that our English word does). In the very beginning of the book, or *Vorrede*, a discourse which precedes discourse, Zarathustra says "I am weary of my wisdom" (*"Ich bin meiner Weisheit überdrüssig"*): we are given a motivation for Zarathustra's descent to men in his desire to impart his wisdom to them. Such imparting is usually a matter of sharing and communicating in which ownership is extended without any loss or dilution. Spinoza sums up the philosophical tradition with his claim that knowledge is a unique good in that it can be commonly owned and need not give rise to any competition. Yet Zarathustra speaks not of extending possession of a good thing, but of emptying himself of something which has filled him to the point of satiation. Not only does *überdrüssig* convey a sense of being sated, but wisdom is metaphorically linked to a bee's uncomfortable superfluity of honey. Wisdom is to be given away, that is, dispersed or possibly exchanged for folly, rather than socialized. Zarathustra does not speak of attaining completion through a community of intelligence as do philosophers from Plato to Hegel, but of a cleansing through surrender, an *askesis* not for the sake of wisdom but *of* wisdom: "Behold! This cup wants to be empty again, and Zarathustra wants to be man again (Z, 39; 4, 12)"[1] Yet such *askesis* does not signal a capitulation of philosophy to poetry. In the chapter "Of Poets" in part two, there is a somewhat parallel disavowal of poetry: "I have grown weary of the poets, the old and the new: they all seem to be superficial and shallow seas." The chapter cited and the book's division into parts will deserve some attention later. It is worth noting now because it sounds a cautionary note against the temptation to see *Zarathustra* as poetry—at least in any simple sense. The texture of *Zarathustra* is indeed highly metaphorical and imagistic. One encounters an apparently endless series of passages like this:

> My glib tongue—is of the people; I speak too coarsely and warmly for silky rabbits. And my words sound even stranger to all inky fish and scribbling foxes.
> My hand—is a fool's hand: woe to all tables and walls and whatever has room left for fool's scribbling, fool's doodling.
> My foot—is a horse's foot. . . .
> My stomach—is it perhaps an eagle's stomach. For it likes lamb's flesh best of all. But it is certainly a bird's stomach.
> ("Of the Spirit of Gravity," 1; Z, 210; 4, 241)

Even allowing for the significance of Nietzsche's revaluation of the body, it is a relief that he did not proceed to the intestines. In any case, the reader may already be tempted to exclaim "*Ich bin der Metaphern überdrüssig.*"

Philosophers and critics often tend to privilege metaphor in their accounts of literature, usually in order to contrast the polyvalent texture of metaphorical language with the aim at clarity and a univocal sense said to be found in philosophy or science. Depending upon one's valuations, the contrast may work to the advantage of either party. Poetry's rich and varied meanings may appear as abundance or vagueness; the universal meanings of philosophy and science are clear or sterile. The contrast is too simple, for even the hardest-nosed and toughest-minded philosophers are hopelessly addicted to metaphor. But the hybrid characterization of some texts—including Nietzsche's—as metaphorical philosophy is not much more penetrating. To view *Zarathustra* as metaphorical could mean one of several things. It might be a way of cautiously praising the work for richly suggesting a variety of insights, while keeping it at arm's length. Alternatively, it is sometimes connected with an attempt to show that Nietzsche carried out in his writings some of his programmatic remarks about the non-referential, musical, and self-contained nature of language. Even those who take the second approach, however, usually fail to come to grips with such messy details of the text as Zarathustra's writing on the walls, horse's feet, and eagle's stomach.

To understand *Zarathustra* is to see how it situates itself in regard to the ancient quarrel between philosophy and poetry. In that conflict it is not simply an object to be classified, captured, or reluctantly surrendered to the enemy; it demands to be read as one of the more self-conscious reconsiderations of the struggle itself. In this connection it is useful to realize that the book's apparent indulgence in the poetic mode is at least partially balanced by a criticism of poetry. In the chapter "Of Poets," to which I will return, Zarathustra criticizes poetry in terms of two fundamental rhetorical dimensions. The poets are said to fail in the realm of thought and feeling by their penchant for vague and indefinite metaphorical constructions— that is, they are deficient in the use of and self-consciousness regarding the tropes or figures of speech. They are also criticized for their excessive vanity which leads them to strut like peacocks for an audience of buffaloes. Whether this extravagant comparison violates Zarathustra's first stricture is an intriguing question which must be postponed. What the two criteria taken together suggest is that a successful text, such as *Zarathustra* is presumed to be, will exhibit a careful handling of tropes and an attention to the nature of its audience, the latter being sufficiently cultured and aristocratic that the writer need not humble himself to be understood. One consequence is that we ought to be cautious in assuming that the peacock's tail of *Zarathustra*'s metaphorical texture is simply identical with the poetic or literary aspect of the text.

Confronted with this apparent contradiction, a number of interpretations are possible. Nietzsche might be accused of careless self-contradiction, except that the very same chapter (as we shall see) invites us to think out what such contradictions mean and imply. Like Jaspers we might take the alternation of views and emphases to be signs of Nietzsche's own restless philosophical activity which avoids the danger of resting content with any singular propositional form of the truth. This seems closer to the spirit of the book. But where Jaspers sees a restless, driven activity which he attempts to illuminate by means of Nietzsche's life, I tend to see the deliberate work of an author. As I have already suggested, referring to Nietzsche's life to explain his writing is a tricky procedure indeed, since Nietzsche views his own life in terms of his writing career. Now it is an elementary lesson of literary criticism that we ought not to identify the viewpoint of a character in a book, or even that of the narrator of a book, with that of the author or of the book as a whole. If Zarathustra contradicts himself or expresses a certain view or is foolish we should treat these matters in the same way as we do the contradictions, views, and foolishness of Captain Lemuel Gulliver. As Nietzsche says, "I am one thing, my books are another." If this sounds too simple it is because we expect a philosophical book to take positions and make claims in a more determinate way than a literary text must. Yet in this case we are dealing with a book which deliberately questions our expectation of finding a single view, an authoritative voice, or a systematic teaching.

The literary structure of *Zarathustra* should remind us that we are dealing with a book which is acutely concerned with its own nature as a written document and its place in the textual histories of both literature and philosophy. Here I want to recall some of the remarks made earlier about the Socratic-Platonic problem of the written versus the spoken word and the distinction between oral and written media. If we are going to read *Zarathustra* as a literary work (keeping in mind that this does not make it a non-philosophical work), then we should be clear about the *kind* of literary work that it is. In his comprehensive study of *Zarathustra*, Harold Alderman has interpreted the book as essentially dramatic, comparing it to the Platonic dialogues; and he takes the chief theme of the book to be one which is appropriate to drama, the search for those possibilities of the human voice which are appropriate to the philosophical life. I think this approach to the book is a significant improvement over those interpretations which would seek Nietzsche's doctrines without regard to the context of his writing, alleging his fragmented style as a reason for providing a structure lacking in the books themselves; nevertheless, it is misleading and I think it will illuminate the present reading if I explain why it is misleading. It seems unexceptionable to say that:

> The dramatic complexity of the book then lies in the encounter of a number of speakers, and in this the book is like philosophy itself which is also the encounter of speakers, of voices, of ideas. Philosophy is, as both Plato and Nietzsche knew all too clearly, a kind of drama: the drama of men speaking out of the experience of their lives in an attempt to make things clear. So, in this minimal sense, at least, the dramatic structure of *Thus Spoke Zarathustra* is also the philosophical structure.[2]

For Alderman this coincidence of literary and philosophical structure is more than minimal, for he concludes his book by reminding us that "Zarathustra is then the teacher who teaches the need to explore the full range of the human voice."[3] Again, an apparently unexceptionable observation. Yet the literary analogies used here are questionable and produce misunderstandings of some of the philosophical concerns of the work. *Zarathustra* is not written for the theater; and the reason for this is more than a reluctance to compete with Wagner on the latter's own turf. In literary terms the book is a narrative, not a drama; it is not just the words of Zarathustra and the other characters which are presented but descriptions of situations, actions, and settings. It is a very complex narrative indeed, replete with echoes and parodies of the Bible, Goethe, and a rich variety of texts. This is more than a stylistic quibble; in any case Nietzsche regards questions of style as of great *philosophical* importance. The comparison with Plato may also be misleading for a number of the important dialogues such as the *Symposium*, the *Theaetetus*, and the *Parmenides* are told from the standpoint of a narrator who either participated in the discussion or heard of it from another. In *The Birth of Tragedy*, where Nietzsche is concerned with sorting out a variety of artistic genres, he says that "Plato has given to all posterity the model of a new art form, the model of the *novel*" (*BT*, 14; *1*, 93–94).

Let me now suggest some of the ways in which the decision to read *Zarathustra* as drama, narrative, or some more specific variety of text is not a philosophically innocent one. The critical categories which we adopt to discuss the drama or other literary genres themselves have a philosophical origin, often obscured, in such thinkers as Aristotle and Hegel. Hegel would agree with Alderman's assumption that the drama is the form in which philosophical and literary form come to coincide most closely and his reasons would be philosophical ones having to do with the way in which drama, by privileging the human voice, provides the greatest possible communication between the author and the audience of a work of literary art. For these same reasons Hegel takes philosophy, that is, a philosophy which abandons literary form and moves in the pure medium of the concept, to be an even better form of communication.[4] But because Nietzsche rejects the possibility of such communication and some of its philosophical presuppositions, he writes a non-theatrical text. *Zarathustra*, and other of Nietzsche's writings after the Wagnerian extravagances of *The Birth of Tragedy*, suggest that the theater is a place which produces the *illusion* of common understanding.

In drama, the central organizing principles are (as Alderman and Aristotle both testify) the plot and the human voice. To read *Zarathustra* as a drama would then involve an implicit commitment to look for consistent characters and a plot with a recognizable pattern of development. But notice how such concerns seem to conflict with some of the book's most obvious concepts. Zarathustra is not a humanist but one who proclaims the *Übermensch*, not a superior or higher man, but one who transcends man. The notion of eternal recurrence is at odds with the idea of a linear, intelligible sequence which is involved in the usual conception of dramatic plot. Later I will suggest that in the context of *Zarathustra* these two themes of *Übermensch* and eternal recurrence taken together imply the dissolution of a consistent sense of self or character—another of the mainstays of drama. Finally, to take the text as a drama rather than as a book to be read and reread is to deemphasize the role of that active interpretation which Nietzsche so often demands of his readers. And, as I will also suggest later, the failure to emphasize the role of such interpretation (*Auslegung*) in respect to Nietzsche's books may also lead us to ignore it in the case of his ontology in which reading, text, and interpretation are central notions.

Zarathustra is sometimes playful, but *Zarathustra* is always a play, a rhetorical *Spiel* which plays with serious affairs of the understanding. It speaks without authority, and so we will be hopelessly confused if we see it as a new gospel and not as an anti-gospel (Nietzsche said once that the gospels should be called dysangels or bringers of bad news.) A few of the poles of this rhetorical play can be specified. We have already encountered the play between philosophy and poetry in which there is a ceaseless alternation. Another is the play between poetry and prose. This may at first appear anomalous, for rhetoric is thought to be concerned with prose rather than poetry, and Nietzsche sometimes describes it so in his writings on rhetoric. Yet even there he notes how *Kunstprosa* (literary prose) can take on an indefinite number of poetic features. More to the point is that there is a larger rhetorical organization which governs the varying textures of the work—which can be designated (in part) as parable, poetry, song, teaching, and silence. The distinction between immediate texture and larger structure appears, for example, when we try to ascertain the role of metaphor in *Zarathustra*. The book's immediate texture is no doubt highly metaphorical. Many of the recent studies of Nietzsche by the followers of Jacques Derrida tend to see all of Nietzsche's works, including *Zarathustra*, as a *Spiel der Metaphern*.[5] Metaphor however can be taken in either a broad or a narrow sense in which it designates, respectively, either any deviation from some linguistic norm or a particular figure of speech which can be contrasted with others. This is a significant distinction because the book is organized around four figures of speech or tropes, which rhetorical theory has tended to recognize as relatively central: metaphor, metonymy, synecdoche, and irony. This organization makes the book surprisingly traditional in certain respects. But the book's structure is not simply a mechanical way of giving a semblance of order to aphoristic writing. Each of the major parts has a dominant tone or mood whose plurality suggests the necessary plurality of language by providing variant contexts for the treatment of themes, situations, and ideas.

In traditional rhetoric such subjects are called *topoi*. *Zarathustra* achieves much of its effect by ringing the changes on a number of recurrent *topoi*. Of these the most intriguing for my purpose is that of language itself; but before turning to that topic it will be useful to sketch the sequence of the book's main parts. The following reservations are to be kept in mind, however. As the later chapters of this study will show, the form of *Zarathustra* is not typical of Nietzsche's works; he says in *Ecce Homo* that each book has its own distinctive style. On a more enigmatic note it should be mentioned that the sorting out of these four parts is not only a temporal or narrative sequence; to whatever extent the book is informed by the idea of eternal recurrence, which attempts to overcome any linear conception of time, it ought also to be opposed to any special temporal priority being accorded to any of these general approaches or perspectives.

The *Vorrede* of *Zarathustra* precedes the main text in a logical as well as a chronological sense. In it Zarathustra attempts to teach the superman to those in the marketplace, but can represent him only as a distant goal. For his audience of contented townspeople he can produce only vague intimations of what lies totally beyond. This is symbolic or prophetic poetry (in Hegel's sense): the vague adumbration of a transcendent or distant object which can be suggested at best indirectly by a negation of the actual and the present. Symbolic discourse, because of its inadequacy to its subject, is in a sense prediscursive; accordingly the action of the *Vorrede* revolves around Zarathustra's failures to communicate to the crowd and their ridicule of him.

Part one of *Zarathustra* consists of a series of metaphorical discourses. The *Vorrede* spoke of man as a bridge, as something to be overcome for the sake of the superman. This talk was starkly abstract, full of plays on *übergehen* (going over, passing beyond) and *untergehen* (going down, perishing), suggesting a sheer up or down movement with little sense of a concrete goal. In part one Zarathustra begins by giving some metaphorical content to the projected notion by teaching the three metamorphoses of the spirit—camel, lion, and child. Metamorphosis—change into another species—is very close to the idea of metaphor as transference of meaning. Childhood is of course an almost unavoidable romantic metaphor for regained innocence and spontaneity, but other parts of the metaphorical complex are more novel. Traditional virtue is sleep, longing after heaven is burying one's head in the sand, and reading and writing are matters of blood and violence. Zarathustra, aware of his own poetic energy, urges his listeners to join him in making new metaphorical identifications: body will be spirit, peace should be victory, the state is a cold monster. The creation of new metaphors and the destruction of old ones is the activity of transvaluation itself, for "all names of good and evil are images [*Gleichnisse*]" and "he who has to be a creator always has to destroy." The richness of metaphor in part one could be detailed indefinitely; Zarathustra's remarks (often confused with Nietzsche's views) about war and women can be seen as metaphorical identifications of freedom and dependence. Yet as Paul de Man suggests, such a rich cluster of imagery "is itself a sign of divine absence, and the conscious use of poetic imagery an admission of this absence."[6] God is absent from the very beginning in *Zarathustra*; but by the time of the extended series of metaphorical discourses in part one, the superman is also absent and there is a frenzied effort to fill his place with poetry. In terms of "The Three Metamorphoses of the Spirit," part one consists of a heavy burden of metaphorical baggage which the camel must bear to prepare it for higher things. The end of this apprenticeship is signaled in the last chapter of this part, "Of the Bestowing Virtue," in which Zarathustra gives a lesson in the hermeneutics and creation of metaphor; the lesson will prepare the reader for the more active tone of what follows and for the greater demands to be placed on the reader's powers of interpretation.

The tone of part two is reductive. The idea of will and will to power are prominent and are employed to set up a series of dualities which present clear choices to the will. The will is said to be the cause of all things and in a stronger sense things are said to be nothing but will. This reduction of effects to causes is metonymical as is the sharp series of contrasts which the will must confront. Paradigmatic for this series is Zarathustra's teaching "On the Blissful Islands": "But to reveal my heart entirely to you, friends: *if* there were gods, how could I endure not to be a god! *Therefore* there are no gods (Z, 110; 4, 110)." The inference is not logical but tropological. When all is reduced to the will, experience becomes a series of oppositions and dichotomies between the will and all of its possible impediments. Some of the polarities are philosophically familiar—god and man, self-denial and self-affirmation, permanence and becoming—but they are given a new twist by the will's repudiation of the traditionally privileged members of these pairs. Other dichotomies are peculiar to the focus on the will. For example, one must choose between revenge (rationalized as justice) and life as continual self-overcoming. Revenge may at first appear to be a strong exercise of the will but in its dependence on the object exciting the revenge it reveals a weakness. Moreover, one of the dichotomies facing the will is apparently ineluctable and seems to condemn the will to a cycle of revenge:

> The will itself is still a prisoner.
> Willing liberates: but what is it that fastens in fetters even the liberator?
> "It was": that is what the will's teeth-gnashing and most lonely affliction is called. Powerless against that which has been done, the will is an angry spectator of all things past.

The will cannot will backwards; that it cannot break time and time's desire—that is the will's most lonely affliction. ("Of Redemption"; *Z*, 161; *4*, 180)

It is appropriate to the trope of part two that the dichotomy is not resolved. There are similar dichotomies which appear in the treatment of poetry and interpretation (even the interpretation of dreams) in this part. The dichotomous structure is even carried into the relation between Zarathustra and his auditors: here there are more questions and problems posed by the listeners, and Zarathustra often abruptly shifts from external address to inner soliloquy.

Part three has often been taken to be the philosophical heart of *Zarathustra* because it contains the idea of the eternal recurrence. This philosophical valuation of part three is a consequence of the governing trope, which is synecdoche, understood as thorough parallelism of microcosm and macrocosm. Synecdoche has normally been the privileged philosophical trope because it produces a sense of totality and comprehensibility—it is not subject to perpetual shifting, as is metaphorical identification, nor to the overly simple reductions and frustrating dichotomies of metonymy. Plato's *Republic* enjoys most of its pedagogical prestige just because of its synecdochic series of concentric circles linking political and individual justice, social and personal psychology, and, of course, the true, the beautiful, and the good. That the concept of the eternal return can be seen as a this-worldly version of Platonic longings for eternity has been perspicuously shown by Heidegger, among others. Yet it is perhaps the synecdochic suggestion of totality which, in general, produces the sense of eternity. In the notion of eternal recurrence, each moment is "baptized in eternity," it brings with it the whole train of past and previous moments. The eternal thing in this perspective is just the eternal ring of becoming itself, so to talk or think about eternity is to be brought back to the cycle of particular moments. Nietzsche himself, in *Ecce Homo*, calls the eternal recurrence the fundamental conception of *Zarathustra*. This may well be, but to read the book in a search for its basic conceptions is already to have privileged the synecdochic and philosophical troping of part three. In the same *Ecce Homo* sections Nietzsche also makes some extravagant claims about the significance of the poetry of Zarathustra, but philosophers have seen little reason to take this as a fundamental clue to the book's meaning. Yet to read Nietzsche either from the perspective of his self-interpretation or from that of his literary accomplishment would seem to require an emphasis on both of these aspects of the book as well as others. If *Zarathustra* is a more or less straightforward philosophical book, then an emphasis on part three is in order; but the status of philosophical doctrines and arguments is constantly at stake in the book; as a text, *Zarathustra* simply does not privilege the philosophical trope. An emphasis on the trope of part three, however, does bring to light other synecdochic motifs which surround the famous idea. Zarathustra's homecoming is a return to origins in which language becomes totally adequate, leaving no residues or accidents. The weighing of the world and the handing down of a new set of law tables amount to a totalistic revaluation in line with the concept of the eternal recurrence.

Part four has been something of a puzzle for Nietzsche's interpreters because of its apparently radical change of tone. Some have suspected, on the basis of its private publication subsequent to the bulk of the book, that it is not a real part of the whole; others have thought, despite Nietzsche's subtitle—"Fourth and Last Part"—and conclusion—"The End of *Thus Spoke Zarathustra*"—that the part must be transitional to others which were never written.[7] Yet tropologically this part is completely in order by contributing to the planned disorder of rhetorical play. The governing trope is irony here, as Zarathustra struggles with his pity for higher men. His answer to a cry of distress leads to the assemblage of a motley collection of guests and petitioners; when the whole gathering (including the last Pope) is about to engage in an ass festival which parodies the Last Supper, Zarathustra parodies the community of god and man by his refrain "Truly, you may all be Higher Men but for me—you are not high and strong enough." Each higher man embodies a misunderstanding or oversimplification of Zarathustra and his teachings, from which Zarathustra distances himself by ridicule. Zarathustra finds all of the praise directed at him by his would-be disciples misplaced and misdirected. When he finally expresses some pleasure in his visitors it is to instruct them regarding their asinine festival: "And if you celebrate it again, this ass festival, do it for love of yourselves, do it also for love of *me*! And in remembrance of *me*!" (Z, 325–26). Surely the ass suggests the absence of God or of anything which could properly take his place. Zarathustra does not want to be worshipped himself, and he will be remembered only by continual dance and play which by its very nature must avoid any centering of a privileged object or person. Even the notion of eternal recurrence is treated playfully in a number of ambiguous references to the confusion of times. That a play upon the tropes should end with irony makes the fact of play itself unavoidable, but it does not leave much standing in the way of straightforward doctrines or teachings—just as the higher men must surrender their desperately gleaned fragments of doctrine to take part in Zarathustra's dances.

The four tropological perspectives of *Zarathustra* are not merely rhetorical devices which present a fixed content in various ways. Each of the major ideas of the text is associated with a distinctive trope. The *Übermensch* is a metaphorical concept, the idea of that which lies beyond man, or past man, and which therefore can be characterized only by figures of speech which reach for what is not yet present. The will to power is a metonymical notion, involving the opposition between any instance of that will and the resisting world or the conflict with other wills. Eternal recurrence is a synecdochic doctrine in which each moment and the entire cycle of becoming become mutually representative, as in the correspondence of microcosm and macrocosm. The irony and carnivalization of the fourth part have not usually been thought to play such a systematic role as do the ideas of the superman, will to power, and eternal recurrence, although they are obvious enough features of its thought. Seeing that they are given a position of equal importance with the thoughts traditionally identified as philosophical may help to show that they are not merely aspects of style in some narrow sense, but are part of the basic structure of the work.

This sketch of the structure of *Zarathustra* may seem opposed to the still-common view of the book as formless, bombastic, and enthusiastic but it does agree with Nietzsche's own standards of literary integrity. Clarity, order, coherence, and *esprit* are the criteria of excellent writing which Nietzsche constantly employs. Two remarks from *The Gay Science* are appropriate here, although they are ostensibly contradictory:

> Those who know that they are profound strive for clarity. Those who would like to seem profound to the crowd strive for obscurity. (*GS*, 173; 3, 500)

> One does not only wish to be understood when one writes; one wishes just as surely *not* to be understood. It is not by any means necessarily an objection to a book when anyone finds it impossible to understand: perhaps that was part of the author's intention—he did not want to be understood by just "anybody." All the nobler spirits and tastes select their audience when they wish to communicate; and choosing that, one at the same time erects barriers against "the others." All the more subtle laws of any style have their origin at this point. (*GS*, 381; 3, 633–34)

Philosophers too often operate with a presupposed and therefore unclarified notion of clarity. Yet as Nietzsche recognizes, the nature of clarity is itself a philosophical problem which in the case of a written text involves rhetorical and generic considerations. A genre is rhetorically determined by its inclusions and exclusions; it does not only generate an audience but functions as a conspiracy of "the happy few" to keep the deeper nature of the text unprofaned by outsiders. A work may be intrinsically clear but initially puzzling to its proper audience and a perpetual possibility of misunderstanding to any others. This describes the form of Nietzsche's writing, especially that of his works from the time of *The Gay Science* on. The rhetorical *Spiel* of *Zarathustra*, with its reverberations of the aristocratic Greek audience willing to savor the troping of topics, is just such a Janus-faced genre. To stop at the level of an aphoristic and epigrammatic reading of Nietzsche is to see the decentered nature of his discourse but to ignore the playing field within which makes such decentering possible and delightful.

II

Like Odysseus, that wisest and most playful of the Greeks, *Zarathustra* is *polytropos*. Almost every topic that emerges in the book becomes the occasion for ringing the changes through the succession of parts. This is especially interesting in the case of discourse itself. The nature of writing, the quarrel between philosophy and poetry, the value of the poetic tradition, the referentiality of language are constant preoccupations in *Zarathustra*. To see what the text does with these themes and to determine in what sense Nietzsche has any final views or positions about them, it is necessary to see how they are handled in a variety of places. I wish to examine several of these places, keeping in mind their situation within the rhetorical structure of *Zarathustra*.

"Of Reading and Writing," in part one, is the first chapter of *Zarathustra* primarily devoted to discourse. It captures the predominant metaphorical tone of that part by a rapid series of images connecting reading and writing with violence, sexuality, and a dancing god. But its rhetorical stance is also metaphorical. It is presumably addressed, like many of Zarathustra's talks in part one, to a vaguely defined group of listeners in the town called The Motley Cow. As a figure of the narrative, Zarathustra is concerned only with the variations of oral discourse— speech, song, and silence. By his *speaking* of reading and writing, especially aphoristic writing which is done in blood, the chapter refers us back to the text itself. It need not be addressed to anyone in particular because metaphorical, symbolic discourse operates on the assumption that its images are concrete universals which are universally accessible. When the *topos* reappears under the other tropes, the nature of the speaker's relation to his audience is much more determinate. Just as metaphorical theories of poetry dispense with rhetorical considerations, the metaphorical presentation here achieves an image of universality by being indeterminately addressed to all and none. The metaphorical chains of the chapter trace the decline of reading and writing while projecting their rejuvenation. Zarathustra's play on the Incarnation gives a capsule history of literary decay: "Once spirit was God, then it became man, and now it is even becoming mob." Augustine, the first great Christian literary theorist, abjured his own rhetorical training in the high and noble style in order to espouse the "holy humility" of the gospels. The Incarnation is a figure for the possibility of spirit entering into the everyday. Hegel and his follower Erich Auerbach have written progressive histories of romantic or realistic literature in which the Incarnation is the watershed after which literature can portray ever larger areas of human experience and can aim, like the Bible, at speaking to all. For Zarathustra this is a degeneration to the reader as the "last man": "He who knows the reader, does nothing further for the reader. Another century of readers— and spirit itself will stink" (Z, 67; 4, 48).

We who are reading these texts are invited to step outside the modern rabble to become part of a drastically narrowed circle of readers and writers. This leap from indeterminate universality to conspiratorial isolation is made possible by the elastic nature of the metaphorical discourse which we are reading. The reader, left on his own, will either meet the challenge or fall back into the mass of "reading idlers." Zarathustra himself makes this connection between the difficult form of the writing and the strength of its readers: "aphorisms should be peaks, and those to whom they are spoken should be big and tall of stature." What this height consists in is spelled out by a series of images which may seem to shift radically away from the *topos* of discourse, but which should be read as expansions of it. The successful reader will understand what's written in blood and rejoice in the danger and thin air which accompanies it. Danger calls up the image of the warrior: "Untroubled, scornful, outrageous––that is how wisdom wants us to be: she is a woman and never loves anyone but a warrior (Z, 68; *4*, 49).'' When we read this reflexively it is reading and writing which are violent assaults. The warrior Nietzsche has in mind is at the opposite pole from Sartre's engaged writer: ''You say it is the good cause that hallows even war? I tell you: it is the good war that hallows every cause'' (Z, 74; *4*, 59). To explore this chain of metaphors further we would need to look at the other discourses in this part on woman and the warrior: to see that these are already metaphorized in the discourse on reading and writing immediately helps to dissociate them from the crude readings of the idling reader who sees Zarathustra or Nietzsche as a simple misogynist and warmonger.

Although God had been sublimated in the descent of writing, he now reappears as *a* dancing god. The indefinite article and the play of the dance suggest an answer to Nietzsche's problematic: How can one write a sacred book when God is dead? The problem of authority in a book that has surrendered both theological guarantees and their realistic substitutes cannot be solved, but only dissolved within play itself. When Zarathustra invites us to ''kill the Spirit of Gravity'' by laughter he traces an ascent to the dance which is the reversal of the descent to the mob of readers:

> I have learned to walk: since then I have run. I have learned to fly: since then I do not have to be pushed in order to move.
> Now I am nimble, now I fly, now I see myself under myself, now a god dances within me. (Z, 68–69; *4*, 49–50)

Surely the repeated ''now'' (*jetzt*) secures the metaphorical identification of Zarathustra's discourse and our reading with the dance.

Passages such as this certainly tend to provoke the view that *Zarathustra* is a metaphorical book. Contemporary philosophical usage is poorer than that of traditional rhetoric and poetics at this point, for philosophers now tend to use ''metaphor'' to designate language which is distinctively literary, poetic, or figurative. *Zarathustra* is metaphorical in this wide sense. Surely Aristotle, who initiated the rhetorical and philosophical discussion of metaphor, uses the term in a broad sense to designate any transference or displacement of meaning. This is significant since I will later suggest that a crucial passage in *Zarathustra* is intended (among other things) as an *Auseinandersetzung*, a confrontation with the Aristotelian conception of metaphor. It is perhaps indicative of the problematic nature of metaphor itself that the attempts in later rhetorical and poetic theory to narrow the concept by distinguishing it from other tropes or figures of speech have fallen into neglect; these attempts, which usually try to tie metaphor down to a concern with similarity or resemblance, have been replaced by a neo-Aristotelian account which again makes central the notion of transference or displacement (or, in terms of contemporary transformational grammar, ''semantic deviance'').[8] Nietzsche himself is conversant with both traditions; he uses metaphor in the wider sense in ''On Truth and Lie'' and in the narrower sense in his lectures on rhetoric. I have already suggested that

Zarathustra is not a predominantly metaphorical book in the narrower sense of metaphor; the analysis of the later parts of the book should provide more evidence that it is not and that metaphor proper is only one of a number of figurative devices employed in the text.

Nevertheless, metaphor proper does play a large role in *Zarathustra* and nowhere more obviously than in this first part. We have seen Zarathustra making a number of metaphorical identifications in his attempt at transvaluing received values. Sometimes these metaphorical identifications are stated as imperatives, as in "May your peace be a victory" (Z, 74; *4*, 59) or "Let woman be a plaything, pure and fine like a precious stone illuminated by the virtues of a world that does not yet exist" (Z, 92; *4*, 85). The general principles behind this kind of metaphorical discourse about the virtues are also stated by Zarathustra. In an important passage which will soon be discussed at length he says "All names of good and evil are images [*Gleichnisse*]." (Zarathustra employs a number of words in such contexts to describe the creation of images, metaphors, parables and the like—*Gleichniss* is the most prominent of them; later I will suggest some reason for thinking that we can treat them all as metaphors.) Such imaging or making of metaphors is often described as the creation of meaning, not only in art narrowly conceived but in the production of value, so that when Zarathustra says that "evaluation is creation" and "He who has to be a creator always has to destroy" (Z, 85) we may take him to be describing his own metaphorizing in the discourses of part one.

Still, Zarathustra's metaphors often cry out for interpretation: Take the chapter on "War and Warriors," for example (Z, 73–75; *4*, 58–60). Initially we might wonder whether Zarathustra is actually praising organized military combat, or some metaphorical analogue of such combat, or both. The two kings in part four who repeat some of Zarathustra's sayings from this chapter take them all too literally, and this probably shows that it is dangerous to put Nietzsche into the hands of kings who are not both philosophers and poets. Surely war is conceived metaphorically and Zarathustra seems to supply the key when he says "if you cannot be saints of *knowledge*, at least be its warriors" (my emphasis). Yet this only opens up more problems of interpretation. For Zarathustra suggests both that war is for the sake of something ("you should wage your war—a war for your thoughts") and that it is for the sake of battle itself ("it is the good war that hallows every cause"). And if we seek consistency by supposing that it is war for thoughts—any thoughts— which is being praised, we immediately run into another impasse. For the warrior is told both to fight for his own ideas and also that his highest virtue is obedience— and Zarathustra has no hesitation in commanding his "brothers in war" to follow the idea that he gives them: "Man is something that should be overcome." In the text we read:

> Let even your commanding be an obeying!
> To a good warrior "thou shalt" sounds more agreeable than "I will." And everything that is dear to you, you should first have commanded to you. . . .

But you should let me dictate your highest idea to you—and it is: Man is something that should be overcome. (Z, 75; *4, 59–60*)

No doubt one might seek a reading which would transcend this apparent contradiction. Or one might simply stop here, resigning oneself to Nietzsche's penchant for the paradox and the contradiction. In fact, while Nietzsche, hating (in Zarathustra's words) "the idling reader," leaves us to admire or puzzle out the provocative discourses on war, woman, and other matters, he does provide us with something like an overview of metaphorical discourse itself which may be of use in our own reading and interpretation. At several crucial points in the book Zarathustra himself turns aside from his role as a speaker and creator of meanings to become for a time a reader and interpreter of his own and others' language. Continuing to think of part one of *Zarathustra* as heavily committed to metaphor proper, such a reflective discourse on the metaphorical principle itself appears, appropriately, in its last chapter "Of the Gift-Giving Virtue" (*Von der schenckende Tugend*) (Z, 99–104; *4, 97–102*). The dramatic setting is significant. Zarathustra is about to take leave of those who call themselves his disciples, so that they will not always be disciples but may use their experience with Zarathustra to discover themselves. In Zarathustra's last address to the disciples in this chapter he declares:

You had not yet sought yourselves when you found me. Thus do all believers; therefore all belief is of so little account. Now I bid you lose me and find yourselves; and only when you have all denied me will I return to you.

I want to suggest that Zarathustra's urging his disciples to become independent of him, here explicit, is also a major motive of his *first* address to them in the same chapter. Ostensibly, that address is concerned with a farewell gift which he has received from the same disciples. It is a familiar kind of occasion, especially for academic audiences, in which students honor a departing or retiring teacher. Beyond expressing his gratitude, however, Zarathustra goes on to suggest a way of interpreting metaphorical discourses of the sort which he has been giving to his disciples up until now. In going beyond particular acts of interpretation to provide a hermeneutical framework he offers his disciples a great gift of his own: the chance to be (in Aristotle's phrase) "masters of metaphor" themselves.[9] Such mastery will involve their being able to see the point or meaning of Zarathustra's metaphors (although as we shall see this meaning will not be a reduction to the nonmetaphorical); more important, it will encourage and prepare them to be creators of such discourses themselves. In narrating this lesson, which encapsulates the ancient quarrel of philosophy and poetry, Nietzsche shows that he is not blindly opting for a poetic mode of writing philosophy but that his writing is sufficiently reflexive and dialectical to give an account of itself. Taken in conjunction with the idea of metaphor developed in Zarathustra's discourse, there is a challenge to the whole rationalist attempt either to subsume poetry within philosophy (as being a deviant or ambiguous way of making prosaic statements, for example) or to exclude it altogether from rational discourse (on such alleged grounds as its emotive character).

Let us see whether Zarathustra's discourse justifies these general claims. The farewell gift is a staff "upon the golden haft of which a serpent was coiled about a sun." The gift is itself a response to Zarathustra's challenge at the end of his last discourse, "Of Voluntary Death." Zarathustra foresees his own death as a consummation of his teaching and hopes that his friends will continue what he has begun:

> Truly, Zarathustra had a goal, he threw his ball: Now may your friends be the heirs of my goal, I throw the golden ball to you.
> But best of all I like to see you, too, throwing the golden ball, my friends! (Z, 99; 4, 95–96)

After showing his delight in the staff by leaning on it, Zarathustra proceeds to interpret its meaning, beginning with the gold orb:

> Tell me: how did gold come to have the highest value? Because it is uncommon and useless and shining and mellow in lustre; it always bestows itself.
> Only as an image [*Abbild*, which also has the meanings of copy or representation] of the highest virtue did gold come to have the highest value. Gold-like gleams the glance of the giver. Gold-lustre makes peace between moon and sun.
> The highest virtue is uncommon and useless, it is shining and mellow in lustre: the highest virtue is a bestowing virtue.

Here we have an elementary hermeneutic situation. Something is *given* to the interpreter, as we say, and Zarathustra is grateful that there are always such givens susceptible of interpretation. In this case that which is given is suggestive of the activity of giving itself. As a teacher Zarathustra's interest in method is of at least equal importance to his interest in substance. It is not only the content of the interpretation which concerns us, but the fact that an interpretation can be given at all, and the principles by which it is achieved. We might think of the staff as a difficult case, one of those troublesome questions which students sometimes pose without quite knowing what they are doing; for it is a visual image rather than an overt piece of discourse. Yet Zarathustra, the master of metaphor, can master even such a difficult case, treating it as if it were possible to interpret it in the same way that one would interpret a bit of language. For he proceeds to give a linguistic account of its meaning and to link his explication to the "names" and "images" (*Gleichnisse*) which are parts of overtly verbal discourse about virtue. The somewhat ambiguous status of the visual image—between nature and language—may suggest that although Zarathustra's disciples have learned enough to be grateful for, they have not yet become strong and independent enough to present their master with the gift of discourse itself (for example, they're not yet able to produce a *Festschrift*). Zarathustra uses the expression *in Gleichnisse reden*—to speak in parables—several times in this address. This is a clear reminiscence of Jesus' speaking in parables; but in Nietzsche's anti-Bible the disciples (or the readers) are to be encouraged to interpret such parables themselves and to have the strength to produce parables of their own.

The gold orb is reminiscent of the sun which Zarathustra praises at the very beginning of the book for its ever-renewed power to give. The gold orb suggests the bestowing virtue, being a metaphor of such virtue. So the staff is not only a gift but a metaphor for gift-giving itself. Zarathustra had begun his speech in the *Vorrede* by a metaphorical identification between himself and the sun; in recognizing that association his students show an understanding of at least one crucial metaphor in their teacher's discourse. By taking possession of the orbed staff, and even more by his interpretation of it, Zarathustra shows himself to be the master of metaphor. Now the particular image of the staff leads to a reflection on selfishness and giving in general. Giving is a virtue in the Greek sense of *arete* or the Renaissance *virtu*; it is a power, to be contrasted with the protective selfishness characteristic of a weak or sick body.

At this point there is a crucial transition in Zarathustra's discourse. He has already passed from talk about the staff to talk about giving and finally to talk about virtue. One might wonder why he should continue, for he seems to have succeeded in showing how the metaphor makes a value vivid and present. Instead he proceeds to speak of the mind and the virtues as *themselves* images (*Gleichnisse*), thus opening up a whole new line of metaphorics:

> Our mind flies upward: thus it is an image of our bodies, an image of an advance and elevation. The names of the virtues are such images of advances and elevations. Thus the body goes through history, evolving and battling. And the spirit—what is it to the body? The herald, companion, and echo of its battles and victories.

There is a new metaphorical relation announced here: the mind and the virtues are metaphors of the body and its "advances and elevations." Rather than interpret this particular metaphor (which is surely not an unusual thought for readers of Nietzsche) let me suggest that we should attend to the way in which it is linked to the previous one of the gold orb as metaphor of the bestowing virtue. The rapid juxtaposition of two metaphors is a rhetorical device recognized at least since Aristotle: the formation of a proportional metaphor. Here the proportion can be represented thus:

$$\frac{\text{gold}}{\text{the bestowing virtue}} = \frac{\text{mind and virtue}}{\text{body (bodily power)}}$$

Gold is to the bestowing virtue as virtue is to the body. Now in such a proportional metaphor two pairs of things each exhibit the same relation; therefore (as the diagrammatic or mathematical representation indicates) the first may also be linked to the third or the second to the fourth. One of Aristotle's clearest examples in the

Rhetoric is "the cup is the shield of Dionysus"; just as the wine cup is the symbol of Dionysus, so the shield is the symbol of Ares.[10] If Zarathustra is constructing a proportional metaphor then we should expect him to link gold with the body or the bestowing virtue with the mind and virtues in general. In fact, looking ahead to the end of Zarathustra's address, we find him coming very close to stating one of these consequences of the proportion: "It is power, this new virtue; it is a ruling idea, and around it a subtle soul; a golden sun, and around it the serpent of knowledge." I say that Zarathustra comes "close" to making gold a metaphor for the body. In doing so he calls our attention back to the visual image which has of course been present to his disciples all through the talk (so far as we can tell from the text Zarathustra is still leaning on it). In this last statement, however, it is actually a new proportion which has been developed, namely:

$$\frac{\text{power (new virtue)}}{\text{subtle soul}} = \frac{\text{golden sun}}{\text{serpent of knowledge}}$$

Now by reinforcing the parallelism between power (clearly a bodily thing both in this passage and in much of Nietzsche) and the golden sun, Zarathustra by means of a *new* proportional metaphor draws out the consequence of the original one. Beyond this he demonstrates the indefinitely generative principle of metaphor and the powerful body themselves.

I have suggested that Nietzsche is in some way or other alluding to Aristotle's conception of the proportional metaphor. But several differences between Aristotle's principles and Nietzsche's practice are evident. In what follows I intend to show that these differences can be elaborated in terms of Nietzsche's critique of the Aristotelian conception of language, metaphor, and the relation of philosophy to poetics and rhetoric. Yet we might note initially that whereas Aristotle favors the compression of metaphorical discourse and of the proportional metaphor in particular, Zarathustra's discourse is quite extended. Aristotle praises Pericles for his saying that the loss of the city's youth during the Peloponnesian War was as if the spring had been taken out of the year; Pericles simply goes to the point. Zarathustra, in the pasage we have been examining, constructs and elaborates many of the kinds of thoughts which would, by Aristotelian standards, be brilliantly suggested in a single striking sentence. Yet this stylistic deviation has its own dramatic, rhetorical, and philosophical purposes. Zarathustra, let us remember, is a teacher who is giving his students (whom he will be leaving for a long time) a farewell lesson of great importance, one of which is designed to liberate them from their subordinate status as students and disciples. Such a lesson needs to be made relatively explicit.

But there are other and more powerful reasons for Zarathustra (and Nietzsche) to be so generous in the gift of metaphorical speech. For the discourse is not only an example of metaphor and a clue to the interpretation by others of Zarathustra's metaphors; it is also an argument for the necessity of metaphorical speech and a critique of those views which would take metaphor to be ornamental or dispensable. One aspect of the proportional metaphor just elaborated can alert us to this. Whereas

in the proportional metaphors cited by Aristotle the relationship between the elements in each pair is fairly straightforward, in Zarathustra's proportion the relations
are themselves metaphorical. So, for example, the youth of Athens and the spring
of the year (in Pericles' speech) are each the choicest parts; if I say "the camel is
the ship of the desert" the relation between camel and desert or ship and sea is the
straightforward one of being a standard or convenient mode of transportation. If a
metaphor can be analyzed only into other metaphorical elements, this suggests (as
Zarathustra also says explicitly) that metaphor is inescapable; and it offers the
beginning of an argument as to why this should be so: because the metaphor cannot
be grounded on a literal level of speech. Now if this were the case in a casual or
peripheral use of metaphor we might not see it as having any great consequences.
But in a context in which Zarathustra is both demonstrating and teaching the mastery
of metaphor, the suggestion requires careful consideration.

As soon as Zarathustra has constructed the proportional metaphor which we
have been examining he proceeds to a general endorsement of metaphorical discourse; in fact he claims that all talk about the virtues and other "spiritual" things
is metaphorical. And for us there is the lesson that we ought not to avoid metaphor:

> All names of good and evil are images [*Gleichnisse*]: they do not speak out, they only
> hint. He is a fool who seeks knowledge from them. Whenever your spirit wants to speak
> in images, pay heed; for that is when your virtue has its origin and beginning.

Now this thought is easily recognizable as one of the main ideas about philosophical
discourse which give rise to Nietzsche's problematic of philosophical communication. Its repetition in this context is methodical rather than gratuitous, for it is
part of the lesson which Zarathustra is giving his disciples. In fact it is both illustrated
in Zarathustra's own metaphorical discourses (including this one) and it is the
consequence of the proportional metaphor linking gold, virtue, and the body.

To see that this is the case we need to focus on the subject and substance of
the proportional metaphor. Far from being simply an illustration of an Aristotelian
rhetorical device, Zarathustra's metaphor, taken materially as well as formally, is
intended as a parody and inversion of a strong tradition about the nature of metaphorical language and its relation to literal discourse. According to one very powerful school of thought about metaphor, there must be one term or element within
the metaphor which is itself non-metaphorical. Quite frequently this is believed to
be something of the nature of thought or spirit, which is said to take on some bodily
clothing.[11] Given the two notions of proportional analogy and of the material or
bodily as the less intelligible form of the intellectual or spiritual, it is not a large
step to construct something like a Thomistic conception of analogical language.
Here the final term of an Aristotelian proportional metaphor would be that which
is supremely intelligible and which makes everything else intelligible. In fact, as
Nietzsche suggests in *Twilight of the Idols* ("How the 'Real World' at Last Became
a Myth") Platonism and Christianity are at one in positing the real world which is
intelligible in itself as existing behind the scenes. Plato's analogy of the sun and
the Good differs from the analogical logic of Aquinas or of Dante's *Paradiso* in

so far as the former is "attainable now for the wise man" while the latter is only "promised" to the virtuous and faithful. The difference here is simply a greater stress on the limits of the human senses and intellect in relation to their ultimate intelligible goal. The development of European nihilism, Nietzsche might say, can be traced both in the realm of metaphorical conception and in that of the philosophical use and evaluation of poetic language. Now since God is dead, Christian poetry which points to an intellectual vision of God must be replaced by a poetry of the body. Or, to stress that the point has implications far wider than Nietzsche's critique of religion, if there is no intelligible and rational ground of things, it is inappropriate to use a philosophical language which employs forms borrowed from the rationalist tradition. Rhetoric and poetics are not philosophically neutral; the remark "I fear that we are not getting rid of God because we still believe in grammar" (T, "Reason in Philosophy," 5) suggests the need for transformations of our linguistic *praxis* appropriate to the realization that the *only* world is that of the body.

To give thoughts a bodily guise is (in the tradition) to express them metaphorically. But to take the body as the final term of the metaphor is to suggest that that which occupies the traditional place of the most intelligible is precisely that which renders discourse metaphorical and incapable of a transparent rational elucidation or of any approximation to such an elucidation. It is important to note that Zarathustra is not implying that the body is really more intelligible than the mind; if he were, then he would simply be proposing to replace logic or onto-theology with physiology. The body is the ground or base of the virtues and of spirit and it is a key to their interpretation, since they are metaphors of the body; but it is not intrinsically intelligible (at least by the standards of traditional science and metaphysics). Elsewhere Nietzsche suggests that the body is itself a very complex social community of wills to power, so that the body as a single thing is a displacement (or metaphor) of something else (*BGE*, 19; 5, 32–3). And there is little reason to think that these wills to power could be understood through an intuition or reason purged of the figurative. They too are to be comprehended metaphorically.

At this point, however, it appears that by eliminating any contrasting concept for metaphor, Zarathustra (or Nietzsche) is himself saying something unintelligible. That is, the view put forward in Zarathustra's address seems to be something like this: a metaphor is always a metaphor of another metaphor which in turn is a metaphor of another . . . *ad infinitum*. Nietzsche could very well accept this translation of his view, although he would have the style to do it in the spirit in which Zarathustra accepts his animals' version of eternal recurrence by mockingly calling it a hurdy-gurdy song. Metaphor, as Jacques Derrida has pointed out in "White Mythology," is not a philosophically neutral term but one which comes laden with the attempts of philosophy to comprehend and subordinate poetry or at least to exclude it from the domain of philosophy proper.[12] Rather than giving us a new theory of metaphor, it might be more accurate to say (following the usage of Heidegger and Derrida) that Zarathustra is placing the concept of metaphor under erasure. We cannot pull ourselves up by our own bootstraps and begin to speak a language untouched by the Western tradition; but we can use that language and the concepts embedded in it artfully, so as to suggest or evoke a different approach. This helps to explain why Nietzsche would deviate from the tradition only in a form which contains a complex critique and parody of the tradition itself. For he has Zarathustra use Aristotle's favorite form of the metaphor to suggest the invalidity both of Aristotle's theory of metaphor and of the views of language, mind, and body on which it is based.

Let me suggest some ways in which the lesson contained in Zarathustra's proportional metaphor bears on two sorts of hermeneutical questions which have already been suggested. These focus on the smaller and larger ends of the continuum of textual meaning. We want to know whether Zarathustra's discourse about metaphor aids in the interpretation of some of the earlier metaphors of part one and also whether it helps to establish the claim that a Nietzschean text has an order and coherence arising from the problematics of philosophical communication itself. The first problem has a priority because if *Zarathustra* can aid in interpreting at least some of its own metaphors, it may also have a more thorough dialectical and self-referential structure.

Now it should be clear that Zarathustra's discourse "On the Gift-Giving Virtue" shows that we should not expect a successful interpretation of his metaphors to yield a reduction or translation into non-metaphorical terms. So in the chapter on "War and Warriors" there is no literal base which can be used to ground the metaphorical complex of combat, risk, and obedience. Thought or idea (*Gedanke*) and knowledge (*Erkenntnis*) are themselves to be conceived as metaphors for elevations of the body and its activities, so that war is a bodily metaphor for intellectual struggle which is in turn a metaphor for something having to do with the body. No reduction of such a metaphor is possible because even the body is a kind of metaphor; just as, significantly, no reduction is desirable because the ability to speak freely in metaphor is itself a sign of the body's desired heightening of power. But it may seem that this oscillation of bodily and spiritual meanings volatilizes the sense of the passage rather than rendering it more determinate. It may be a progress in understanding, however, just to be relieved of the necessity of finding either a spiritual or physicalistic interpretation of such passages. In fact the interpretation suggests the degree to which we must keep in mind that for Zarathustra it is only the metaphorical expressions of the body in spirit which have value and, conversely, his insistence that we cannot lose sight of the bodily ground of these values.

Like the staff given him by his disciples, the gift which Zarathustra gives them in return is a glowing collection of metaphors surrounded by a wisdom which encircles or is tied to the metaphorical itself. Jacques Derrida has elaborated upon this centrality of the golden orb or bestowing sun in the classical theory of metaphor and Bernard Pautrat has suggested its importance within Nietzsche's imagery in a variety of his texts. Derrida's aim is to show that philosophy fails in its aim of subsuming metaphor within the conceptual because the very terms in which it attempts to do this are parts of an obscured but ineluctable metaphorical complex. Whether or not this is true of the tradition, what Nietzsche is attempting here is an explicit inversion of that tradition which anticipates Derrida's reading of the implicit deconstruction which the tradition is supposed to exercise upon itself. Nietzsche has found the language appropriate to the point which was made so much more awkwardly and inconsistently in the essay "On Truth and Lie." Besides that, he has put metaphor in its place as one typical mode of language which needs to be supplemented by others in a comprehensive treatment of the possibilities of discourse. Such a play and array of linguistic modes unfolds in the other parts of *Zarathustra*.

III

As Nietzsche records in *Ecce Homo* and in his letters, each part of *Zarathustra* was written during a brief period of inspiration. Nevertheless the book was planned earlier and anticipated in the last sections of his previous book, *The Gay Science*. Each part was published separately, with one part appearing before the next was complete. Since the planning, composition, and publication of the book stress the importance of its division into parts the reader ought to be aware that each of these divisions may have a distinctive tone, purpose, and strategy. The opening of part two is different from anything which has preceded it and alerts us to the new emphasis which it gives to Zarathustra's career. Having preserved his solitude again for "months and years" he awakes with a start from a dream:

> Why was I so frightened in my dream that I awoke? Did not a child carrying a mirror come to me?
> "O Zarathustra," the child said to me, "look at yourself in the mirror!"
> But when I looked into the mirror I cried out and my heart was shaken: for I did not see myself, I saw the sneer and grimace of a devil. Truly, I understand the dream's omen and warning all too well: my teaching [*Lehre*] is in danger, weeds want to be called wheat! My enemies have grown powerful and have distorted the image [*Bildnis*] of my teaching, so that my dearest ones are ashamed of the gifts I gave them.
> My friends are lost to me; the hour has come to seek my lost ones! (Z, 107; 4, 105–106)

While the first part began with Zarathustra's metaphorical identification with the sun, the second begins with an image of self-division. Zarathustra has been split into two parts—one true and one false. Earlier he had narrowed down an indifferent audience for his teaching to a select group of students; but this selection has had the consequence of making him one thing for his students and something else for all the others. To have friends, Nietzsche often suggests, is also to have enemies, a fact which is mystified by all of those universalistic ethical views (such as Christianity, utilitarianism, and socialism) which do not recognize how crucial are such things as loyalty, affiliation, and opposition.

In this part of the book Zarathustra will be concerned with the will and the obstacles which it encounters in attempting to will itself. This is quite different from part one's stress on the importance of creative valuation. Metaphorical and artistic efforts to produce a style of values are not sufficient by themselves; they are countered by such things as the "enemies" and so require acts of will. So Zarathustra's interest in willing here is motivated by an experience which he has had in his career as a teacher. It would be a mistake, however, to see this shift as a stage in an irreversible temporal sequence; it is rather that Zarathustra's wisdom which again pains him by its abundance is too great to be compressed into any single form of language. It has no single authoritative interpretation in the language of men, so there is a need to suggest its susceptibility to a variety of different turnings and readings. Or as Zarathustra says:

> I go new ways, a new speech comes to me; like all creators I have grown weary of the old tongues. . . . How I now love anyone to whom I can simply speak! My enemies too are part of my happiness. (Z, 108; 4, 106–107)

Who are Zarathustra's enemies? Most immediately they are those denounced by name (or category) throughout this part of the book. While the first part of *Zarathustra* can be compared in some ways to the beatitudes of the gospels, this one recalls the condemnations of the Jewish prophets. The enemies include the priests, the rabble, the men of culture, believers in pure knowledge, famous wise men, and the scholars; they are not simply Zarathustra's enemies but paradigms of what it is to be an enemy since their deepest motive is that reactive hostility which is elsewhere called *ressentiment*. Perhaps the clearest form of such vengefulness is described in Zarathustra's talk "Of the Tarantulas." The vengeful profess a concern for justice and equality; in fact they are frustrated seekers after power who, unable to directly impose their own will on others, have turned to a strategy which aims at insuring that no one can rise *above* their level.

Such a reaction may also be called envy (*Neid*), an attitude which Zarathustra had already encountered in "Of the Tree on the Mountainside." There Zarathustra had come upon a youth who deliberately avoided him. Such avoidance, it emerges, is due neither to indifference nor to anger but to envy, which can be defined as hostility toward the good of another so great that one wishes the other's good destroyed even if it will bring no gain (and even, possibly, a loss) to oneself. As Zarathustra explains, envy operates like the wind. Both forces are invisible, providing the spectacle of action at a distance. One avoids the object of envy only in a superficial way; envy which is not expressed tends to grow in isolation, just as the imagined grandeur of the envied one will grow in such conditions. Envy is the inverse and sometimes the consequence of noble aspiration:

> Now it is with men as with this tree. The more it wants to rise into the heights and the light, the more determinedly do its roots strive earthwards, downwards, into the darkness, into the depths—into evil. (Z, 69; 4, 51)

If one wants to fly but compares oneself unfavorably with those who do, one's envy takes the form of a fear (and hatred) of flying. (In the immediately preceding section, "Of Reading and Writing," Zarathustra had boasted of his own agile climbing, flying, and dancing.) Now the youth confesses:

> My contempt and my desire increase together; the higher I climb, the more do I despise him who climbs. What do I want in the heights?
> How ashamed I am of my climbing and stumbling! How I scorn my violent panting! How I hate the man who can fly! How weary I am in the heights! (Z, 70; 4, 52)

Zarathustra's advice to the youth is reassuring. He throws his arm around him and takes him for a walk, telling him that he must not fear his own noble aspirations and suggesting that he still has the youth and energy to keep his highest hope holy (Z, 71).

Perhaps this rather simple solution justifies Walter Kaufmann's calling this chapter "advice for adolescents" in his brief commentary. The forms of envy and *ressentiment* which Zarathustra encounters in the second part of the book are more strongly rooted and institutionalized, as their names suggest (e.g., "Scholars," "Education," "Famous Wise Men"). Moreover, all forms of envy are intensified by the death of God. While God lives (that is, while belief in God is still possible), envy can be minimized by insisting that all men are equal before God. In other words, the distance between all men and God is so great that any differences among us must seem very minor by comparison. Before God, as the saying goes, all men are equals or brothers. If God is dead, the only scale remaining is the one which measures differences *among* men and these are capable of being infinitely magnified by the envious eye or, more simply, "the evil eye." In the first part of *Zarathustra*, Zarathustra is in all ways the opposite of the envious person. If the latter is comparable to a black hole which seeks to destroy all which comes within its range, Zarathustra is like the sun or the glowing orb which he praises in "Of the Bestowing Virtue." Some people are simply stars, always radiating strength and expressing themselves fully in metaphor.

Yet every black hole was once, however briefly, a star. This is the lesson that Zarathustra must learn when he confronts his own envy in "The Night Song" of the second part. There the teacher who had confidently accepted the gift which identified him with the glowing sun laments his own radiant brilliance. Being nothing but a star is too limiting; even such a sun can experience envy:

> Light am I: ah, that I were night! But this is my solitude, that I am girded round with light.
> Ah, that I were dark and obscure! How I would suck at the breasts of light! . . .
> I do not know the joy of the receiver; and I have often dreamed that stealing must be more blessed than receiving.
> It is my poverty that my hand never rests from giving; it is my envy that I see expectant eyes and illumined nights of desire. (Z, 129; 4, 136)

The truth of Zarathustra's dream which opens part two is that he harbors enemies within himself. All limitation seems an excuse for envy and vengefulness.

After confronting his own enmity, Zarathustra goes on to sing "The Dancing Song" in which he confesses that he finds Life—personified as a woman—unfathomable, and Wisdom—also a woman—as perhaps even more seductive and elusive. Zarathustra is presumably shaken by the discovery of his own mutability and so hopes that Life, at least, will be constant despite her changing appearances. When she confesses her own mutability—"I am merely changeable and untamed and in everything a woman and no virtuous one"—Zarathustra refuses to believe her. Zarathustra's Wisdom, or strictly speaking an unidentified voice within, prods him with questions: "Why? Wherefore? Whereby? Whither? Where? How? Is it not folly to go on living?" (Z, 133; 4, 141). Having acknowledged his own envy and enmity, finding no secure counter-balance in the constancy of life, Zarathustra wonders if there can be any point in living in a world that is so resistant to his attempts to understand it. He is unable to see that Life was merely speaking the truth about herself and that a mutable world can still be understood by means of the idea of will to power. Before he can see that, Zarathustra moves from the sadness which comes over him at the end of "The Dance Song" to a fuller form of despair. For the thought of death has propelled him into an elegy for those who are already dead:

> O, you sights and visions of my youth! O, all you glances of love, you divine moments [*ihr Blicke der Liebe alle, ihr göttlichen Augenblicke*]! How soon you perished! Today I think of you as my dead ones. (Z, 133; 4, 142)

It may not be immediately apparent just whom Zarathustra is mourning here. The dead ones are simply the moments (*Augenblicke*) of his own past, his "youth's visions and dearest marvels" (Z, 134). To see one's own past as a collection of dead friends is in keeping with the fragmentation of the self characteristic of this metonymical section of the book. Although Zarathustra and the moments "were made for one another . . . made for faithfulness like me, and for tender eternities" they have been stolen in a crime worse than murder. Why *worse* than murder? To kill a man is not, by itself, to produce an agonizing internal division for him. But to send the lovely moments of a man's past to their graves, to render them irretrievable while the man still lives, is to produce a painful and inescapable split between the man's past and his present.

Who are these enemies? Zarathustra does not name them here, and one might suppose that they are roughly identical with the catalogue of enemies denounced throughout part two. Yet it might be more accurate to say that Zarathustra is suffering from a generalized rancor against what he later calls "time and its *it was*" (Z, 161) which he will discover to be the source of all revenge. So while some of the responsibility for the death of the beautiful *Augenblicke* must be attributed to those who represent specialized vengefulness of one sort or another, he himself is also the enemy and the murderer to the extent that he has acquiesced in, moralized, and rationalized the simple binary division of time into the living present of experience and the dead time of the past.

In the chapter "Of Redemption" Zarathustra develops his thoughts about "time and its 'it was' '' in a series of speeches. They are addressed first to a hunchback, then to his disciples, and finally to himself; the whole sequence suggests how the problems of time and revenge are bound up with the search for the philosophically appropriate way of speaking to specific audiences. The hunchback challenges Zarathustra to make the cripples whole again, promising him their belief if he does. Zarathustra's reply is concerned with the nature of fragmentation. The truly fragmented person is not the one who is missing a bodily part, but the one whose spirit (*Geist*) has been fragmented by the atrophy through disuse of some of its chief capacities. One who is spirtually nothing but a walking ear has less chance of being a great man than does one who is simply missing an ear. Turning away from the hunchback to his disciples Zarathustra attempts to explain why men are fragmented and confesses his own fragmentation. Men are everywhere "shattered in pieces and scattered as if over a battle-field of slaughter" and it is this painful sight which Zarathustra admits is his "most intolerable burden." These visions of dismembered and fragmented bodies are emblematic of Zarathustra's experience of opposition and self-division in this part. To "walk among men as among fragments of the future" is one way to overcome the burden of past and present. In psychoanalytic terms, this is the contrast developed by Melanie Klein between the acknowledgement of the whole body and the obsession with independent bodily parts. Yet even if one has such hopes for the future how can one redeem the past?

> To redeem the past and to transform every 'It was' into an 'I wanted it thus!'—that alone do I call redemption! . . .
> Willing liberates: but what is it that fastens in fetters even the liberator?
> 'It was': that is what the will's teeth-gnashing and most lonely affection is called. Powerless against that which has been done, the will is an angry spectator of all things past.
> The will cannot will backwards; that it cannot break time and time's desire—that is the will's most lonely affliction. (Z, 161; 4, 179–80)

When the will comes up against the ineluctability of the past it becomes wrathful and ill-tempered. Even if all of the other occasions and excuses for revenge could be overcome, the will would still be so frustrated from its impotence over the past that it would seek revenge upon anyone who does not seem to share its own wrath and distemper. But not being able to admit its own vengefulness the will represents its own activities and time's "perpetual perishing" (in Locke's phrase) as punishment for some offense. Turning against itself—for it must recognize that it is as subject to the punishment of temporal existence as any other object of its revenge—it imagines the only possible redemption as the surrender of the will itself. " 'Except the will at last redeem itself, and willing become not-willing—': but you, my brothers, know this fable-song of madness!'' (Z, 162; 4, 181). Now Zarathustra will soon be immersed in a struggle with his most abysmal thought of eternal recurrence; that thought offers a way of transforming the obstinate "it was" into the creative "But I willed it thus!" We too will have to attempt to understand what eternal recurrence means for Zarathustra and for ourselves. At this point in the text, however, we are brought back to Nietzsche's concern with language. The theme is made explicit by the hunchback; he has been eavesdropping during the long address and now asks why Zarathustra spoke to him differently from the way he spoke to his disciples.

> Zarathustra answered: "What is surprising in that? One may well speak crossly [*bucklicht reden*] to a hunchback [*Bucklichte*]."
> "Very good," said the hunchback; "and with pupils one may very well tell tales out of school.
> "But why does Zarathustra speak to his pupils differently—than to himself?" (Z, 163; 4, 182).

Divided against himself by the will's collision with time, Zarathustra's speech is also fragmented. Zarathustra's own account of this (which the hunchback has overheard) is that "It is difficult to live among men because keeping silent is so difficult. Especially for a babbler [*für einen Geschwätzigen*]." But to the extent that one is dominated by the binary oppositions with which Zarathustra is concerned here, silence may just not be possible. Zarathustra has been brought into polemical discourse with a whole range of purported forms of wisdom; these discourses illustrate the structure of duality essential to all revenge. Such talk will always be "talking at." We might imagine Zarathustra as having been silent during this series of confrontations. But because he shares in the general structure of envy and enmity such silence would in fact be a two-sided conversation in need of external mediation in order to be brought to a more fruitful level of exchange. Such an internal duality would be like the one that Zarathustra himself has described in "Of the Friend":

> "One is always too many around me"—thus speaks the hermit. "Always once one—in the long run that makes two." I and Me are always too earnestly in conversation with one another: how could it be endured if there were not a friend? (Z, 82; 4, 70)

Zarathustra also knows that the desire for a friend may mask an inadequacy of our own; specifically we often "want only to leap over envy with our love." It is better to work through and express that envy than to be torn apart through the dualities of the internal conversation or to seek a friendship for which one is not yet ready.

The language of internal division is articulated in two chapters which deal with two modalities of discourse: the contest between philosophy and poetry ("Of Poets") and the interpretation of dreams ("The Prophet"). "Of Poets" begins as an elaborate and playful scholastic exercise on that old chestnut, the liar's paradox:

silence would have as its fruit an internal polemic between the different aspects of the self. The aggressive tone of this whole part of the book is inseparable from its leading thoughts and its rhetorical situation. In such a situation even Zarathustra is susceptible to revenge, and revenge will lead to the inadequate, world-denying language of priests, scholars, or poets. The language of internal division becomes even more prominent in two other chapters; in "Of Poets" Zarathustra confesses to being a poet who is at war with poetry while "The Prophet" presents us with a dream and its interpretation. Following Freud, we can read this last dream as a compact text which comments on the larger one.

"Of Poets" is an elaborate play upon the poetic version of the liar's paradox: the poet, Zarathustra, says that poets lie, proceeding to parody the famous final chorus of *Faust* and to attack the metaphorical principle itself. This reductive treatment of poetry is startling when juxtaposed with Zarathustra's earlier metaphorical attempts to empty himself of his wisdom, but it is thoroughly in keeping with the reductive metonymies in this section. Just as the will founders on the ineluctability of the "it was," so the poetic principle collapses when interrogated through dialogue; its attempts to bridge the gap between earth and heaven are exposed as fabrications. This is Nietzsche's version of the Platonic critique of poetry in the *Republic*; but Zarathustra, unlike Socrates, acknowledges that he himself is a poet. The structure of the chapter is itself dyadic: in the first part Zarathustra converses with a disciple and then, in the second, abruptly turns to the soul's converse with itself. And the tone of both conversations is set by the larger *Auseinandersetzung* (confrontation) between Zarathustra's discourse and Goethe's poetry, which is taken to be representative of the whole poetic tradition.

Zarathustra's initial remark seems to regard poetry as simply a collection of doctrines one of which happens to clash with his own reduction of spirit to the body:

> "Since I have known the body better," said Zarathustra to one of his disciples, "The spirit has been only figuratively [*gleichsam*] spirit to me; and all that is "intransitory"—that too has been only an "image" [*"und alles das 'unvergängliche'—das ist auch nur ein Gleichnis"*]. (Z, 149; 4, 163)

The parody of the *Faust* chorus is continued through the chapter, and it parallels a more serious critique of poetry's metaphorical longings for the eternal ("we desire even those things the old women tell one another in the evening. We call that the eternal-womanly in us") and its vain desire for an audience. That *Faust* should be the basis of the critique shows that Zarathustra is ready to take on the big guns of poetry, as Socrates declared battle against "Homer and all his tribe." Goethe is usually taken to be the supreme German poet and *Faust* to be his masterpiece; the final scene in heaven, ending with the mystic chorus, can be regarded as his last poetic testament. It records Faust's salvation by stressing the priority of the eternal. Zarathustra aims at reducing such poetic metamorphoses to the pathetic fallacy and at exposing the surreptitious introduction of the eternal into poetry. Poets, says

Zarathustra, imagine that their impressions when lying in the grass are nature's speech to them; emboldened by these imaginary secrets they project their fantasies into the heavens: "we set our motley puppets on the clouds and then call them gods and supermen" (Z, 150). Apparent metaphorical unities can be reduced to the metonymic opposition of poet and nature, or poet's fantasies and imaginary eternity. Metaphor (*Gleichnis*) is here connected with metamorphosis—but such metamorphoses must be *only* imaginary. If we first missed the point that the critique applies to Zarathustra's own metaphorical chains, the self-critique is underscored by the lumping together of "gods and supermen" as "motley puppets."

Zarathustra's critique of unitary metaphor occurs in a dialogue with his disciple; in a play upon binary structures, his analysis of the poet's vain need of an audience comes when he turns away from the disciple to talk to himself. *Faust* is still the appropriate example because of Goethe's dramatic inclinations (even if *Faust II* is unactable). Richard Wagner's universalistic aspirations are undoubtedly in the background; the Hegelian dialectic which sees drama's universalism and its community of author, actors, and audience as the high point of all art and poetry may be there as well. Zarathustra's deflation of such community takes place by means of images, mirroring his attack on metaphor through dialogue with another. The false unity of the poetic peacock with his audience of buffaloes (rhetorical fiction) is just the other side of those illegitimate metamorphoses (metaphorical tropes) which attempt to bridge the gap between heaven and earth. Zarathustra's repeated exclamation of his weariness of the poets who can carry on such subterfuges continues the pastiche of Goethe by transforming his "*Ach, ich bin des Treibens müde!*" into "*Ach, wie bin ich der Dichter müde!*" ("Oh, I'm weary of doing" into "Oh, how weary I am of the poets"). If there is any hope for the poets it lies in their own weariness of themselves. Zarathustra prophesies the appearance of such self-conscious figures who will have grown out of the poets and calls them "penitents of the spirit" (*"Büsser des Geistes"*). This prophecy of poetry's self-overcoming is still parody for it refers back to the penitents at the end of *Faust*. What the poets of the future are to give up are not earthly things but fictions of metamorphosis and common understanding with their audience. They are to turn inward, as Zarathustra has turned away from his disciple and as he will turn further inward in the next major section of the book (part three). Yet Zarathustra's discourse here is not the self-consciously hermetic and difficult modernism which he sees coming; it is itself a play upon the opposition of prose and poetry which heightens their tensions. Much of Nietzsche's *Gay Science* revolves around this same tension and helps to clarify "Of Poets." The book's very title is duplicitous, referring both to the Provençal term for the art of poetry and to the more prosaic idea of science only to set up another incongruity by the addition of gaiety or joy. The text itself alternates between poetic and prosaic passages. In one secton Nietzsche suggests the fruitfulness of the tension:

> Good prose is written only face to face with poetry. For it is an uninterrupted, well-mannered war with poetry: all of its attractions depend on the way in which poetry is

continually avoided and contradicted. Everything abstract wants to be read as a prank against poetry and as with a mocking voice; everything dry and cool is meant to drive the lovely goddess into lovely despair. . . . *War is the father of all good things*; war is also the father of good prose. (*GS*, 92; *3*, 447–48)

In "The Prophet" Zarathustra hears the melancholy refrain of nihilism: "Everything is empty, everything is one, everything is past!" (Z, 155). At odds with himself, since he has not resolved the will's opposition to time, one side (at least) of Zarathustra is deeply affected by this speech. Feeling his own teaching in danger of being engulfed by the sadness of nihilism "Zarathustra went about grieving . . . in his heart; and for three days he took no food or drink, had no rest and forgot speech. At length it happened that he fell into a deep sleep." (Z, 156). This is Zarathustra's greatest experience of silence in this very dialogical and polemical part of the book, so we expect its product to be important. On awakening Zarathustra relates a dream to his disciples; his voice comes to them "as if from a great distance" indicating that his separation from himself has still not been healed. In the dream, which Zarathustra says is still obscure to him, he has renounced all life and become "a night-watchman and grave-watchman yonder upon the lonely hill-fortress of death." Guarding the glass coffins of "life overcome" Zarathustra at first finds the silence terrifying, but eventually drifts off to sleep. Awakened by three startling blows on the heavy door he finds himself unable to open it.

Then a raging wind tore the door asunder: whistling, shrilling and piercing it threw to me a black coffin: And in the roaring and whistling and swirling, the coffin burst asunder and vomited forth a thousand peals of laughter and from a thousand masks of children, angels, owls, fools, and child-sized butterflies it laughed and mocked and roared at me. (Z, 157; *4*, 174)

Zarathustra was then sufficiently terrified to shriek himself awake.

Only in this part of the book does Zarathustra need another to tell him the meaning of his discourse. His talk here is a dream-story. One who cannot understand his own dreams is suffering from a self-division of some kind. This is also evident from the content of the dream which, if the disciples' interpretation is to be trusted, represents Zarathustra as both death and life, the night-watchman and the raging wind with a thousand varied masks (we might think of Brueghel or Bosch here). Nietzsche has much to say about dreams which throws light on the dreams and visions which occur in *Zarathustra*. Although he regards dreams in general as paradigms of the confused causal thinking of everyday life, the successful dream is different:

The dream. Our dreams are, on the rare occasions when they are for once successful and perfect—usually the dream is a bungled product—chains of symbolic scenes and images in place of the language of poetic narration; they paraphrase our experiences or expectations or circumstances with such poetic boldness and definiteness that in the morning we are always astonished at ourselves when we recall our dreams. In dreaming we use up too much of our artistic capacity—and therefore often have too little of it during the day. (*HAH*, II, II 194; 2, 639)

Zarathustra's dream, or at least the dream as told, consists of both symbolic scenes and images and a narrative poetic language. It is the dream of a philosophical artist representing his own spiritual condition to himself. In this case it is a dream eminently susceptible to a structuralist analysis, based as it is on those binary patterns so congenial to the structuralist method. Life and death, sleeping and waking, noise and silence, the open and shut door, darkness and the colorful profusion of the thousand masks all contribute to the main effect. The very dualities between sleeping and waking, between the dream and its absence are themselves prominent. As the night-watchman, Zarathustra falls into a dreamless sleep, only to be awakened by the noise at the door; once awake (so he dreams) he beholds the waking dream of the thousand masks. Then he awakens into the world which he shares with the disciples. All is unmediated transition in this symbolic expression of Zarathustra's straddling the domains of passive and active nihilism and his inability to effect a continuity between the dead past and the living present.

This dream is thus an elaboration of that first dream of the hideous mirror image with which part two began. The concern with duality was never a matter of an opposition simply between oneself and one's enemies conceived as substantial selves. As this latest dream shows, the war of hostile parts may occur within the "same" person (that is, one conventionally identified as the same); as the parable in "Of Great Events" confirms, many may also become one (in the state) in a spirit of opposition to that which is other (the individual as such or other states). The presiding theme on which Nietzsche has been playing variations is what Charles Peirce called Secondness—the sense of raw shock, clash, and opposition. Yet since this is the governing thought of only one part of *Zarathustra* it would be a mistake to found an interpretation of will or will to power on the tone of these passages alone; unfortunately too many of Nietzsche's commentators have done just that.

Zarathustra's disciple interprets the dream as a vision of Zarathustra's life. His teacher is said to be "the wind with a shrill whistling that tears open the doors of the fortress of death" and the "coffin full of rotten wickedness and angel-masks of life." Yet if this were the whole account of the dream, Zarathustra would not be as slow as he is "to leave his bed and his sadness" (Z, 158). When he finally does get up he jokes about letting the prophet drown in the sea. The difference between my interpretation of the dream and that of the disciple is that, on the view offered here, Zarathustra is closer to the prophet's nihilism than the disciple realizes and so dreams himself as divided between the night-watchman of life and the vivifying wind. The disciple's final words are thus a little too glib:

Truly, you have dreamed *your enemies themselves*: that was your most oppressive dream!

But as you awoke from them and came to yourself, so shall they awake from themselves—and come to you! (Z, 158; 4, 175)

That Zarathustra has dreamed his enemies is true. But in the world of *Thus Spoke
Zarathustra* dreams and visions are not to be dismissed as mere fantasies; they are
as significant as any of our other experiences. To have dreamed one's enemies
gives one no automatic power over them unless one has power over one's dreams.
In order to gain such power Zarathustra needs a different orientation toward "time
and its 'it was' " and a transformation of his pity and disgust for mankind. What
Zarathustra needs to do is to take a more active role in his dream life. Here he is
the dreamer and another, his disciple, is the interpreter. In the next part of the book
we see Zarathustra debating with a figure in his visions (the dwarf) and using these
visions in order to rehearse his waking activities (the riddle of the shepherd and
the snake). These performances require that Zarathustra become both dreamer and
interpreter at once. In the last section of part two "The Stillest Hour," Zarathustra
is, not surprisingly, at odds with himself as to whether he has a teaching yet to be
spoken and whether he is the one to speak it. The self-divisions that can infect
language and the speaker have been explored in dialogue, song and dream; the
reader should be ready now for a new mode of discourse.

THREE

Homecoming, Private Language, and the Fate of the Self

(Zarathustra III)

Zarathustra III has frequently been taken to be the culmination of the dramatic action of Nietzsche's book as well as its philosophical center. Many critics have argued that the book might properly end here and that *Zarathustra* IV is an embarrassing afterthought. Certainly it is here that there is explicit discussion of the eternal recurrence, which Nietzsche, in *Ecce Homo*, is believed to have called the fundamental idea of the book. Yet we must note some qualifications to this view at the outset. It is Zarathustra's animals who speak explicitly of eternal recurrence, rather than the supposed teacher of the doctrine. When they do venture to tell Zarathustra what he believes and teaches he retorts that they have turned his thoughts into a "hurdy-gurdy song" and retreats even from his animals for a more solitary series of songs in which eternal recurrence is treated symbolically and allusively; and since the songs are not overheard they do not teach that thought to anybody.

What Nietzsche says literally in *Ecce Homo* is that the thought of eternal recurrence is the *Grundconception* of *Zarathustra*. He says this in a discussion devoted to explaining the personal circumstances and surroundings that led to the conception and composition of the book. These are the highly stylized reminiscences of an author relating "Why I Write Such Good Books." In that context it may be significant that Nietzsche speaks not of a *Begriff* or *Idee*, the usual German philosophical terms for a comprehensive thought or idea; instead he refers to a *Grundconception*. This is the language of the artist or writer who lets us in on the genesis of a work, what Henry James called "the germ of a story," rather than the philosopher explaining the interconnection of his major thoughts. For a *Konzept* may be a sketch or plan and is frequently used to describe a preliminary outline by a visual artist or draftsman. A *Konzeptbuch* is a sketch-book. In any case Nietzsche's expression is hardly unambiguous. In reading *Zarathustra* III, then, we ought to be guided by the language and presentation of the text and its articulation with the rest of the work rather than by the hermeneutics of the animals or by an interpretation of one of Nietzsche's later remarks about the genesis of his work.

To see how we ought to situate the eternal recurrence and some of the other themes and events of the third part we need to see what kind of language is being employed there. That is, we need to ask what its fundamental categories are, to whom it is addressed, and how it is connected to the other forms of discourse in the book or to the more prosaic types of discourse into which it is so tempting to translate it. The dominant linguistic move of part three is the exploration of the possibility of a private language; in the material mode it is Zarathustra's quest for his authentic or genuine self. I will have more to say about these somewhat suspect categories and their connection later but let us begin by reading part of Zarathustra's first speech in this part. Climbing a mountain which lies on the way that will take him away from the Blissful Islands Zarathustra speaks to himself:

> I am a wanderer and a mountain-climber (he said to his heart), I do not like the plains and it seems I cannot sit still for long.
> And whatever may yet come to me as fate and experience—a wandering and a mountain-climbing will be in it; in the final analysis one experiences only oneself.
> The time has passed when accidents could befall me; and what *could* still come to me that was not already my own?
> It is returning, at last it is coming home to me—my own self and those parts of it that have long been abroad and scattered among all things and accidents. (Z, 173; 4, 193)

"In the end one experiences only oneself": this is the formula of a phenomenology of solitude. What the passage announces is a search for the self to be undertaken by a method that excludes going beyond the self.

It soon becomes clear, however, that *what* Zarathustra has to say about the self here must determine the *way* in which he says it. The movement of this part of the book is a flight *from* public speech to the deepest and most mysterious reaches of the self—even perhaps to the point of discovering that it is just one more illusion of the public language. Zarathustra's voyage home is one in which the public dimensions of language are abandoned one by one. During the journey, which has chapters on both land and sea, Zarathustra speaks to his fellow sailors and to "Zarathustra's ape" when the latter confronts him in a city he is passing through. Once he has arrived home, however, Zarathustra either is silent or speaks to himself. His speech to his animals is part of this speech to himself which is characterized variously as his speaking "to his rejoicing conscience" (Z, 181; 4, 203) as the "stillest hour" speaking to him (Z, 182; 4, 204) or as the long address to the sky beginning "You abyss of light" (Z, 184; 4, 207). Public speech must be conducted in the public foum, but that forum is poisoned by the "enemies"; that is, *ressentiment*, the thirst for revenge, rules wherever the binary structure of linear time has not been rethought. In "The Homecoming" Zarathustra sums up this distinction between public and private speech by emphasizing the emptiness and vanity of the former:

> Down there, however—all speech is in vain! There, the best wisdom is to forget and pass by; I have learned *that*—now! . . .
> Everything among them speaks, nothing prospers and comes to an end any longer. Everyone cackles, but who still wants to sit quietly upon the nest and hatch eggs?
> Everything among them speaks; everything is talked down. And what yesterday was still too hard for time itself and its teeth, today hangs, chewed and picked from men of today. (*Z*, 204; *4*, 233)

In this mood Zarathustra views all public speech as gossip and idle chatter. As in Heidegger's analysis, the last man, man who has become small (*das Man*) is the man of idle talk (*Gerede*). Nietzsche's account is more historical than Heidegger's, although the difference is not especially relevant at this point. What Zarathustra is interested in here is the rhetorical basis of this chatter; it is a way of evading the task and problem of being human and living in time. But while Heidegger presents such idle talk as a kind of game which we play in order to hide from our own anxiety, Nietzsche focusses on the importance for public speech of envy and its derivatives. This envy is derived from *ressentiment*. Public language, even the language of the scholars, is directed at making the great appear small; this is part of the general strategy by which people seek to be revenged for "time and its 'it was,' '":

> Their stiff sages: I called them sagacious, not stiff—thus I learned to swallow words [*Worte verschlucken*]. Their gravediggers—I called them researchers and testers—thus I learned to confound words [*Worte vertauschen*]. (*Z*, 205; *4*, 234)

"The Homecoming" is a turning point because it marks Zarathustra's arrival at a place where he can comfortably and articulately use the language which is truly his own. It will be worthwhile to look at this chapter in some detail in order to understand both Zarathustra's gradual abandonment of ordinary language and the singing of new songs which follows his discovery of his own form of language. "The Homecoming" plays on a rich theme in German poetry: being alone when one is at home. (One thinks of Novalis's solipsistic "*immer nach Hause*" and of Holderlin's "*Die Heimkunft*," which, as Heidegger points out, has to do with the strangeness and distance of homecoming).[1] Here Zarathustra's soul covers with itself joyfully and from the beginning. True homecoming is not simply returning to one's geographical origins but is experiencing solitude (*Einsamkeit*) as bliss. The speech of this chapter is a dialogue between Zarathustra and his home—and his home *is* solitude—that revolves around the meaning of solitary language and its distinction from the discourse of a false community. This internal colloquy is sufficient unto itself; it is a microcosmic version of a poetic cosmos. It offers a distinct alternative to the indefinite metaphorical union with an audience of all or none projected in "Of Reading and Writing" or the metonymical opposition of teacher and disciple or inner and outer discourse found in "Of Poets." *Einsamkeit* is not *Verlassenheit* (loneliness) which one can very well experience in company. Zarathustra's solitude would reassure him that "Here all things come caressingly to your discourse and flatter you: for they want to ride upon your back. Upon every image [*Gleichnis*] you here ride to every truth" (Z, 202; 4, 231). Talk in solitude is wholly adequate to things—Zarathustra can speak to them now and they will speak to him. He has overcome the detours of loneliness which forced him to speak to an other. His speech will now be a *Dinggedicht*, a poetry of things, unlike the speech "down there" where speech is not heard in a deep sense, but simply cheapens and betrays. The inauthentic speech "down there" is constitutive for ordinary morality and knowledge. Those who *call* themselves "the good" are actually "poisonous flies." Life among those who conceal their weakness with such words leads to pity—and pity leads to the confusion of names, as when gravediggers are called investigators and scholars. In part one Zarathustra would have metaphorically identified scholars as gravediggers; now that he has his *own* language of solitude he can say that gravediggers are by confusion called scholars among themselves. Given the adequate circle of one's own language there is no need to produce a metaphorical chain to move from older meanings to new.

Zarathustra's solitude is the conscious recognition that his quest is an internal one. There is a subtle distinction between the gaps and obstacles of mundane, external speech and the differences within identity of solitary discourse. The crudity of conceptual and referential speech among the many involves a play on the German philosophical tradition: "He who wants to grasp [*begreifen*] everything human would have to grapple with [*angreifen*] everything. But for that my hands are too clean (Z, 203; 4, 233)." As in Kant and Hegel one understands things by means of concepts (*Begriffe*). Nietzsche's punning brings out the overtones of grasping with the hands which still cling to this understanding of understanding. Speaking and thinking which are assaults on things necessarily encounter unpleasant objects that one would rather not touch, and only two unsatisfactory possibilties are then open: by greedily grasping everything to oneself all room for the play of thought and discourse is destroyed (Hegel), or else speech must always run up against an impenetrable other (Kant). Here, however, Zarathustra and his solitude, Zarathustra and his animals, Zarathustra and things belong to one another without collapsing into an unqualified identity.[2] It is in terms of this self-contained play of a language adequate to one's whole world that we can understand the emphasis on the eternal recurrence as Zarathustra's *own* teaching. It is not an abstract doctrine that can be passed from mouth to mouth or hand to hand; its home is in Zarathustra's solitary silence or song, not in being seized or conceptually understood (*angriffen* or *begriffen*).

Home is where we all speak our own private language. Each of us has a shorthand system for registering our typical emotional nuances, our tastes, our sense of what is appropriate and what is jarring. This does not sound like the strict untranslatability which Wittgenstein, for example, would use to describe his concept of a private language. For it seems as if my feelings, even if rather esoteric, can be communicated to you; I can begin to provide rough translations of some of my categories and perhaps I can even produce a sort of line-by-line translation of my most intimate fantasies and emotions. In this case however translation *is* betrayal, for the very shorthand of my own language, its feeling natural for me, is what allows me to move rapidly over a number of experiences. The translation is ponderous: to perform it is both to stop playing with the web of connections and to fail to provide the sense of that play for the reader of the translation. The question is not just about the ability to provide a lexical equivalent of phrases but also has to do with the much more difficult task of conveying the style of the primary language. Nietzsche's frequent metaphor in *Zarathustra* for successful language is the dance; to translate a private language would be like providing a schematic representation of a dance in a written notation. Each would be useful but it would be a mistake to confuse either with the full sense of the original.

We see more of the point of Zarathustra's discovery of his own language by seeing the stages of that discovery itself. In "Of the Vision and the Riddle" Zarathustra mediates between his own visionary experience and an audience of sailors on the boat which is taking him home. As Zarathustra says, this is a discourse for adventurers and explorers, for it relates his own search on uncharted paths. The experience narrated by Zarathustra is characterized as a vision that occurred during two days of silence on the boat. It is comparable in some ways both to the dream of life and death interpreted in "The Soothsayer" and to the silent experience which precedes the animals' proclamation of the eternal return. In some of his earlier writings Nietzsche describes the vision (*Gesicht*) as the primary experience of which the dream is a derivative. It is a clear perception of forms in which we poetically see and construct some important aspect of our lives. Zarathustra's vision here is distinguished from the earlier dream in several ways. Unlike his disciple, the sailors offer no interpretation of the experience; Zarathustra presents it to them as a riddle. If he has not solved it for himself he will do so soon enough, on completing his homecoming, when he arises from the seven days' silence of his convalescence. This hermeneutic situation parallels the action of the two parts of the vision. In the first part Zarathustra disputes with the Spirit of Gravity; in the second he breaks his appalled silence to shout at the shepherd to bite off the head of the snake which is choking him. The dream of the prophet was a dream of immobility. There Zarathustra's ego, the night-watchman, was helpless before death and the life which was an unrecognized part of himself. He lacked that strength to say "It is a dream! I will dream on!" which Nietzsche praises. Here Zarathustra directs the content of his own vision. The dwarf (the Spirit of Gravity) is a heavy force, but he does not prevent Zarathustra from climbing to the top of his path and confronting the dwarf's nihilism at the gateway marked "Moment" (*Augenblick*) But he can climb to that gateway only by bearing the weight of the dwarf's "every stone that is thrown must—fall!" Zarathustra describes his experience of that climb as that of "one sick whom his wicked torture makes weary and who as he falls asleep is awakened by a still more wicked dream" (Z, 177; 4, 198). Dreaming is a waking up within sleep and some are not strong enough even for the dream.

Zarathustra however is not such a dreamer, but perceives himself as like the dreamer. He has the courage not to end the dream scene but to dream on, and he does this by taking command of the dream scene with his courageous "Dwarf! You! Or I!" (It should be noted that Zarathustra's short address on courage is spoken not to the dwarf in the vision but to the sailors to whom he is relating the vision.) What courage requires is "Was that life? Well then! Once more!" Courageous vision or dreaming requires a continuation of the vision or dream. The dwarf's reply to Zarathustra's questions about time takes his own abysmal thought for granted and dismisses it with a "so what?" But Zarathustra *instructs* the dwarf and explains a crucial aspect of eternal recurrence. The dwarf says that truth is crooked and "time itself is a circle" (Z, 178; 4, 200). What the dwarf is missing is the lightness and mobility of time's circle. Time's circularity ought not to be conceived as a weight imposed on it (a punishment perhaps) which would prevent it from ever getting away from its origins. It should be thought of, as in Zarathustra's query, as becoming and process: "And are not all things knotted together so firmly that this moment draws after it *all* that is to come? *Therefore*—itself too" (Z, 179; 4, 200). Here Zarathustra stops speaking to an other and falls into a reverie about some early memories; within the dialogue of the dream, he seeks a greater privacy. But he suddenly finds, in an awakening experience, that the dwarf and the whole scenery of that vision have vanished. "Was I dreaming then? Was I waking up?" he asks himself.

The vanishing of the dwarf is significant. Zarathustra remains in the visionary state and is able to continue dreaming after he overcomes this oppressive weight of the other. The dreamer has taken control of the world of vision and dream; that world is a potentially rich field for self-exploration but is also subject to distortion by the envy and revenge of the public world. To have awakened at this point would have been to have had a dream successful in itself; yet the real power of dreaming is manifested in the production of new dreams without having to wake or to fall back into sleep. In this second part of the vision Zarathustra sees the shepherd choked by the snake and after an agony of disgust calls out to him "Bite! Bite!" After spitting out the loathsome head the shepherd jumps up "a transformed being surrounded with light, *laughing!*" (Z, 180; 4, 202). Here again Zarathustra successfully takes command of his own dream. He is on his way to accomplishing the same in his waking life by making its speech thoroughly his own as he has already mastered the hieroglyphics and the drama of the dream.

On his way home Zarathustra speaks mainly to himself except for an encounter with his ape, the man who has learned to imitate him but lacks his spirit. Zarathustra's ape "had gathered something of his phrasing and cadences [*Satz und Fall der Rede*] and also liked to borrow from the treasures of his wisdom" (Z, 195; 4, 222). This ape or mimic is found in the metropolis, for it is the rhetorical aspect of Zarathustra's speech which he has learned. Rhetoric requires an audience, so the ape cannot leave the great city which he spends so much energy denouncing.

The ape's talk is worth considering if only because it resembles so closely the popular image of Nietzsche as a no-saying prophet:

> The God of Hosts is not the god of the golden ingots; the prince proposes, but the shopkeeper—disposes! . . .
> Here all blood flows foul and tepid and frothy through all veins; spit upon the great city that is the great rubbish pile where all the swill scum froths!
> Spit upon the city of flattened souls and narrow breasts, of slant eyes and sticky fingers. (Z, 197; 4, 223–24)

The ape has become immobilized in the language of enmity which Zarathustra is in the process of leaving behind. If he had the self-knowledge of Caliban, he could say "You taught me language, and my profit on't is, I know how to curse."

But Zarathustra also *overhears* the language of others. He is on his way to thinking the most godless thought of eternal recurrence and so is interested in hearing the last attenuated version of the language of religion and theology. Many of those who once had the courage to reject God have become pious again. Passing through a city Zarathustra hears some of these who have become night-watchmen who "know how to blow horns and to walk about at night and to awaken old things that had long gone to sleep" (Z, 200; 4, 229). We might plausibly think of these night-watchmen as those who have once experienced the death of a living religion but now want to hold on to some vestige of religious consciousness. They know that there is no empirical evidence which would make their belief in God probable but wish to insist on the importance of their thoughts and talk about him. Zarathustra reports that he heard this conversation among night-watchmen:

> "For a father he does not look after his children enough; human fathers do it better."
> "He is too old! He no longer looks after his children at all"—thus the other night watchman answered.
> "Has he any children? No one can prove it, if he doesn't prove it himself. I have long wished he would prove it thoroughly for once."
> "Prove it? As if *he* has ever proved anything! He finds it hard to prove things; he thinks it very important that people should believe in him."
> "Yes! Yes! Belief makes him happy, belief in him. Old people are like that! So shall we be too!" (Z, 201; 4, 229)

Like Zarathustra's achieved language of this part, the talk of the night-watchmen is not referential in any ordinary way. Their discourse is the talk characteristic of passive nihilism. What is important for these people is to keep on talking, to tell a satisfying story which will while away the darkest hours of the night. They are like many existentialist theologians who argue that faith is more heroic and blessed the more absurd and unverifiable its object of belief. Perhaps they resemble even more closely one of the positions adumbrated in John Wisdom's essay "Gods" in which the dispute about whether a bit of land is a tended garden turns into a kind of ultimate aesthetic choice about two competing forms of language or life. It would be a mistake to conflate this language with Zarathustra's; as the incident suggests, the stories told by the night-watchmen are the last and most tenuous justifications of a way of life and speech which serves only to maintain the equanimity of the elderly. Zarathustra has his own story to tell about the gods: they died of laughter when one of their number was impudent enough to suggest that he was the *only* god. Zarathustra's story is his and he recognizes it as such; it is told for the sake of a laugh, and it parodies the ethereal scholasticism and the guesses about the unknown that we have just heard. If language is to loosen its connection with the world, why bother to refine the old stories when we could be devising new ones? And why should we have to adjust our speech to those who tell such stories? Why should I accept a private language designed by a committee?

On his way home Zarathustra has shown his increasing mastery of his own language in the dream and has observed the emptying out of metaphysical language. Metaphysical language is here understood as all discourse which introduces trans-phenomenal entities. To speak one's own language is to speak of one's experienced world; this is Zarathustra's phenomenological move in part three. Once this phenomenological limitation or opening is understood, there should be little temptation to construe eternal recurrence as an impersonal cosmological idea. Consider, for example, Zarathustra's praise of chance in "Before Sunrise":

> Truly, it is a blessing and not a blasphemy when I teach: "Above all things stands the heaven of chance, the heaven of innocence, the heaven of accident, the heaven of wantonness."
> "Lord Chance" ["*Von Ohngefahr*]—he is the world's oldest nobility which I have given back to all things; I have released them from servitude under purpose. (Z, 186; *4*, 209)

Although Zarathustra contrasts chance with purpose here, his description of the spontaneity of experience is also opposed to any deterministic reduction of experienced chance to an epiphenomenon of a world of non-experienced scientific objects and laws. Zarathustra's opposition to metaphysical language includes the attempts of both religion and science to introduce a world behind the scenes. In the *The Genealogy of Morals* Nietzsche will show the nihilistic affinities between religion and science while demonstrating how scientific language can be made to contradict and overcome itself. The eternal recurrence may now appear even more paradoxical than it did before. Surely, it seems, the cycle of events must be determined if it is to repeat itself, and yet Zarathustra praises the chance quality of events. Of course the phenomenological experience of what is novel and surprising would *itself* be one of the experiences repeated in eternal recurrence.

The presentation of eternal recurrence in the chapter "The Convalescent" is set within the context of Zarathustra's search for his own thought and his own language. As with some other difficult philosophical ideas it has been placed at a distance from its author. It is described in the text as Zarathustra's thought, rather than Nietzsche's; and even Zarathustra's affirmation takes place in a complex narrative context. In this respect it is tempting to compare the presentation of the thought with Plato's presentation of Diotima's teaching about *eros* in the *Symposium*. In the *Symposium* there are several stories embedded within one another, the last being Diotima's mysterious teaching about love. Socrates spoke with Diotima, then spoke with others at the drinking party and those who were there passed it on to others who have finally passed it on to us. Plato's indirectness is congruent with his conception of the distinction between human and divine wisdom. The embodied soul is limited in its ability to recall its most illuminating experiences, so writings about such things should remind us of the need for greater progress in dialectic and vision. There is nothing intrinsically mysterious or unknowable about love, or gods, or the soul. It is just that such matters cannot be fully understood by us while still embodied, and even our highest human insights about them are in danger of being distorted by written communication.

The situation in "The Convalescent" is quite different. While the shadowy figure of Diotima suggests the need for continual progression in moving from human to divine understanding, Zarathustra's struggle with his thought and his affirmation of it do not point beyond themselves. No authority is mentioned; there is no talk of an otherworldly experience. Zarathustra's unusual method of communicating his thought arises from the strangeness of the thought itself and from its being very much *his* thought. As the most godless and this-worldly of thoughts, the one which affirms the world of the senses, becoming, and the body, it must not refer us to a religious or scientific source that would introduce a transphenomenal level behind what William James called "a world of pure experience." While Plato's language can point to its own deficiencies in comparison to a purified intellectual intuition, neither the teacher of eternal recurrence nor his author can consistently suggest the inadequacy of the language they employ. If the teaching of recurrence remains unspoken it is because Zarathustra has reached that vanishing point in the search for his own language at which any form of public communication would be stultifying. Zarathustra's talk is not designed to give us a sense of an important truth which has been seen vaguely. What he has thought and seen has been all too clear and overwhelming. It is very much his own and paradoxical in several ways which we have yet to canvas. Zarathustra's most intimate experience, like disembodied intuition in Plato, is beyond the reach of public language; the first is the most this-worldly of experiences and the second the most otherworldly.

Zarathustra's wrestling with eternal recurrence in "The Convalescent" is only possible after he has achieved his own language in "The Homecoming." In the intervening chapters he must exercise his new linguistic freedom by calling things by what seem to him to be their true names. This is accomplished in Zarathustra's revaluation of sensual pleasure, lust for power, and selfishness in "Of the Three Evil Things" and in his comprehensive "Of Old and New Tablets." We might expect, then, to hear a long discourse on Zarathustra's most abysmal thought soon. But in "The Convalescent" Zarathustra speaks of this thought only very indirectly. Just where we might expect the most important of discourses we find silence, the rebuke of others, and apparent asides that concern not the thought itself but some of Zarathustra's problems in accepting it. Or, looking at the text of the chapter in more detail, we can note that it is Zarathustra's animals who speak of the eternal recurrence while he responds to them; yet his response is never on their level of more or less prosaic explanation. Rather than discussing the philosophical thought, Zarathustra comments on the metaphilosophical problems of communicating it. Too many readers and commentators have taken the animals' exposition of the idea here to be identical with Zarathustra's comprehension of it, and almost all have then had no hesitation in identifying Zarathustra's thought with Nietzsche's. This is to ignore the dialogue which takes place between Zarathustra and his animals as well as the problem of private language which surrounds everything said in this part of the book.

Let us read the text of the chapter as a dialogue held against the background of the private language problem. This sounds as if it verges on the absurd, for one cannot conduct a dialogue in a private language; by definition there can be (at most) one speaker. The dialogue is not *in* this questionable language, however, but *about* it. Throughout this part we should take Zarathustra to be approaching this private language, and indicating some of its problems, rather than speaking in it. Or, more precisely, we should think of him as speaking in it only to himself, and only when he is said in the text to be silent. This of course implies that there is a point at which the most developed form of linguistic capability becomes the same as silence; this is one of the many paradoxes which I think the text does indeed seem to suggest. In another sense, this dialogue is very private indeed, for it takes place between Zarathustra and his animals. The cunning serpent and the daring eagle are aspects of Zarathustra; they are some of his virtues in an embodied form. They are with him, even when he is described as solitary, with the exception (discussed below) of his artful desertion of them in part four.

Zarathustra awakes one morning to wrestle with the abysmal thought, which he treats as a body lying in his bed. He calls upon the abyss to *speak*, and when it seems to be doing so, he collapses with a cry of disgust. After lying for a while as if dead he maintains a seven-day silence, after which his dialogue with the animals begins. It is suggested then that the abyss has spoken to Zarathustra in some form which no one can overhear, and that he has pondered its sayings in a thoughtful silence which is likewise incommunicable. Zarathustra himself does not break the silence, but he does finally reach out for an apple; at this gesture of life "his animals thought that the time had come to speak with him" (Z, 233; 4, 271). They invite him to step out into the garden of the world, assuring him that all things will help him to recover from his oppressive experience. We also see that they have not shared his experience during the silence when they ask "Has perhaps some new knowledge come to you, bitter and hard?" (Z, 234; 4, 272). In fact this gap between the experiences of Zarathustra and of the animals comes as no surprise, for we have already been told that during the wrestling with the thought the animals were merely spectators, while during the seven days' silence they watched over him, solicitous of his welfare.

Zarathustra replies to the animals and attempts to move the discussion into the linguistic mode:

> "O my animals," replied Zarathustra, "chatter on like this [*schwätzt also weiter*] and let me listen! Your chattering is so refreshing: where there is chattering, the world is like a garden to me. How sweet it is that words and sounds of music exist: are words and music not rainbows and seeming bridges between things eternally separated?
>
> "Every soul is a world of its own; for every soul, every other soul is an afterworld.
>
> "Appearance lies most beautifully among the most alike for the smallest gap is the most difficult to bridge.
>
> "For me—how should there be an outside-of-me? There is no outside! [*Es gibt kein Aussen!*]. But we forget that, when we hear music; how sweet it is, that we forget!
>
> "Are things not given names and musical sounds, so that man may refresh himself with things? Speech is a beautiful foolery: with it man dances over all things.
>
> "How sweet is all speech and all the falsehoods of music! With music does our love dance upon many-colored rainbows." (Z, 234; *4, 272*)

The animals had invited Zarathustra to be healed and soothed by the things of the world; he moves the conversation into the linguistic mode by praising the soothing music of their invitation. Yet he does not answer their question about his new knowledge, unless we take that knowledge to be (at least in part) the denial of the outside and the idea of language as an illusory musical bridge. "Every soul is a world of its own." Whatever form one's communion with one's own soul takes, it is not communicable to another. Yet we all have a need for the appearance of community and this appearance is fostered by speech. Whatever the cognitive pretensions of speech it can at least function as music which will impart something of the form of what is most one's own and the feelings connected with the attempt at communicating it.

The animals, however, seem unable to grasp the problem of language; in Zarathustra's world an animal may be able to talk but it cannot reflect on its own talk in a metalanguage. The serpent and the eagle begin their stubborn pursuit of the thought of eternal recurrence, explaining an idea which they assume that they share with Zarathustra. Their exposition of the idea is concise, clear, and formulaic: "In every Now, being begins; round every Here rolls the sphere There. The center is everywhere. Bent is the path of eternity." While Zarathustra had compared the animals' earlier invitation to the most beautiful music, he now gently rebukes them for this prosaic exposition of his thought; he calls them "buffoons and barrel-organs" and accuses them of having already made his thought into a "hurdy-gurdy song [*ein Leier-Lied*]" (Z, 235; *4, 273*). Zarathustra is still affectionate with his animals, but makes it clear that there is something missing from their account. Again he shifts the attention away from the thought to his own experience in thinking it and to the animals' role in watching him. Zarathustra suggests that there is no disinterested contemplation: whatever the animals learned while watching him was colored by their feelings about the scene that took place before them. He even wonders whether they could have been enjoying the spectacle of great pain as men so often do. (In *The Genealogy of Morals* Nietzsche suggests that most forms of discourse can be understood as internal or external theaters of cruelty.) This is an invitation to the animals to reflect on the rhetorical background of their own interpretation of Zarathustra's thought and his mission. This thought about men's cruelty leads Zarathustra to explain his own great struggle with the thought: his disgust with the small man, whose cruelty is always petty and yet must recur eternally. Zarathustra had to break through that disgust in order to think his thought and the memory of that disgust makes him shudder even now. Solicitous once more, the animals tell him to speak no more but to learn singing from the songbirds: "convalescents should sing; let the healthy talk" (Z, 236; 4, 275). In fact Zarathustra will spend most of the remainder of this part of the book dancing and singing. Yet even this late realization by the animals of the linguistic theme of the conversation is not perspicuous, Zarathustra indicates. "That I have to sing again—*that* comfort and *this* convalescence did I devise for myself: do you want to make another hurdy-gurdy song out of that, too?" The prose of the animals must be inadequate to Zarathustra's own silent times with his thought and to the way in which song issues out of that thought. But the play of opposition between their prosaic version of the experience and his own comprehension of it is necessary. It saves the text from total silence while indicating the problems connected with any linguistic version of the idea.

Heedless of Zarathustra's subtleties the animals rush ahead to explain why "new lyres are needed for your new songs [*Zu deinen neuen Liedern bedarf es neuer Leiern*]" (Z, 237; 4, 275). The animals are now confident that they know *who* Zarathustra is and *what* he teaches: "behold, *you are the teacher of the eternal recurrence!*" Yet Zarathustra will teach recurrence only through song and play.[3] The animals conclude this long discourse and "expected that Zarathustra would say something to them: but Zarathustra did not hear that they were silent" (Z, 238; 4, 277). The conversation has already broken off and the animals' conception of Zarathustra as a teacher has been shown to be faulty, for he does not speak in the way that they had expected. The outcome of their speech, in other words, shows its failure of understanding. Throughout, the animals have concentrated on the thought as Zarathustra's own; it is what *he* will teach, not simply an idea in the public domain. If he were to die now, they say, he would exclaim "I spoke my teaching, I broke upon my teaching: thus my eternal fate wants it—as prophet do I perish!" Now there is an irony in these words put into their master's mouth which is not evident to the animals. In order to see it more fully, however, we must approach the thought of eternal recurrence from another angle.

As Zarathustra's ownmost thought, eternal recurrence exhibits the problems of private language. The attempts to translate it into a more common language exhibit how paradoxical the thought is. That is, any version which we might try to formulate (in a language more or less continuous with that of the animals) will violate some of our most deeply held principles. As soon as we attempt to elaborate upon the animals' version of the thought—to speak it—we must encounter these problems.

There may indeed be some other approach to the thought which Zarathustra indicates several times by the expression "thinking the thought" (rather than speaking it), but for now we are concerned with the problem of articulating the idea in ordinary language or even in any standard form of philosophical language. One of these paradoxes has to do not with what we might call the content of the thought, a thought "for all" without reference to particular persons, but with the thought as held by or thought through in the fullest and deepest sense by an individual thinker.

First let us attend to the thought in so far as it is addressed to all. As Nietzsche himself has described the thought, it is such that it produces the greatest tension. This tension lies not only in the difficulty of affirming even the most repulsive and disgusting aspects of existence by bestowing an eternal value on them, but in the logical contradictions of the thought itself. Most of these have been pointed out by philosophical writers on Nietzsche, so I will not recapitulate their work here.[4] But it may be valuable to summarize what these problems with the thought are from the standpoint of the prosaic consciousness.

By making temporal sequence into an eternally repeated process, the thought suggests a collapse of the distinction between time and eternity. Now while there may be nothing illogical in denying either temporal becoming or an eternal realm (Parmenides and his many followers deny the first while historicists deny the second), the absolute identification of the two is puzzling, to say the least. The eternal world is just the world of becoming, according to this thought. It may be, however, that this is not a logical problem and that Nietzsche has put his finger on a sloppy assumption characteristic of that metaphysical thinking which supposes the separateness of the temporal and the eternal. In any case there are more serious problems of a logical sort with eternal recurrence. Consider the ways in which the thought seems to combine fate and free will as well as freedom and determinism. Both Zarathustra and his animals, at various points in the book, refer to the way in which a given event or set of circumstances will draw all of its succeeding events along with it. This suggests an inevitability or fate which requires that once X has occurred Y must occur, where Y is the successor of X; and once Y has produced Z and Z has produced A and so on, eventually the "first term" X (and any term may serve arbitrarily here as first term) will be produced once more and it will draw with it an exact repetition of the entire cycle. In Nietzsche's notes there are some attempts to describe this repetition as determined by physical constants such as the finitude of energy and possible energy-states in the universe. This physical determinism is not explicit in *Zarathustra* and I have already suggested some reasons for not associating it with the presentation of the thought there. But these deterministic speculations are useful reminders that even in *Zarathustra* a kind of necessity is ascribed to the repetitive cycles. What needs to be noted now is that the book also insists on the chance character of existence (cf. the discussion of "Before Sunrise") and on a voluntarism of some kind in which every "it was" can be transformed into a "thus I willed it" (cf. Z, 163). On a certain construction of the thought of eternal recurrence the element of chance might be supposed to be *only* an appearance due to our ignorance of what is coming next in the cycle; and this ignorance itself is a contingent fact about the cycle, for we can imagine cycles in which some or all of the agents know (at one or all points in the cycle) some or all of the events which, at that point or points in the cycle, have yet to occur. Yet this attempt to reconcile an apparent conflict in Nietzsche's thought is not true to his insistence that the thought is intimately connected with the dissolution of any distinction between the true and the apparent world (cf. *Twilight*, "How the True World Became a Fable"). And the appeal to the very distinction between contingency and necessity which the thought may be putting in question is of doubtful value in determining whether or not the thought must put that distinction in question.

Even if some way of evading these apparent conflicts were devised, there would be another logical objection to the thought of eternal recurrence. The problem is in the conception of an event or series of events being exactly the same as and yet distinct from another event or series. There is no discernible way in which any event can be distinguished from its repetition; but then, by the identity of indiscernibles, those two events (or two series) are the same event (or series). Yet if they are precisely the same thing, how can we differentiate them, as talk of recurrence seems to presuppose? The eternal recurrence collapses the distinction between the one and the many by suggesting that a single integral thing—the sequence of all events—is many things. Equally it suggests that the many repetitions of an event are just one thing, "the same." Bernd Magnus has argued that the thought of eternal recurrence does indeed violate the principle of identity.[5] But he assumes somewhat hastily that this incoherence of the thought shows that time cannot be cyclical. This is perhaps a bit misleading, for we can conceive of a non-repeated circle of events each of which is continuous either in a causal sense, or in a phenomenological sense, or both with its immediate antecedents and consequences. It would be an "eternal cycle of becoming" but not an eternal *recurrence*. This thought may be close to that of the Spirit of Gravity while that of recurrence is Zarathustra's.

I am reviewing the difficulties connected with a prosaic reconstruction of eternal recurrence in order to suggest that Nietzsche has good reasons for not putting any such version of the thought into Zarathustra's mouth. One might agree with some of the above criticisms but attempt to shift the perspective by arguing that even if the thought is absurd, Nietzsche's interest is not in securing our contemplative acceptance of it but in having us confront the possibility of *willing* it. It is that thought which produces the greatest tension in us because it asks us to affirm the infinite and eternal importance of each of our experiences. It could thus be understood as a practical imperative: live each moment *as if* it were of infinite importance. This interpretation is also open to question and further interpretation. It attempts to preserve the value of the thought by shifting from the prose of understanding to the prose of action. Yet the thought resists translation into any prosaic form. Taking the thought as an "existential imperative" (in Bernd Magnus's useful phrase) supposes some things about who acts on imperatives and what it is to act on an imperative. An imperative is addressed to someone by someone. In some cases, as in that of Kant's categorical imperative, the one who lays down the imperative (the "imperator") is identical (in some sense) with the one to whom the imperative is addressed (the "imperatee"). So there is a certain plurality which is always present in such giving of orders and obeying, whether or not more than one "person" (in the conventional sense) is involved in the process. Nietzsche suggests that any willing or commanding involves something of such a plural character:

> Philosophers are accustomed to speak of the will as if it were the best-known thing in the world. . . . Willing seems to me to be above all something *complicated*, something that is a unit only as a word—and it is precisely in this one word that the popular prejudice lurks, which has defeated the always inadequate caution of philosophers . . . let us say that in all willing there is, first, a plurality of sensations, namely, the sensation of the state "*away from which*," the sensation of the state "*towards which*," the sensations of this "*from*" and "*towards*" themselves. (*BGE*, 19; 5, 31–32)

In the same section Nietzsche goes on to argue that " 'freedom of the will' is essentially the affect of superiority in relation to the one who must obey: 'I' am free, 'he' must obey.'' If willing is essentially plural, however, what becomes of an imperative in which the conception of *my* action is central? That is, if "I'' am seen as a plurality of some kind, the insistence on designating certain actions as just *mine* becomes a troublesome one. Now *interpreted as an imperative* the eternal recurrence does seem to accord such a special status to my actions and my experiences. In this respect it involves a concentration on the self that is not typical of all imperatives. Those issued by religious authorities typically prescribe or proscribe certain acts but they do not necessarily require an attention to each of one's actions and experiences as specifically one's own. Even Kant's categorical imperative has to do with treating all rational beings (including oneself) as ends; the emphasis is not so much on the continuity and quality of *individual* experience but on having intentions of a certain *general* form.

Now it is just this stress on the *mineness* (one might think here of Heidegger's *Jemeinigkeit*) of my experience in the thought of eternal recurrence that renders it practically paradoxical. For the thought, when thought through, is not congenial to that conception of a unitary and constant self which is required in order to support such an emphasis on mineness. Soon I will be suggesting that the many figures suddenly introduced in part four of *Zarathustra* are partial selves and that Zarathustra's distancing himself from the higher men is also a way of refusing to be tied down to any determinate, atomic identity. But now we are more concerned with the thought as a thought and the implications which that thought has for the notion of personal identity. We have already noted that the crucial confrontation with the thought is deliberately set within the context of an exploration of the possibility of a private language, yet if the thought is in some way inimical to a conception of personal identity, must it also be inconsistent with the ideal of a purely private language? This is the bullet (or snake) which Zarathustra must and does bite. The results should not be surprising to those who have considered Wittgenstein's remarks about solipsism (in the *Tractatus*) and his discussion of private language (in the *Philosophical Investigations*). For in each case the point is that the most extreme insistence on the mineness of all my thought, experience, or language renders questionable the very notion of the individual self. When all is mine there is no longer the possibility of distinguishing myself from another or what is mine from what is not; so that "I," "mine" and so on, when pushed beyond a certain limit, cease to have any meaningful application. The same point is made by Hegel in the first chapter of *The Phenomenology of Spirit* where he shows that the absolute insistence on the inevitability of my experience being "my experience of this, here and now" makes not only the indexical terms "this," "here" and "now" abstract and useless, but shows the "I" and the "my" to be similarly absurd.[6] Now before discussing the analogous dialectical movement in Nietzsche's text it should be noted that the attitude taken toward this insight there is quite different than Wittgenstein's or Hegel's. Those philosophers saw the point as a *reductio ad absurdum* of the notion of an absolute self with a private language; having seen the absurdity, we are to turn with relief to the more concrete and actual uses of language or to the more determinate categories of science. Zarathustra, on the other hand, joyfully accepts the idea of the dissolution of the self. He (and Nietzsche) do not retreat to common sense or to systematic philosophy but welcome this strange avenue to a radical dissolution of selfhood.

To see these radical implications of the thought of eternal recurrence, it will be useful to consider another view which takes a somewhat more conventional view of the thought's purpose. The interpretation I wish to examine somewhat critically is that of Alexander Nehamas who argues that the point of the thought, for Nietzsche, is to provide the one who thinks it with a means of strongly integrating all of his or her experiences, that is, of attaining an organically unified self. Like some other recent philosophical writers on Nietzsche, Nehamas approaches his work through its concern with literary and textual models and analogies. For him the thought of eternal recurrence must be understood in terms of "Nietzsche's overarching metaphor of the world as a text that is to be interpreted."[7] In this case the text would be that of one's own life, and the point of teaching eternal recurrence would be to urge the thinker to seek that interpretation of his or her own text that would lead to seeing the text of the life as completely integrated and definitive. As Nehamas says, this view "assimilates the ideal person to an ideal literary character and the ideal life to an ideal story."[8] Like Nehamas I have been relying heavily on Nietzsche's use of textual models; unlike him, however, I have been focussing attention, especially in the case of *Zarathustra*, on the actual development and articulation of Nietzsche's text, rather than constructing a general view of what Nietzsche thinks about textuality. By tracing some difficulties in Nehamas's treatment of eternal recurrence I hope to show some of the radical questions and possibilities that Nietzsche's texts are designed to lead us to confront. In the process I also want to suggest that Nietzsche's conception of text and interpretation does not lend itself to the Aristotelian or Hegelian idea of organic unity which governs Nehamas's construction; Nietzsche's own conception, as writers such as Deleuze, Klossowski, and Derrida have suggested in various ways, is deconstructive and dispersive rather than totalizing and integrating.

So I will be arguing that the aim of the thought of eternal recurrence is just the opposite of what Nehamas sees as its point; to take the thought of eternal recurrence seriously is not to aspire to a deeper, more profound integration of the self, but to confront the disintegration and dissolution of the ordinary self rather than its ideal unification and transfiguration. It is this attack on the integrated self which renders Nietzsche's thought truly uncanny and abysmal (*abgrundlich*—lacking a foundation).

As Nehamas says, it is possible to distinguish Nietzsche's flirtation with cosmological arguments for recurrence from his deeper interest in the psychological meaning of the thought for the one who thinks it. On this question it is significant that Nietzsche did not publish the sketches of a cosmological argument for the doctrine which later appeared in *The Will to Power* and that his first treatment of the idea, in *The Gay Science*, has to do with the immense burden presented by the thought and its power to transform the thinker (*GS*, 341; *3*, 570). But what sort of transformation does Nietzsche have in mind? On Nehamas's view, I (who am thinking the thought) must first realize that it is foolish to think about my having a life related to, but different from, my actual life. That is, if what eternally recurs for me is just this actual life, I should not hope for a better or fear for a worse one; moreover, all counterfactual thoughts about my past and present are rigidly excluded. Since my life is just what it is, I am at best wasting time and at worst wallowing in self-deception by thinking to myself thoughts of the "if only" variety, e.g. "if only I had been born rich," "if only I had made the right social contacts at the right time." So far I still agree with Nehamas who sees Nietzsche here as challenging us to accept or reject our lives as a whole: since each part of my life is bound up with all the others, rejection of any one would entail rejection of the whole. Ordinarily one does regret at least part of one's past, and Nietzsche suggests that resentment of one's own past may be the deepest root of envy, *ressentiment*, and other attitudes which he deplores. What eternal recurrence challenges us to do is to overcome such resentment.

Nehamas suggests that the way in which Nietzsche believes we can overcome resentment is through an active process of interpreting and reinterpreting our lives as if we were fictional characters. He finds support for such a view in Nietzsche's early declaration that "it is only as an aesthetic phenomenon that existence and the world are eternally justified" and in his continued exaltation of the artist's power to transcend the banalities of life (*BT*, 5; *1*, 42–48). The model by means of which each of us can become an artist of his own life is that of the literary character. Literary characters, like any person as understood from the perspective of eternal recurrence, inhabit a world that "does seem to be exhausted by the descriptions of what actually happens in the stories in which they are found." Nehamas suggests that in following out the thought of recurrence we should strive to see ourselves as such characters, for they offer us a way of seeing how a life can be both necessarily what it is and at the same time coherent, integrated, and aesthetically satisfying. The claim is that this model also illuminates a problem for Nietzsche's thought by showing in a perspicuous manner how it ascribes a priority to the aesthetic over the moral: a fascinating literary character—like Melville's Ahab or Proust's Charlus—"may be a perfect character but (represent) a dreadful person."[9]

I believe that the model of the "ideal character" in an organically unified text is not helpful in understanding the psychological intent of eternal recurrence. Let us consider this at first indirectly by looking at Nehamas's description of the process whereby one might decide whether one's own life approximated that of an ideal character *sub specie aeternitatis*. The question facing such an interpreter of his or her own life would be whether or not every aspect of it can be integrated in such an ideal.

> Nietzsche tries to suggest how intense and painful a self-examination is necessary before one can even begin to answer the demon's question affirmatively. But it is still the case that the desire for *nothing* to be different presupposes that *everthing* has been faced, and there is no independent way of establishing that this has been done. The problem is even more urgent because there seems to be no clear sense in which the totality of our actions can ever be faced: is it even possible to speak of "the totality" of a person's actions? The process of self-examination . . . may have no end.[10]

Consider the consequences of an open-ended process of interpretation which will decide the question of whether or not I can accept eternal recurrence. Eternal recurrence now becomes a regulative rather than a constitutive idea (in Kantian terms). I may never know whether I am worthy of recurring eternally, let alone "once more." Like the Christian who painfully interrogates his own state of sin or grace, the Nietzschean would live in anguished uncertainty about his or her future redemption. This parallels that dichotomy between the world of experience and the true world which Nietzsche constantly criticizes.

Nehamas then, has produced such a "Christian" version of eternal recurrence by relying upon a view of textual interpretation as tending toward a definitive understanding of an organically unified text. Such a model, it is true, has a very wide following; it receives a classical formulation in Hegel's *Aesthetics* and it is the working model of the American New Critics. As the German and French philosophical reception of Nietzsche and Nietzsche's authority for the deconstructive movement in art and literary criticism suggest, however, Nietzsche's own model of textual interpretation is congenial to the opposed concepts of difference and plurality. His celebration of the plurality of interpretations ought not to be read as if each interpretation, to be an acknowledged member of the plurality, had to conform internally to the standard of organic unity. That is, his pluralism is more radical than simply allowing that (contra Hegel and the New Critics) there can be many equally valid interpretations which exhibit organic unity. He is claiming that an interpretation—even a strong and vitalizing one—need not present us with an organically unified manifold. From an aesthetic point of view this can be seen in the praise of the Dionysian. From a more general hermeneutical perspective we can think of Nietzsche's operative principle in *Toward a Genealogy of Morals*: "only that which has no history can be defined" (*GM* II, 13; 5, 317). Hegel supposed that the hermeneutic circle of interpretation could be closed and that the person of the interpreter could be added as a footnote to the text. Nehamas appeals to this Hegelian model in citing as an example of the self-interpretation necessary for the affirmation of eternal recurrence Proust's *Remembrance of Things Past*. There the hero comes to see the earlier moments of his life, which had originally appeared to be disjointed and wasted segments of time, as finally coming to form "parts of a unified pattern, the result of which is his determination to begin at last his first book,"[11] i.e., the novel in which his readers read just this. Since Proust's narrator Marcel is a literary character, he has no future beyond the conclusion of his book and so he would, on Nehamas's view, be worthy of affirming eternal recurrence. The consequences for the actual historical individual Marcel Proust, who died while still revising his novel, are somewhat different. If Proust was also worthy of affirming eternal recurrence it could only be because he had no future at that point; that is, there were no possible events in his future which could shake the self-interpretation he had produced of himself as having lived "a perfect life." Notice that this transforms the doctrine of eternal recurrence into another version of Solon's "count no man happy until he is dead." On the contrary, Nietzsche has Zarathustra suggest that for the affirmation of eternal recurrence it is enough if we "say yes to one joy" (Z, 331; 4, 402). Significantly, the one character in *Thus Spoke Zarathustra* whom Zarathustra helps to affirm the eternal recurrence, "the ugliest man," says that he so affirms because of the joy of "one day, one festival with Zarathustra" (Z, 326; 4, 396). It is of more than coincidental interest that the Hegelian reading of Proust to which Nehamas appeals has been challenged by contemporary theorists of narrative. Although the model of loss and recapture of the narrator's self in which the narrator in the text comes to coincide with the author is understandably generated in a reading culture that is governed by a regulative ideal of organic unity, some recent critics have demonstrated that other readings of Proust are possible in which this identification does not occur.[12]

Let me now turn to an alternative account of the psychological ramifications of eternal recurrence which, I think, is closer to Nietzsche's intentions and texts. On this view the primary focus of attention is not on the question of whether or not I am worthy of eternal recurrence, but rather on the *consequence* of my thinking the thought seriously. The result of such thinking ought to be a dispersive rather than an integrative conception of the self. First, such a result would be compatible (as Nehamas's is not) with Nietzsche's frequent critiques of the conception of a substantial self. Typical of such critiques is the polemic in the first part of *Beyond Good and Evil* in which Nietzsche says that we must "declare war" against an atomistic or individualistic conception of the soul and should, in its place, entertain pluralistic hypotheses according to which the soul or self is composed of a multiplicity of psychic entities (*BGE*, 12–23; 5, 26–39).

Let us now see whether the thought of eternal recurrence does support this reconstruction of its import. Keeping our distance from the text long enough for this investigation we will then be able to return to it refreshed, as Zarathustra does after his own period of silence. We can begin by putting the point in a relatively weak and minimal form. The thought of eternal recurrence, unlike typical ideas of religious and philosophical importance, does nothing at all to strengthen the identity of the one who understands, accepts, or affirms it. Usually the acceptance of a major religious or metaphysical belief is seen as marking an important transition within the life history of a continuous individual, or it is regarded as a watershed separating his earlier illusions from a new and conscious identity with his or her deeper, truer, or eternal self. So (to begin a partial and schematic survey of such views), Platonism includes both the idea that reality is an unchanging world of forms and also (as in the myths of immortality) the notion of an eternal soul which can know these forms. In a historical religion such as Christianity, one's life is divided by the experience of being "born again" which exhibits the before and after of a spiritual quest. In Hegel, who attempts a synthesis of the temporal and the eternal, it is through a progression in time that one arrives at one's true and eternal identity as part of Absolute Spirit. In all of these cases knowledge of or faith in a certain principle is seen as strengthening both one's commitment to the principle and one's identity in so far as one is a knower or believer. It should be noted that the importance of these views for the individual is dependent upon either a linear notion of time or a distinction between the temporal and eternal worlds (or both).

Now the idea of eternal recurrence excludes the possibility of structuring my life in terms of a linear sequence marked by the affirmation of the idea itself, for the thought declares that my experiences before my realization of the thought and those which I might have after forgetting it or temporarily ignoring it are of equal importance with those which I have in the most serious meditation upon it. According to the thought *all* my experiences are of infinite significance. Just as I cannot subordinate my past ignorance to my present or future knowledge, so I cannot subordinate a temporal world of error and illusion to an eternal, enlightened world. This may help to explain Nietzsche's frequent praise of the healthfulness of forgetting, in contrast to the Platonic enterprise of *anamnesis*.[13] Yet it might be supposed that within a single cycle of my life the thought of eternal recurrence could play an integrating role for me, allowing me to see my life as a meaningful progression. But to the extent to which I affirm the thought I affirm also my error and ignorance of it; for in affirming the whole of my life I must affirm all of those moments before I knew of the thought, or when I rejected it, or when I was considering it, as well as those (possible) moments of my future when I may forget it or (for whatever reason) cease to affirm it. And in such periods of error, ignorance, or backsliding the thought cannot play a major role for me because I will not be affirming it. Any attempt to use the thought in order to make my life history into a meaningful development runs into the danger of complicity in that general revenge which the human race yearns to practice upon "time and its 'it was.' " That is, such an attempt amounts to segmenting my life into a "before" and an "after," such that I would be permanently fragmented and split, like the fragmented persons that Zarathustra describes in "Of Redemption" as the real cripples of this world.

I introduced these reflections by suggesting that they would establish the minimal point that the thought of eternal recurrence does not reinforce one's conception of oneself or help one to find one's true self. The point can now be put more emphatically. The thought of eternal recurrence invites me to affirm all that occurs and so it invites me to affirm all of my actions and experiences. But it does not suggest that I affirm these because of any special order or development which they possess; indeed they may be discontinuous in a number of ways, as reflection on the fact of forgetting suggests. In accepting eternal recurrence, therefore, I accept all that is contingent and accidental about myself. But surely, someone will say, all these experiences are mine, whether or not my life exhibits a meaningful career and whether or not I hold fast to the thought of eternal recurrence. Yet if we look more closely, what the thought affirms is the moment (*Augenblick*) or rather the entire sequence of moments which constitutes a cycle of the universe or of what we call an individual life. As in Hume or Buddhism or Whitehead, the moments become primary. As Zarathustra has already suggested, the purpose of his most abysmal thought is to provide deliverance from the complex of guilt, revenge, and responsibility in which human beings are generally caught. One of the constant themes of Nietzsche's work, explicit from *The Dawn* through his last books, is the connection between our idea of a constant, responsible agent, that is, the ego as classically understood, and this complex of guilt and revenge. In *Twilight of the Idols* there is an important section entitled "The Four Great Errors." All of the alleged errors are mistakes made in ascribing independent agency and responsibility to the self. All the errors are construed as motivated by the revenge of "the theologians, who continue to infect the innocence of becoming with 'punishment' and 'guilt' by means of the concept 'moral world-order.' " In contrast Nietzsche declares that "our teaching" must be that "the fatality of [a human being's] nature cannot be disentangled from the fatality of all that which has been and will be . . . *nothing exists apart from the whole*!—That no one is any longer made accountable . . . this alone is the great liberation—thus alone is the *innocence* of becoming restored."

We have travelled some distance from the text in attempting to think through the thought of recurrence. I have suggested one line of thought according to which this thought is inconsistent with the romantic heroism and individualism so often ascribed to Nietzsche and his most memorable character, Zarathustra. I have also attempted to place Zarathustra's confrontation with this thought within the context of the quest for a private language in which one can say that which is truly one's own. If both the placement of the thought in this context and the interpretation of the thought's anti-individualism are valid, then Zarathustra's thinking of this thought (or more precisely Nietzsche's narration of it) is best seen as a metaphilosophical demonstration of what happens when one explores one's very own thought in one's very own language. The eternal recurrence is said to be the most godless thought; it is not difficult to suppose that Nietzsche might think of the most godless thought as also the most individual one. What may not be so apparent is that the death of God must also be the death of the individual as such. For God represents simply the most egregious form of a central organizing principle that would explain the presence of order and value in the world; the idea of an independent ego is simply one more variation on this principle, as are all forms of atomism. If eternal recurrence is the most abysmal or groundless (*Abgrundliche*) thought, it may be because it lacks the basis of a single thinker as its *Grund*; it cuts away its own apparent support. In *Zarathustra* Nietzsche suggests that the look into the abyss can be joyous rather than terrifying if we surrender the search for such a ground where there is none. This, I think, is the import of eternal recurrence, rather than the attempt to become one's own foundation by means of an interpretation of oneself as absolutely coherent and integrated. The point is not to restore foundationalism by ceaselessly looking for a final interpretation of one's own text, but to explore a world in which the quest for foundations has been surrendered.

A text from the spring of 1881, before the "discovery" of eternal recurrence, states the theme with some passion.

> *The main idea!* [*Hauptgedanke!*] It is not nature that deceives us, the individuals, and furthers her goals through deceiving us: rather the individuals explain all of existence according to individual, that is false, criteria; we want to be just and consequently "nature" [*die Natur*] must appear as a "deceiver" [*die Betrugerin*]. In truth there are no *individual truths*, but rather individual *errors; the individual* itself is an *error*. Everything that happens in us is in itself *something other* that we do not know: we first put intention and deception and morality into nature.—I make a distinction however between the imaginary individuals and the true "life-systems," of which each of us is one—one throws both together into one while "the individual" is only a sum of conscious sensations and judgments and errors, a *belief*, a small piece of the true life-system or many pieces thought and fabled as together, a "unity," that has no rank [*Stand*]. We are blossoms on a tree—what do we know of that which can become of us in the interest of the tree! But we have a consciousness as if we would and should be *everything*, a fantasy of "I" and all "not-I." *To stop feeling oneself as such a fantastic ego!* To learn gradually *to throw away the supposed individual!* To discover the errors of the ego! To realize that egoism is an error! Not to understand its opposite as altruism! That would be the love of *other supposed* individuals! No! Beyond "me" and "you"! To feel cosmically. (9, 441–2)

When Zarathustra finally turns away from his animals, seeming to them to be asleep, he is actually conversing with his own soul. Such interior conversation is a constant theme of the third part of *Zarathustra*. But this conversation of the soul with itself (recalling Plato's definition of thinking) and the songs that follow the self-communion bring a new tone to the internal colloquy. The title of the chapter which records the conversation is "On the Great Longing" (*Von der grossen Sehnsucht*); *sehnen* and its derivatives suggest not merely desire but more specifically desire from afar that involves the tension of distance. This element of distance becomes constitutive of the picture that Zarathustra draws of his own soul, for he describes it as stretched out, spanning all distances, temporal, spatial, and spiritual:

> O my soul, I taught you to say "today" as well as "once" and "formerly" and to dance your dance over every Here and There and Over-there.

O my soul, I rescued you from all nooks. . . .

O my soul, now there is nowhere a soul more loving and encompassing and spacious [*umfangender und umfänglicher*]! Where could future and past be closer together than with you? (Z, 238–39; 4, 278–9).

The soul has been through a process of purification or convalescence that has resulted in its transformation. It is "rescued from all nooks" in so far as it is no longer limited to a precise location. The thought of eternal recurrence is such as to expand the soul's boundaries to the furthest possible extreme. Zarathustra's praise of his own soul here (or his love-song to himself) is not the triumphant cry of the hegemonic, imperial self but the joy felt upon release from the constrictions of a narrowly defined identity. Whereas in Plato the soul's conversation with itself reveals it to be a desiring being that longs for its own completion through the fulfillment of desire, the soul praised by Zarathustra is one which is already overfull in its very openness to things. As Eugen Fink suggests, the great longing is simply openness to the world (*Weltoffenheit*). Such a longing is content to live with distances, we might say, because it does not *have* to go anywhere. Its desire is not directed toward any specific objects in their specificity; the desire is rather to dance or play over the many things of human space and time that are separate from one another. Dioynsus is also invoked (although not by name) in this address as the master of that golden marvel, the boat of free will, and as:

the vintager who waits with diamond-studded vine knife,
your great redeemer, O my soul, the nameless one for whom only future songs will find a name! (Z, 240; 4, 280).

Dionysus, the god of intoxication who is continuously torn apart and yet reasserts himself, is the god appropriate to a soul that lacks simple location and dances "over every Here and There and Over-there."

Zarathustra's insight into eternal recurrence cannot be communicated in the prosaic manner that the animals first attempted. In the last three chapters of part three, we find Zarathustra poetically addressing his own soul (in "The Great Longing"), engaging in "The Other Dancing Song" with Life, personified as a woman, and, in a vatic mode, pronouncing the mysteries of "The Seven Seals" whose dark images are meant to protect and enclose the most abysmal thought. Both "The Other Dancing Song" and "The Seven Seals" are love songs suggesting how the thought of recurrence can lead to "the lineaments of gratified desire." In the first of these, Life is a woman with whom Zarathustra plays a flirtatious game (Life and Wisdom have already appeared as women in "The Dance Song" of part two). She is jealous of his Wisdom and surprised to hear that Zarathustra knows that it is impossible to leave Life for good (he has whispered his knowledge of recurrence to her). Here, too, Zarathustra brings into play the notorious whip which the old woman told him of secretly in part one ("Are you going to women? Don't forget the whip!"); the actual use of this metaphor, which has been left out of play for so long, does not suggest the sadism that it has been taken to imply when read out of context. Here it is used for keeping time in a dance.

Each part of "The Seven Seals" ends with a refrain expressing the eroticism of eternal recurrence:

> Oh how should I not lust after eternity and after the nuptial ring of rings, the ring of recurrence?
> Never yet have I found the woman from whom I wanted children, unless it be this woman whom I love: for I love you, O eternity!
> *For I love you, O eternity!*

The appearance of the erotic here may seem out of place if we think of the recurrence as an impersonal cosmological doctrine. We may even be tempted, knowing of Nietzsche's shyness and his frustration with women, to interpret these love songs as the expression of what has been repressed. Certainly in a world where everything returns there will also be a return of the repressed. Yet I think it is possible to see a closer connection between the thought of recurrence, the dissolution of the narrowly constructed self, and the eroticism of these songs. From the beginning of his convalescence, Zarathustra knows that song is the best expression of the thought of recurrence. He says that song or music creates bridges which overcome solitude, if only in appearance. Now as I have been reading the development of Zarathustra's thought in part three, he has sought the most profound solitude only to find that there is no genuine distinction between an absolute solipsism and a view of the world in which the boundaries of the ego are radically expanded or dissolved. Erotic love is traditionally celebrated as such a dissolution of the boundaries of the self, in so far as the self has been conceived as a distinct being with its own principle of identity. This makes the love song a somewhat anomalous genre of literature. On the one hand, as a lyric it expresses the individuality of the singer; on the other its content suggests a dissolution of that individuality which is its formal premise. Now this is precisely the paradox of Zarathustra's long search for a philosophically and rhetorically appropriate mode of speech in part three: he seeks that which is most his own but discovers, in the process, that the condition of being absolutely at home with himself is one in which the self can no longer be discriminated as a single subject in contrast with others and with an objective world.

We may, for a moment, take seriously Heidegger's suggestion that Nietzsche is the completion of the Western metaphysical tradition which has its beginning in Plato. Then we may note that Zarathustra's love songs, expressing as they do his most groundless thought of recurrence, are in some way parallel to those Platonic myths of Eros in the *Symposium* and the *Phaedrus* that speak in parables of the soul's ascent to an eternal ground. In both cases the genuine object of desire is eternity, although Plato construes the eternal as outside of *this* world and, therefore, its pursuit is endangered by too great a concern with the erotics of this world. There is, however, something parallel to the pattern of self-dissolution which we have found in Nietzsche. The erotic ascent of the soul is one in which it casts off those features which individuate it (traceable in the final analysis to the body) and becomes or merges with soul as such. At the higher Platonic altitudes we use "soul" not to individuate your psyche from mine, but as a mass-word which designates a single stuff like water in which there are no intrinsic divisions. Nevertheless, when soul in its purity completes its Platonic marriage with the eternal, it is quite thoroughly differentiated from that world of appearances and bodies, which Plato describes contemptuously as consisting of animals who can think of nothing but "grazing and mounting each other."[14] Nietzsche identifies *this* world, the world of experienced joys and sorrows, as the eternal world; so Zarathustra's marriage with Eternity is not *merely* a parable or myth but expresses the eroticism involved in seeing *this* world as the genuine object of desire. The loosening of the boundaries of the self then has to do with a dispersion into the multiplicity of recurrence rather than with an ascent to a refuge beyond space and time.

In his reading of Heidegger on Nietzsche, Jacques Derrida points to Heidegger's omission of sexuality in his attempt at a monumental exegesis. Specifically, he notes that in reading Nietzsche's "How the True World Finally Became a Fable: the History of an Error," Heidegger does not recognize (let alone comment on) Nietzsche's italicized "stage direction" for the third, or Christian phase of the error's history: *"it becomes woman [es wird Weib]."*[15] This is indeed a surprising omission since Heidegger emphasizes the continuity of the development from Plato to Nietzsche. Yet the omission is typical. Although one often finds slighting references to Nietzsche's supposed misogyny, there has been little concern with the fact that at one of the crucial points in *Zarathustra*, Life, Wisdom, and Eternity are all celebrated as women and that Zarathustra hopes for a marriage with Eternity. Eugen Fink suggests that all of "The Seven Seals" may refer to the ancient cosmogony of Father Heaven and Mother Earth.[16] This may well be; in any case, each part of this chapter has an erotic concern that contributes to its songs of love consequent on the thought of recurrence and its transformation of the self. The fifth of these seals has to do with the eroticization of space, for example (I omit the refrain reproduced above):

> If I love the sea and all that is sea-like, and love it most when it angrily contradicts me:
> if that delight in seeking that drives sails towards the undiscovered is in me, if a seafarer's delight is in my delight:
> if ever my rejoicing has cried: "The shore has disappeared—now the last fetter falls from me,
> "the boundless roars around me, far out glitter space and time, well then, come on! old heart!" (Z, 246; 4, 290)

The sea is a fairly constant object of love in *Zarathustra*. By itself it suggests the boundlessness of space and the proliferation of adventurous possibilities, as when Zarathustra praises the sailors of the sea in "Of the Vision and the Riddle." Here those same features of the sea are celebrated and there is a special emphasis on the boundless (*das Grenzlose*) and the glittering of space and time. The boundless sea is not so much a place as the condition which makes all places possible (to speak with Kant for a moment). Space is not just a system of coordinates but the lived space of a perpetual possibility of adventure. The imagery of this verse of the song suggests that space and time, the two forms of the Kantian transcendental aesthetic, have been collapsed into the single form of space, for "far out glisten space and time." Nietzsche's poetic conception of space here is that of a sheer boundlessness giving access to all objects of desire; he calls the heart to participate in the voyage. It is this conception of space as pure openness which Rilke seems to have derived from Nietzsche, as Heidegger notes.[17] Zarathustra says to his soul that eternal recurrence allows it "to say 'today' as well as 'once' and 'formerly' and to dance [its] dance over every Here and There and Over-There." Now it is space, not the linear time of the Kantian transcendental aesthetic, which offers the sheer availability of all places. Time, as ordinarily understood, is unidimensional; it is constantly eliminating possibilities through what Locke called its "perpetual perishing." It is the dichotomous aspect of ordinary time which Zarathustra laments in his "Funeral Song." The spatialization of time is not, in this context, a philosophical error, but an achievement that becomes possible only with great thought and love.

FOUR

Festival, Carnival, and Parody

(*Zarathustra* IV)

With the fourth part of *Zarathustra*, Nietzsche's writing displays an obvious transformation of style, tone, and thought; and the change, most of the critics have
argued, is not for the better. Since Nietzsche had the fourth part printed privately,
distributed only some of these copies to a few friends, and then attempted to retrieve
those, the case against giving serious attention to this part of the text acquires some
circumstantial plausibility. But the question of whether Zarathustra's adventures
with the higher men, the "last supper" that they share, the worship of an ass, and
the odd songs that are sung in this part contribute something of significance to
Nietzsche's "greatest gift" to mankind must finally be settled by a careful look at
what he has written. Eugen Fink, whose book on *Nietzsche's Philosophy* is an
illuminating and lucid statement from a generally Heideggerian perspective, makes
the case against the fourth part on immanent grounds, and he does so, in part, by
appealing to considerations of narrative tone and style:

> With the fourth part new stylistic elements arise; the story [*Fabel*] that acts only as a
> light connective in the first three parts . . . now stands out more strongly, even com-
> pellingly; there are poor and painful transitions; the entire fourth part is a sudden crash
> [*Absturz*]. Somehow the poetic vision seems exhausted. This fourth part is tacked on
> like a bad and malicious satyr play to this work that offers a new tragic vision of the
> world. The fourth part is supposed to show the incommensurability of Zarathustra's
> greatness with all previous forms of human greatness, and his transcendence of all types
> of "higher men." But this fails and remains merely an attitude. . . . *Zarathustra* is
> strong and has an original power of language and thought so long as Nietzsche philo-
> sophizes, that is, so long as he develops his thoughts of the *Übermensch*, the death of
> God, the will to power, and the eternal recurrence. But when, as in the fourth part, he
> wants to create an image of existence, when he wants to embody the type of Zarathustra,
> the work loses its high tone; Nietzsche is powerful, so long as he speaks and teaches *as*
> Zarathustra—he becomes weak when he speaks *about* Zarathustra. He is not enough of
> a poet for that.[1]

Fink is right in pointing to an abrupt change of tone, but I think it is a mistake to see such a change as unique to this part; I have been claiming that each of the book's major parts represents something of a new departure in style, language, and thought. While there is an intensification of narrative outline, it is important to ask what the genre of this narrative is; and I suggest it is one in which the abrupt transitions of which Fink complains are completely appropriate. Fink is closer to the themes of the text in suggesting that *Zarathustra* IV is a satyr play than in his view that what Nietzsche is aiming at here is an image of the form of Zarathustra's existence, or an existential model.

Nietzsche himself suggests a literary and philosophical category that is appropriate to understanding the fourth part of *Zarathustra* in his explication of the possibility of carnivalizing the history of culture. Earlier Zarathustra had spoken "Of the Land of *Bildung*" (education or culture; actually the notion is a deeply embedded cultural ideal, for the comprehension of which English speakers require the mediation of a thinker such as Gadamer). This is a chapter that must arouse some fear and trembling in anybody who would venture to teach Nietzsche, that is to make his thought an assimilable part of a common culture. For there Zarathustra attacks the historicist ideal of the nineteenth century, comparing its men to motley collections of fragments from many times and places, portraying them as masks. "Written over with the signs of the past and these signs overdaubed with new signs; thus have you hidden yourselves well from all interpreters of signs" (Z, 142; 4, 153). By turning themselves into universal interpreters of all of the human record the men of culture think that they, as the transmitters of that record, are themselves not susceptible to interpretation. But the hermeneut is not beyond all interpretation; he seems so only because of his temporary monopoly of the disciplines of culture. Should Nietzsche's anticipation that one day a chair will be endowed for teaching of his works ever be realized, its occupant may shudder when he expounds Zarathustra on *Bildung*; for he will wonder whether or not he has simply added Nietzsche to the great collection of masks and disguises that constitute so much of the standard repertoire of what we call the humanities. Are we not all caught up, to some extent, in this historical spirit? Are we colorless skeletons underneath the motley trappings of our learning? I want to suggest that *Zarathustra* IV is a celebration in which the motley and the over-inscribed can become transvalued. The key to this transvaluation is the eternal recurrence and its accompanying weakening of the identity of the self, but the specific nature of the transvaluation can be understood when we look at a section of *Beyond Good and Evil* in which Nietzsche, after a description of the "hybrid European" and his "historical spirit," suggests how we can find

advantage even in this despair: again and again a new piece of prehistory or a foreign country is tried on, put on, taken off, packed away, and above all *studied*: we are the first age that has truly studied "costumes"—I mean those of moralities, articles of faith, taste in the arts, and religions—prepared like no previous age for a carnival in the grand style, for the laughter and high spirits of the most spiritual revelry [*zum geistige Fasching-Gelächter und Übermut*], for the transcendental heights of the highest nonsense and of

Aristophanean mockery of the world. Perhaps this is still where we shall discover the realm of our *invention* [*Erfindung*; seemingly a rhetorical term], that realm, in which we, too, can still be original, say, as parodists of world-history and carnival clowns of God [*Hanswurste Gottes*]—perhaps, even if nothing else today has any future, our *laughter* may yet have a future, (*BGE*, 223; 5, 157)

I propose that the fourth part of *Zarathustra* can be read as a commentary on this passage, for it is a product of Nietzsche's highest philosophical and poetic invention—the model of a "carnival in the grand style" (*Karneval grossen Stils*) and a consummate parody during which *Zarathustra* himself becomes the *Hanswurst*, the buffoon or carnival clown.

Yet the atmosphere of carnival is hardly present at the very beginning here. Zarathustra, we are told, has grown older and his hair has turned white. Living in the mountains, he no longer needs to develop his own vision or to confront the established views and powers of the world "down there." Rather he proposes to become a fisher of men while remaining on the mountain, suggesting that he will have the best of the two worlds which were incompatible for Jesus. Jesus was tempted by the devil with the things of the world and the promise to be "lord of the earth" high upon a mountain from which one could survey as much of the world as possible; Zarathustra is invited by his animals at the beginning of part four to "climb a high mountain" today where "one sees more of the world today than ever before" (Z, 251; 4, 296). Unlike Jesus Zarathustra does not need to give up the charms or the visions of the world in order to spread his message through becoming a fisher of men. Part four then *begins* as parody and eventually reaches heights of comedy and burlesque in an ass-festival that mocks the Christian sacraments. Zarathustra's great struggle in this part is with his tendency to feel pity; again this is an inversion of the pity which Jesus feels for suffering humanity. The motley collection of higher men who are assembled finally at Zarathustra's cave for a parodic version of the Last Supper are not meant to form the nucleus of a church. To the extent that they form a temporary group, their goal is to overcome the illusions of false community associated with institutions such as churches. This theme of dissolution is carried further insofar as the action of part four does not affirm even an integral individual as opposed to the communal or institutional world. This, of course, is a continuation, or enactment, of the revision of individuality which has been accomplished by the thought of eternal recurrence. Not one of the higher men who appear in this part could be called an integral individual; each is a fragment, a type, or an allegorical personage. If Zarathustra presents a contrast to this collection of his guests he does so not by way of being a stable and well rounded figure but by always being in motion, that is, by always ironizing in relation to the higher men.

There is some truth, then, to the suggestion that part four is analogous to the satyr-play which followed the tragic performance at the Greek theater or festival of Dionysus.[2] Yet this observation could also be misleading. First, it is incorrect to suppose that the first three parts of *Zarathustra* form an unbroken stylistic continuity which leaves only an exceptional fourth part to be explained. Each part turns upon its own distinctive mode of thought and language, as I have already claimed, perhaps too frequently. There is also the more subtle danger of an error in literary or generic classification here. The fourth part of Zarathustra is not a comic or satyric drama because it is (like the other parts) not a drama at all, but a narative. That is, it is a story which is being told to us, rather than performed before us; it is not mimetic, but diegetic. In this respect it is like Plato's *Symposium*, to which it bears some other striking resemblances, in being neither tragedy nor comedy but a narrative that contains them. In fact *Zarathustra* IV playfully calls attention to itself as a narrative, as in this passage from "The Drunken Song":

> The old prophet, however, danced with pleasure; and even if, *as some of the narrators [Erzähler] think*, he was full of sweet wine, he was certainly fuller still of sweet life and had renounced all weariness. *There are even those* who tell that the ass danced at that time: For not in vain had the ugliest man given it wine to drink. Now *it may have been so or otherwise*; and if in truth the ass did not dance that evening, greater and stranger marvels than the dancing of an ass occurred. In short, as the proverb of Zarathustra says, "What does it matter?" (Z, 327; 4, 396, my emphasis)

This same uncertainty about the legitimacy and origin of the story being told to us is found at the beginning of the *Symposium*, another drinking party which assembles a variety of "types" and includes the *eiron* Socrates, and where we learn that the story has been filtered to us through a succession of narrators. This is of course a classical device to call attention to the irony of a discourse and to alert the reader to the artfulness of the story's telling. In the case of the *Symposium* the indirection at the beginning of the narrative parallels Socrates' need, within the story, to present the nature of love by resorting to the fictitious figure of Diotima who must herself resort to mysteries and obscure language. Here the device emphasizes the allegorical nature of the narrative which we are reading and its many parodic relations to Plato, the Bible, and other texts.

As Fink says in dismissing this part of *Zarathustra*, one significant variation from what has been encountered so far has to do with the progression and structure of the story. We are much closer to conventional narrative here than in the rest of the book. A purpose is announced (Zarathustra will be a fisher of men; he will resist the temptation to pity); one by one the higher men make their appearance on Zarathustra's mountain and deliver themselves of their various allegorical messages; finally they are shown in assembly, celebrating the last supper and the ass-festival; at the end Zarathustra declares himself contented when he takes sight of the laughing lion and the flight of birds, which had been predicted as meaningful signs. Zarathustra, then, is no longer speaking to an amorphous group or to himself, but to a continuing cast of characters who will not only form part of a determinate action of his, but who will also eventually become significant actors for each other. At the same time the culminating events of this last part are in certain respects non-narrative or anti-narrative; the last supper and the ass-festival recall the carnival and the popular feast in which the hierarchies and distinct identities that we require in narrative are challenged and dissolved. In literary terms it is as if a Rabelaisian celebration were superimposed upon an allegorical medieval romance. Yet this is not a sign of artistic or philosophical ambivalence; it is a way both of recognizing the claims of the aspirants to Zarathustrean wisdom (including the reader) and of teaching those aspirants a lesson about the rather tenuous character of the official public self or the allegedly integral deeper self of otherworldly philosophy and religion.

The key is clearly sounded in the first episode, "The Honey-Offering." Zarathustra is discontent, complaining that his animals don't understand him. In their conversation there is much bantering about the proper metaphor to describe Zarathustra's condition. Gazing out from his cave at the sea and winding abysses (already identified in part three as metaphors for self-dissolution), Zarathustra's melancholy is puzzling to the animals. Solicitously, they attempt to remind him that he should have no cares because he lies in "a sky-blue lake of happiness."

> "You buffoons [*Schalks-Narren*]," answered Zarathustra and smiled, "how well you chose your metaphor [*Gleichnis!*] But you know too that my happiness is heavy and not like a liquid wave: it oppresses me and will not leave me, and acts like molten pitch."
> (Z, 251; *4*, 295)

Zarathustra had called his animals buffoons once before when they had attempted to tell him the meaning of eternal recurrence. It seems that they have still to learn that "*es gibt kein Aussen*" (there is no outside). The controversy about the appropriate metaphor shows that metaphors cannot be simply assigned, as they were in part one; the "radiant virtue" of the master of metaphor leads to incomprehension rather than strength. Moreover, even though Zarathustra is at home, and his animals are in some sense an extension of himself, there is no longer a pre-established harmony of the sort suggested in "The Homecoming" between the metaphors of home and one's own feelings. The "sky-blue lake of happiness" is an inept image; as opposed to the unbounded sea at which Zarathustra had been gazing, the lake is limited and self-contained, with no suggestion of the abyss. If the issue of happiness is to be raised metaphorically it might as well be likened to sticky molten pitch, for Zarathustra has reached a point at which he is stuck and in need of a change. But for his own purposes Zarathustra hits on an image which is less fluid than water but more congenial than pitch: "What is happening to me, happens to every fruit when it grows ripe. It is the *honey* in my veins that makes my blood thicker and my soul calmer." Yet this last metaphor is a deception; metaphor itself has become problematic for Zarathustra because he sees how variable and undependable it is; he ironizes metaphor. By introducing the image of honey, he is able to leave his animals at the summit of the mountain, ostensibly so that he can perform the (necessarily solitary) ritual of the honey-sacrifice. Once his animals have left, Zarathustra is proud that he has concocted a bit of cunning "and, verily, a useful folly. Up here I may speak more freely than before hermits' caves and hermits' domestic animals."

Zarathustra's animals, his snake and his eagle, are aspects of himself, his cleverness and pride. When Zarathustra discourses with his animals, especially in part three, he is moving within the circuit of self-contained language. To leave part of himself through deception is part of an ironic movement which continues throughout part four. Every expectation that Zarathustra has reached a final, determinate conclusion of some sort is attacked in the text. Zarathustra's own approach to the honey-sacrifice recalls his need, announced in the *Vorrede*, to pour out his wisdom (which is likened to honey there): "Offer—what? I squander what is given me, I'm a squanderer with a thousand hands; how could I call that—an offering? (Z, 252; 4, 296)."

Zarathustra lacks the stability required for the almost contractual arrangements implicit in sacrifice. His honey (wisdom) cannot be parcelled out to preserve such stability. Instead it will be "bait" to catch "the queerest human fish." Zarathustra's ironic movement in this part is already present in outline: it involves a distancing from the self, a mocking attitude toward his own wisdom, and the idea of snaring others in order to force them to come up to his own level. The last process will, of course, never be completed because Zarathustra is always climbing higher in a game of catch-me-if-you-can.

Because of this constant movement, there is no single chapter or episode in this part which offers a sustained treatment of the *topos* of discourse. The point of the ironic trope which prevails here is just to explode any appearance of centrality. In his long episodic series of meetings with the higher men Zarathustra sees nothing but parodies, misunderstandings, and fragments of himself. His conversation with each emphasizes his distance from all of them, so that the only community and solidarity attainable is the comic and parodic ass festival in which the higher men begin to see that wisdom is also folly. Zarathustra's great struggle in this part is with his own pity for the higher men. As Aristotle points out, pity presupposes community and identification; we can only feel sorry for those who are somewhat like ourselves. Zarathustra does not begin from such community but he is concerned not to be seduced to it. His defense is not the fear which, as Aristotle says, drives out pity, but a laughter which celebrates distance. In his series of conversations with the higher men Zarathustra exhibits his own self-overcoming by making it clear that he cannot be identified with any of these versions or parts of himself. He does this not to suggest some substantial self or ego which underlies these partial selves, but in order to exhibit the need to revise and dissolve our desire to find substance in the self.[3]

Why does the fourth part continue by intensifying the ironic movement that Zarathustra began by leaving his animals? Rhetorically and dramatically we could say that this part of Nietzsche's text is the satyr play following the tragic trilogy; or, to use Northrop Frye's categories, it is the satiric mode which follows those of romance, tragedy, and comedy; or that it is the traditional completion of the four classical rhetorical tropes identified by Kenneth Burke and Hayden White: metaphor, metonomy, synecdoche, and irony. Yet irony is also a first way of understanding eternal recurrence, which is affirmed at progressively deeper levels in *Thus Spoke Zarathustra*.

Now it is, in general, the purpose of the thought of eternal recurrence to destroy, or at least to weaken, a central or integral conception of the self. As Nietzsche suggests to his reader in *The Gay Science*, "if this thought gained power over you, it would transform you as you are or perhaps crush you." Unlike all the other "great thoughts," whether of Christianity, Marxism, or other faiths, eternal recurrence does not offer a convenient way of dividing one's life into a before and an after. For the moments (*Augenblicke*) of all my past are as eternal, as significant, as all of my future. In affirming recurrence I will all those moments in which I had never suspected that there was such a thought. So the thought requires us to will its own forgetting. Rather than providing a technique of self-integration it emphasizes the eternity of each of those many *Augenblicke*, those "twinklings of the eyes." These moments, we recall, are personified in "The Tomb Song" as having lives and deaths of their own.

The expression of this loosening of the self, this weakening of the boundaries of the ego, is laughter—the laughter which Zarathustra foresaw once in a riddle that followed a vision. Zarathustra asked many questions about the riddle but that which lured him most was the laughter:

> O my brothers, I heard a laughter that was no human laughter—and now a thirst consumes me, a longing that is never stilled.
> My longing for this laughter consumes me. (Z, 180; 4, 202)

We misunderstand Zarathustra's laughter so long as we fail to understand his conception of the self and the dissolving tendency of eternal recurrence. Philosophers who themselves exemplify the spirit of seriousness, like Hobbes, will presuppose the separation of individuals and the singleness of the laughing selves in their accounts of laughter. According to Hobbes's reductionistic formula,

> The passion of laughter is nothing else but *sudden glory* arising from some sudden *conception* of some *eminency* in ourselves, by comparison with the *infirmity* of others, or with our own formerly. . . . It is vain glory, and an argument of little worth to think the infirmity of another, sufficient matter for his triumph.[4]

In *Beyond Good and Evil* Nietzsche suggests that there may be

> an order of rank among philosophers depending on the rank of their laughter—all the way up to those capable of *golden* laughter. And supposing that gods too, philosophize, which has been suggested to me by many an inference—I should not doubt that they

also know how to laugh the while in a superhuman and new way—and at the expense of all serious things. (*BGE*, 294; 5, 236)

Nietzsche's notebooks show an association of the thought of recurrence and the festival or carnival as early as his first notes on the former idea. For just a few pages after the entry dated "the beginning of August 1881 in Sils Maria, 6000 feet up and much further than that beyond all human things!" he says "I want to teach a higher art against the art of artworks: that of the invention [*Erfindung*] of festivals" (9, 506). Hans-Georg Gadamer makes a similar observation in the course of a critical analysis of the aesthetic consciousness. Attempting to account for the nature of artistic time in which multiple performances or experiences of a work of art are neither copies nor deviations from an original, he suggests, in the spirit of Nietzsche's last remark, that the festival might be a more inclusive and adequate category than that of the supposedly autonomous work of art:

> We know this kind of highly puzzling time structure from festivals. It is in the nature, at least of periodic festivals, to be repeated. We call that the return of the festival. But the returning festival is neither another, nor the mere remembrance of the one that was originally celebrated. The originally social character of all festivals obviously excludes the kind of distinction that we know in the time-experience of the present; memory and expectation. The time-experience of the festival is rather its celebration, a present time *sui generis*.[5]

The festival then is a higher art than the art of artworks because of the sense that it provides of the return of the same. Of course the periodic celebration of the "same" festival within a lifetime or an historical epoch will not exhibit the *exact* recurrence of the same which, according to Nietzsche, characterizes the cycles of eternal recurrence. But in attempting to tell a story that suggests what life might be like if one were to affirm that thought, it is appropriate to think of the temporality of festivals as exhibiting a certain analogy to the temporality of recurrence. The use of an analogical pattern of thought here, diverted from its traditional ends, is similar to Nietzsche's inversion of the traditional metaphysics of analogy that is implicit in his account of metaphor (see above, chapter 3).

The figures whom Zarathustra encounters and invites to his festival on a single long day of travelling through his own mountains and forests are partial reflections or refractions of some aspects of himself. The first is "the prophet of the great weariness" whom we have met before; he teaches that "it is all the same, nothing is worth while, seeking is useless, and there are no blissful islands anymore" (Z, 256; 4, 302). In part this is Schopenhauer, but it is also the side of Zarathustra which is overcome with the great nausea of mankind; Zarathustra, we remember, once dreamed himself as this prophet (in "The Prophet," part two). Knowing that he can resist pity as he has overcome nausea, he invites the prophet to wait for him in his cave, telling him that he will become Zarathustra's "dancing bear" before the evening is over. The other meetings are similar. The two kings, it turns out, are confusedly seeking Zarathustra and the higher man, mouthing imprecations against the mob (which sound less like Zarathustra's than his ape's). They recite his words back to him ("It is the good war that hallows every cause") in such a way as to provoke "no small temptation to mock their eagerness" (Z, 260–61). Just as the sad prophet will be turned into a dancing bear, so the kings must return to Zarathustra's cave to wait as if they were courtiers.

Perhaps the most suggestive of these encounters is the one with the Enchanter (*Zauberer*). The Enchanter, like Zarathustra and like some of the other partial selves of part four, is an author of sorts. As several attentive readers of Nietzsche have recently suggested, the Enchanter can be seen as Nietzsche's own incursion into the text of *Zarathustra*. Like Nietzsche perhaps, the Enchanter claims an indifference to any audience in his first song, where he pretends to be alone; yet this charade is enacted for Zarathustra's sake. Later, the Enchanter will entertain the group of higher men (in Zarathustra's absence) with a long song of melancholy in which he professes to be "only a fool, only a poet." He thus parodies the author who writes "for all and none"; in seeking to manipulate Zarathustra and the higher men he embodies a traditional conception of the author as one who achieves a mastery of men's consciousness through the mastery of his text.

Zarathustra rejects such claims to authorship in his response to the Enchanter's first song. That song purports to be a lament addressed to the unknown god whom the magician has somehow disposed of or dispensed with. He would rather have his god back, with all his torments, than the pain of solitude.

> No! Come back,
> With all your torments!
> Oh come back!
> To the last of all solitaries!
> All the streams of my tears
> Run their course to you!
> And the last flame of my heart—
> It burns up to *you*!
> Oh come back,
> My unknown God! My *pain*! My last—happiness! (Z, 267; 4, 316–17)

Zarathustra, as audience and critic, is stronger than this author who could regret his own banishment of God, and responds not to *what* is said—he has no use for gods or their lamenters—but to the *manner* of the singer. As Fred Allen says in another context, the audience rose as one man—which it was—and struck the wailing man with with a stick "with all his force" and "with furious laughter." This thrashing is already a carnivalesque ritual in which the apparent king is dethroned and then beaten. Such thrashing, as Mikhail Bakhtin the student of carnival says, "is as ambivalent as abuse changed into praise. . . . The one who is thrashed or slaughtered is decorated. The beating itself has a gay character; it is introduced and concluded with laughter.''[6] Zarathustra may have forgotten his whip, but he has not forgotten his umbrella (the umbrella would be an appropriate prop for the performance of this scene).[7] The Enchanter confesses his imposture, admitting finally that he was playing the ''penitent of the spirit'' whom Zarathustra had described earlier. But Zarathustra and the Enchanter have somewhat different understandings of what it is to be a ''penitent of the spirit'' (*Büsser des Geistes*). In ''Of Poets,'' Zarathustra denounced the poets for their rhetorical craving for an audience and their use of metaphor in an attempt to attain the unattainable: ''Alas, how weary I am of all the unattainable that is supposed to be reality! [*Ach, wie bin ich all des Unzulanglichen müde, das durchaus Ereignis sein soll!*] (Z, 150; 4, 165).'' Zarathustra seems to be thinking of the new poets as reformed rhetoricians and metaphorizers. They will write poems of this world which give up the vain quest of fame and the concern with any form of the beyond. Here we might think of Mallarmé, or Rilke, or the various forms of the *Dinggedicht*. But the Enchanter emphasizes the bad conscience of the *Busser* rather than his reformed product:

> ''*The penitent of the spirit*,'' said the old man, ''It was he I played: you yourself once invented this expression—the poet [*Dichter*] and sorcerer [*Zauberer*] who at last turns his spirit against himself, the transformed man who freezes through his bad knowledge and bad conscience [*bösen Wissen und Gewissen*].'' (Z, 268; 4, 318)

But Zarathustra replies that this confession is ''not nearly true enough and not nearly false enough for me!'' because it masks a sense in which the magician is charged with insufficient irony; for the genuine ironist's sayings are both true and false, not simply the false disguises of a true reality. The unmasking theme in which we find out the truth behind the poet's song means one thing in the first reductive appearance of the *topos* and something quite different in this ironic conclusion. We should note that the Enchanter has expressed his own bad conscience through a rhetorical form (he is playing to an audience, if only of one) and by means of outlandish metaphors suggesting his torture by the unknown god. In attacking the magician Zarathustra is attacking the illusion of authorship. Those who have thought of the magician as an analogue of Wagner are right to the extent that for Nietzsche Wagner does represent an artist with the highest pretensions to mastery. But Nietzsche has these pretensions himself; unlike Wagner he at least occasionally allows his creations to rebuke him for such megalomania. Nietzsche and Zarathustra—but *not* Wagner— could say with Rimbaud ''I is another''; and Nietzsche *does* say ''I am all the names of history.''

What Zarathustra aims at with the Enchanter is a more undecideable and ironic language. Eventually, the higher men will produce a genuinely playful and undecideable discourse of their own. This happens only some time after they have all assembled together at Zarathustra's cave and issued a mighty collective cry of distress which brings him back from his wanderings. Zarathustra now recognizes them as the higher men, but he plainly takes them to be not yet capable of living up to their name:

> But it seems to me you are ill adapted for company, you disturb one another's hearts, you criers of distress when you sit here together? First of all someone else must come— someone to make you laugh again, a good, gay clown [*Hanswurst*], a dancer and breeze and madcap, some old fool or other. What do you think? (Z, 290; *4, 347*)

Zarathustra says, in effect, "I will be that someone else," "I will be another." While Zarathustra is telling the higher men that they need to be liberated from their melancholy and despair he is also tendering them a formal greeting. The formality is marked by the courteous silence at the end of Zarathustra's address and by the delegation of one of the kings to make a reply in the name of the entire group. The king praises Zarathustra and predicts that more and better men will soon be seeking him out: "all the men of great longing, great nausea, of great disgust" (Z, 292; *4, 349*). Zarathustra concludes the formal greeting by replying that the higher men are simply not high enough for him; they are not the "children" who will one day be his. Now this greeting is ambiguous; Zarathustra is himself carried away a bit by the despair of his guests at the same time that he is proposing to enliven them by playing the clown. What seems to be happening here is a radical shift in the narrative from the mode of allegory to that of carnival and festival. As individual allegorical figures, each of the higher men is in despair in one way or another. The last pope is like a retired servant who has nothing to do, now that God is dead, but honor the memory of his departed master. The conscientious man of the spirit who pursues scientific inquiry by concentrating on an increasingly smaller area (he has now dedicated himself to the brain of the leech) is living through the ascetic renunciation which accompanies such self-restraint. The Tolstoyan voluntary beggar has found no human audience for his message and is reduced to preaching the virtues of rumination and vegetarianism to cows. Each one of their histories, and those of the other higher men, is a moral vignette, much like Dante's separate encounters with the figures in the *Divine Comedy*.

Yet the narrative act of bringing the higher men together leads to a very different kind of story. The components of this second story follow a carnivalesque pattern: a great communal dinner (mockingly called "The Last Supper"), an invigorating talk (Zarathustra's "Of the Higher Man"), a series of songs punctuated by bantering; a festival in honor of the ass, which parodies both Christ and Zarathustra at the same time; and the general frenzy at midnight which is the setting for Zarathustra's "The Drunken Song." The whole series, and the book, is then brought to an end by a brief chapter in which Zarathustra finds his signs fulfilled (the bird flight and the laughing lion) and so knows that his children are near. Now such a series of events has its antecedents in the popular culture of the late middle ages. It is the comic spectacle or the festive play that Mikhail Bakhtin has reconstructed in his study of *Rabelais and His World*. If this identification seems implausible at first, consider Nietzsche's use of the following themes which Bakhtin notes as belonging to the popular carnival: the "sacred parody," often in a form centering around an ass; song and dance; a great indulgent meal; a general attitude of playfulness; and an emergence of sexuality. So far most of these features have already been noted in Nietzsche's narrative; it might be worth observing that his great meal also does double duty as religious parody. Zarathustra's party is a bit short on explicit sexuality, although there is a long and important sexual after-dinner song sung by Zarathustra's Shadow. In his other writings, beginning with *The Birth of Tragedy*, Nietzsche was much concerned with Dionysian festivals, Saturnalias, and other ways which human society has for periodically loosening its restraints. In a note of 1888 Nietzsche lists some things which have been harmed by the church's misuse, among which are "the festivals" (*die Feste*):

> One has to be very coarse in order not to feel the presence of Christians and Christian values as an oppression beneath which all genuine festive feelings go to the devil. Festivals include: pride, exuberance, wantonness; mockery of everything serious and philistine; a divine affirmation of oneself out of animal plenitude and perfection—one and all states which the Christian cannot honestly welcome. The festival is paganism *par excellence*. (*WP*, 916)[8]

In *The Genealogy of Morals*, as we will see in the next chapter, Nietzsche makes the spectacle or festival into an important structural principle for the understanding of history.

One apparent and striking distinction between the traditional carnival form and Nietzsche's use of it must be clarified. The traditional carnival is a popular and democratic form which is opposed to the official hierarchical life of the middle ages, especially to the hierarchy of the church. Accordingly its proper locale is in the marketplace and during carnival all distinctions of social or ecclesiastical rank are inverted. It is "a world turned upside down" (*die verkehrte Welt*), in which, as in Breughel's painting of carnival time, both social and conceptual distinctions are reversed.[9] In the version of the festival found in *Zarathustra IV*, the participants form a small group whose tastes are far from democratic and the setting is far from that marketplace where Zarathustra first announced the *Übermensch*; they include kings and a pope and all are there because of their admiration for Zarathustra. Yet the carnivalesque spirit still reigns. At Zarathustra's party no social distinctions are allowed; as the ironic master of the feast instructs his guests, "whoever would join in the eating must also help in the preparation, even the kings. For at Zarathustra's even a king may be a cook" (Z, 295; 4, 354). Even in their first appearance the kings and the pope are the *dethroned* kings and popes who are *mocked* at the carnival. The Pope is out of a job, the kings have no apparent power, the voluntary beggar lacks a human audience for his preaching. So they are all examples of the carnivalesque destruction or inversion of hierarchy. The carnival is not only a democratic form but one whose democratic tendencies are part of an opposition to established structures in so far as they are seen as repressing a vital and spontaneous life. Now in Zarathustra's (and Nietzsche's) assessment, the contemporary world is becoming increasingly constricted in these ways; "the last man" is a regimented democrat.

Part of the point at issue here is captured by the distinction between the measured pleasure of the last man and the comic laughter of Zarathustra's festival. The last men "have their little pleasure [*Lüstchen*] for the day and their little pleasure for the night; but they respect health. 'We have discovered happiness,' say the last men and blink" (Z, 46; 4, 19). The disparaging sense of *Lüstchen* is to be contrasted with the genuine *Lust* or delight of which Zarathustra sings, as in "*alle Lust will Ewigkeit*" ("all delight wants eternity"). This is the contrast between a measurable and predictable pleasure, on the utilitarian model, which can be associated with specific objects, and a more general sense of delight which is expansive and does not reinforce the narrow ego associated with the last man. In French one would speak here of the distinction between *plaisir* and *jouissance*. Nietzsche's carnival is at one with the traditional form in seeking a delight which undercuts established divisions and repressions.

In his long talk to his mock-disciples at the Last Supper, Zarathustra connects the self-overcoming of the *Übermensch* with the carnivalesque spirit of song and laughter. This discourse "Of the Higher Man" deals successively with three themes. At the beginning Zarathustra reiterates the connection between the death of God and the demise of the doctrine of equality; when it is no longer possible to say that we are all equal before God we should recognize the superiority of the *Übermensch*. For this to happen, man must become "better and more evil" (Z, 299). In the second part of his talk, however, Zarathustra moves downward from talk of the superman to advice to the higher men themselves. Here he tells them to "will nothing beyond your capacity" (Z, 300) and even more surprisingly to

> Follow in the footsteps of your fathers' virtue! How would you climb high if the will of your fathers does not climb with you?
>
> But he who wants to be a first-born should see that he does not also become a last-born. And you should not pretend to be saints in those matters in which your fathers were vicious!
>
> He whose fathers passed their time with women, strong wine, and roast pork, what would it be if he demanded chastity of himself? (Z, 302; 4, 363)

One could read such advice as reflecting a realistic and humanistic side of Nietzsche's teaching. This is no doubt accurate so far as it goes, but we must not forget the context of Zarathustra's talk. He is celebrating with the higher men at a feast which mocks Christianity by its glorification of the body. Bakhtin observes that it is part of the atmosphere of carnival to praise the "lower stratum of the material body," that is sexuality, procreation, and eating. An appropriate talk at such a feast then will be a eulogy of "lower" rather than "higher" things. We can read Zarathustra's talk as a parodic inversion of Socrates' speech about love in the *Symposium*; he moves *downward* to the body rather than *upwards* to the spiritual mysteries of Diotima.[10]

The last part of Zarathustra's address is an accelerating incitement to laughter and dance. Zarathustra claims to be "the laughing prophet" who has "canonized laughter" (Z, 305; 4, 366). It was a saying of Pliny, well known during the Renaissance (and likely to be known to the classicist Nietzsche) that Zarathustra (or Zoroaster) was the only man who began to laugh as soon as he was born; this was taken as a sign of his prophetic mission.[11] Zarathustra becomes the leader of the feast of fools. As the born leader of the feast of fools and the *Hanswurst* whom the higher men need, he declares that the clowns of the mob have all become sad. In effect he is claiming that the carnival and its spirit have died out among the people and that only he and the higher men are now capable of embodying it. He exhorts his audience to be "foolish with happiness" and to "learn to laugh" (Z, 306; *4*, 367–68). Yet Nietzsche's rejection of the people fails to appreciate those carnivalesque outbursts of the counter-culture that have punctuated our history from the French Revolution to the days of the late sixties and which will doubtless recur. In his *Eighteenth Brumaire of Louis Napoleon*, Marx has given a fine analysis of the inevitable turn to farce and parody in the bourgeois state, an absurdity typified by the comedian or actor at the center of power.

Here again Bakhtin is helpful in describing the nature of carnival laughter and its ontological meaning. Such laughter, which Zarathustra participates in and provokes here as the *Hanswurst* of his own carnival, is festive, universal, and ambivalent. It is festive in the sense of being responsive to the gaiety of the entire occasion, rather than directed at a specific object or isolated comic event. It is universal because directed at all by all; the distinction between audience and spectator does not apply here and one laughs at oneself as well as at others. It is an ambivalent laughter because it is simultaneously triumphant and affirmative, on the one hand, and mocking and deriding on the other. In all these respects carnivalesque laughter must be distinguished from a satiric attitude which would be directed toward a specific object other than oneself. Such satiric laughter perhaps deserves the low valuation Thomas Hobbes placed upon it. Now Zarathustra has spent a good deal of time attempting to convince the higher men that they are not of great eminence; certainly the laughter which he provokes is not directed against the mob (there the emotion to be feared is nausea) but is a function of the festive context. He will be the catalyst of the situation, the *Hanswurst*, who sees to it that the occasion itself is rich in laughter. Carnival laughter of the sort described cannot leave intact a conception of the self as an isolated and independent being with its own integral history. The tradition represented by Hobbes can envision laughter only as the expression of such a self's implicit measurement and comparison of itself with others. Laughter which is festive, universal, and ambivalent suggests a quite different conception of the world. Jacques Derrida has given a rather explicit account of the ontology of carnivalesque laughter in his essay "From Restricted to General Economy" (formally a commentary on the writing of Georges Bataille). The standard philosophical tradition (which for Bataille and Derrida is represented by Hegel) has no place for such laughter because it depends upon the effort to conserve a definite ground or base, such as Hobbes's independent ego or the Hegelian life which must be enriched and *aufgehoben* through the confrontation with death. The enemy of a generalized laughter, and therefore of a "general economy" that would not depend on the conservation of a fixed self or meaning, is an ontological one.

It is the belief that there is something which is or ought to be *present* (the self or Absolute Knowledge, for example) and which therefore must be preserved at all costs. But in Derrida's formulation it is just this effort which is comical (in the satiric sense):

> What is laughable is the *submission* to the self-evidence of meaning, to the force of this imperative: that there must be meaning, that nothing must be definitely lost in death, or farther, that death should receive the signification of "abstract negativity," that a work must always be possible which, because it defers enjoyment, confers meaning, serious-ness, and truth upon the "putting at stake". . . . Absolute comicalness is the anguish experienced when confronted by expenditure on lost funds, by the absolute sacrifice of meaning: a sacrifice without return and without reserves. [12]

Here we must think of the measured enjoyment of the last man with his little pleasure (*Lüstchen*) for the day and for the night and his high regard for health. The regu-larization of such little pleasures requires a "restricted economy." Genuine delight (*Lust*), on the other hand, in its desire for eternity knows that all is lost, that there is no final return on one's investments, and that the ego itself cannot maintain its strict and conserved identity in the flux of becoming.

Just as the established structures of a philosophy concerned with maintaining presence and an economy devoted to the conservation of investments presents an obstacle to the advent of a general economy of delight, so Zarathustra's carnival has its own obstacles in the resistance of some of its all-too-serious participants. As soon as the Last Supper is completed and Zarathustra is through with his talk he rushes out into the fresh night air, oppressed, as he says, by the smell of his guests. Yet at the same time he is playing the ironic clown; he deserts his own party so as to avoid being placed in a position of mastery. For the carnival spirit to be realized he must be at least as much clown as he is host. Now when Zarathustra leaves it is the melancholy Enchanter who cannot resist doing battle with his clown-ish host. Before beginning his "Song of Melancholy" which is a spell designed to subdue the spirit of carnival, the Enchanter explains his ambivalence toward Zara-thustra in his unexpected role of *Hanswurst*:

> I also know this monster [*Unhold*] whom I love despite myself, this Zarathustra: he himself often seems to me like the beautiful mask of a saint.
> Like a strange new masquerade [*Mummenschanze*] in which my evil spirit, the mel-ancholy devil, takes pleasure—I love Zarathustra, so I often think, for the sake of my evil spirit.
> But already he is attacking me and compelling me, this spirit of melancholy, this evening-twilight devil. (Z, 307; 4, 370)

The Enchanter then would place the responsibility for his melancholy on some exterior melancholy spirit, presumably the same unknown god to whom his earlier duplicitous song was addressed. But as the narrative remarks, he is always disingenuous in such claims, for he "looked around cunningly and then reached for his harp." The suggestion is, then, that the spirit of melancholy is indeed his *own* spirit, the bad conscience which he had previously confused with a reformed conception of poetry.

Since the Enchanter's song will soon be followed by another, sung by Zarathustra's shadow, the whole sequence should be seen as a poetic *agon* that manages to combine the laughter of the carnival with a reminiscence of the comic succession of speeches in praise of love in the *Symposium*. The latter analogy becomes more compelling when we notice that both songs have to do with desire, the first being concerned with the poet's desire and the second with the impotent desire of the European skeptic among Oriental girls. The Enchanter's song is a seductive lament. He addresses himself or, we might say, his own poetic genius, recounting the history of the poet's desire. The first form which that desire took was a boundless craving for truth that can now be recollected with some tranquility in the quiet and dew of the evening:

> Do you remember then, do you, hot heart,
> How once you thirsted
> For heavenly tears and dew showers,
> Thirsted, scorched and weary,
> While on yellow grassy paths
> Wicked evening sunlight glances
> Run about you through dark trees
> Blinding, glowing sunlight-glances, malicious? (Z 308; 4, 371).

But the high desires of the poetic soul were smashed when he was subjected to a skeptical jeering (perhaps like the one administered by Zarathustra in "Of Poets"):

> "The wooer of *truth*? You?"—so they jeered—
> "No! Only a poet!
> An animal, cunning, preying, creeping,
> That has to lie,
> That must knowingly, willfully has to lie:
> Lusting for prey,
> *Motley-masked [Bunt verlart],*
> *A mask to itself,*
> A prey to itself—
> *That*—the wooer of truth?
> No! Only a fool! Only a poet!
> Only speaking motley [*Nur Buntes redend*],
> Crying out of *fools-masks*,
> Stalking around on deceitful word-bridges." (Z, 308–09; 4, 371–72)

The charge which is levelled against the Enchanter is the same which Nietzsche had made earlier against all human language. In "Truth and Lie in an Extra-Moral

Sense'' he had argued that our language, despite its claims to correspond with reality, is in fact all creation and fabrication, nothing more than a "movable host of metaphors, metonymies, and anthropomorphisms: in short, a sum of human relations which have been poetically and rhetorically intensified, transferred, and embellished."[13] When Zarathustra turned against the poets he had also charged them with using "deceitful word-bridges" and making false connections

> On motley rainbows,
> Between a false heaven
> And a false earth.

So the Enchanter, under such attack, is making one more attempt to be a *Büsser des Geistes*. He will give up the search for truth, in general, but he wants to stimulate our pity for his loss and renunciation by dramatizing his melancholy. Moreover, he will give up more than he had in his earlier attempt, which Zarathustra had brought to an end by assaulting him with a stick. The Enchanter no longer pretends to be unconcerned with his audience but sings quite publicly. It is this public side of his performance which he refers to, in part, by using the language of carnival that Zarathustra had introduced. For he recounts the charge that he is dressed in motley (*Buntes*), speaks motley, is masked in motley and stalks around on motley rainbows. This may be the point at which to note that *Buntes* is a crucial term in *Zarathustra*, and not exclusively in its fourth, carnivalesque, part. The tightrope walker whom the people in the marketplace took for the *Übermensch* that Zarathustra had announced was toppled from his rope by "a fellow in motley clothes, looking like a jester" (Z, 47; 4, 21). This might suggest that the serious, all-too-serious, attitude of Zarathustra in the marketplace, an attitude expressed in his linking himself to the tragic tightrope walker, is in need of correction.[14] When Zarathustra returns to speak to a few, he sojourns in the town called "The Motley Cow" (Z, 56; 4, 31). The modern polity, Zarathustra tells us in his criticism of education and culture, is a mixed, motley collection of styles and forms; it is not one thing. The transvaluation of this condition is the transformation of a liberal, historicist pluralism into the vital world of carnival.

For the Enchanter, to be dressed or masked in motley is to appear as merely the clown or fool (*Narr*) at the carnival, one whose purpose is amusement rather than truth. To be "Only a fool! Only a poet!" (*"Nur Narr! Nur Dichter!"*) is to be reduced to a sideshow entertainment after pretending to the highest wisdom. Yet the Enchanter's way of recounting Zarathustra's charge shows that he has not understood the idea of carnival laughter in the way that Zarathustra has. For Zarathustra is far from dissociating the carnival and truth. Carnival laughter is congruent with the truth of eternal recurrence, although not with the narrow sense of truth as correspondence to an unknowable reality which lies at the origin of the epistemological attack on poetry to which the Enchanter alludes.[15] The Enchanter, let us recall, has just confessed that he is perplexed and attracted by Zarathustra's "masquerade'' although he does not comprehend it. If he did, he would welcome the carnivalesque epithets rather than regarding them as a new critique of his vocation.

Since the Enchanter does believe that his poetic dignity is under attack he replies by giving an alternative account of poetic desire. If the desire for truth must be abandoned, he suggests, then let the poet be filled with the strong and aggressive desires of the jungle cat or the eagle. Rather than build a beautiful statue of a god and guard it before the god's temple, the poet will become an

> enemy to such statues of truth,
> More at home in any wilderness than before temples,
> Full of cat's wantonness
> That you may run,
> Sinfully-healthy and motley and fair,
> In jungles among motley-speckled beasts of prey . . .
> Or like the eagle staring
> Long long into abysses,
> Into *its* abysses
>
> . . . .
>
> They pounce on *lambs*,
> Headlong down, ravenous
> Lusting for lambs
>
> . . . .
>
> Thus,
> Eaglelike, pantherlike,
> Are the poet's desires,
> Are *your* desires under a *thousand masks*,
> You fool! You pet! (Z, 309–10; 4, 372–73)

The Enchanter, then, is attempting to reverse what he sees as Zarathustra's attack on poetry. Characteristically, he praises his own lusty courage and aggression only with Zarathustra safely gone from the gathering, just as he had previously pretended to be alone while seeking pity from Zarathustra whom he knew to be listening to him then. If all language is nothing but the expression of animal desires, then the poet will not be content to be a contemptible fool; under the mask of the fool he will be lurking ready to pounce:

> You saw man
> As God and sheep:
> To rend the God in man
> As the sheep in man,
> And in rending to *laugh*. (Z, 310; 4, 373)

The Enchanter's fantasized laughter is destructive, spiteful, and envious; it has none of the celebrating depth of the carnival spirit. That this is a vengeful and a spiteful laugh becomes clear in a final extended image and one last claim to truth, despite all previous renunciation. In the extended image the Enchanter returns to the motif of the landscape of evening with which he began, and suggests that the moon is green with envy at its enemy the day. The point of the image is that the poet too sank, like the moon, from his delusion of truth.

> Weary of day, sick with light,
> Sank downwards, down to evening, down to shadows,
> Scorched and thirsty with one truth
> . . . .
> *That I am banished*
> *From all truth,*
> *Only a fool!*
> *Only a poet!* (Z, 311; 4, 374)

The Enchanter has indeed become more ironic since his meeting with Zarathustra; yet while Zarathustra's irony has deepened into a carnivalesque laughter, the Enchanter's has frozen and hardened into the irony of resentment that clings enviously to its one truth and goes on the attack because it cannot be productive and radiant. Envy, based on invidious comparison, is parallel to Hobbesian laughter and is the antithesis of carnival. The Enchanter has allowed the poet's ancient playful difference (*diaphora*) with philosophy to turn into an envious quarrel. After his first song we heard that his eye shot a "green lightning bolt" at Zarathustra; in the second he sees himself as a moon green with envy of the sun.

The Enchanter's spell is almost completely successful, for "all who were gathered there went unwittingly as birds into the net of his cunning and melancholy lust" (Z, 311; 4, 375). Appropriately the sham abandonment of truth-seeking by an ambiguous *Büsser des Geistes* is caught and ridiculed by the *Gewissenhafte des Geistes* (the Conscientious Man of the Spirit). He is genuinely interested in truth, and although unable to seek it outside the confines of his research on the brain of the leech, he angrily contests the right of the Enchanter to claim any truth at all. He gives a good rhetorical analysis of the Enchanter's irony: "you are like those whose praise of chastity secretly invite to voluptuous delights"; and he rebukes the higher men for having given up their freedom "like men who have been gazing long at wicked girls dancing naked." It may not be immediately clear why the Conscientious Man's accusation should take on this apparently prurient tone. The suggestion is that there is something self-indulgent about the melancholy, self-pity, and resentment of the Enchanter's song, and that this self-indulgence is like that of men who are bewitched by a sexual spectacle. So it is not so much chastity as such that is being praised (although the Conscientious Man certainly intends to praise a chastity of the intellect); rather the point is to distinguish both chastity and a life of active desire from the slinking and cunning melancholy of those who watch sex shows or fantasize about how they *could* be great poets. The Conscientious Man of the Spirit offers science as the alternative to this melancholy, claiming that it is the only security in a world of fear. Although he says that science is embodied in Zarathustra, the object of his praise repudiates the obsession with fear and calls for "courage and adventure, and joy in the unknown" (Z, 313; 4, 377).

None of these interchanges is decisive but they do heighten the atmosphere of playful contest. So far the pretentious and deceptive song of the Enchanter still holds the field. Now Zarathustra's Shadow enters the fray by seizing the Enchanter's harp and singing a song of his own. It is an after-dinner song, which relates an old memory; it was devised, he claims, to please Oriental girls like the ones described in the song itself; so its first audience and its subject (in part) are the "Daughters of the Desert" of the chapter's title. Some commentators have seen this as an obscure poem, worthy of metaphysical commentary.[16] In fact it is a song full of erotic imagery which, in competing with the song of the Enchanter, carries poetic self-parody a step further. At the same time, it adroitly picks up the theme of desire which motivated the Enchanter's song and, enlightened by the literary criticism of the Conscientious Man, attempts to deflate that desire with a more playful song. The song does not lend itself to a somber reading of the sort that Heidegger practices on Hölderlin; it is part of a playful *agon* with some echoes of the song-contests in *Die Meistersinger* and *Tannhauser*.

The form of the song of Zarathustra's Shadow, like that of so many of Nietzsche's poems outside of *Zarathustra*, a parody of a recognizable poem or genre. In this case the genre is one with which English-speaking readers will have little familiarity. It is the self-consciously exotic and romantic poetry of the Orient written by Europeans in the late nineteenth century.[17] Such "Oriental" poems tend to celebrate the passion and mystery of the East, contrasting it with the boredom or exhaustion of the West. The Oriental poem is a poem of desire; more specifically, of a desire for the strange and foreign as seen through an erotic and fantastic haze. In this respect it is an appropriate rival to the Enchanter's "Song of Melancholy"; Zarathustra's Shadow offers it as an after-dinner song, a piece of occasional poetry designed for an occasion of self-indulgence. What had been implicit in the Enchanter's song becomes rather explicit here. Self-indulgence is no longer disguised, as it was by the "cunning" Enchanter, as the vitality of the panther and the eagle. Here it is expressed as the passive desire of the "European under palm trees" who basks luxuriously while the desert maidens perform their erotic dance for him:

> Here I now sit
> In this smallest oasis
> Like a date,
> Brown, sweet, oozing golden,
> Longing for a girl's rounded mouth,
> But longing more for girlish,
> Ice-cold, snow-white, cutting
> Teeth: for these do
> The hearts of all hot dates lust. Selah. (Z, 316; 4, 382)

The oral imagery is extended by the suggestion that the European has been swallowed by the tiny oasis in the way that Jonah was swallowed by the whale, so that he has not only been taken in by the mouth but rests content in the belly:

All hail to his belly
If it was
As sweet an oasis-belly
As this is: which, however, I call in question,
—since I come from Europe,
Which is more sceptical than
Any little old wife.
May God improve it!
Amen:

Here the European links his fantastic self-indulgence to his skepticism. This skeptical impotence is the truth of European imperialism; it is the condition of the Flaubertian hero whose sentimental education includes a sexual tour of the East. The confession of impotence becomes explicit in the last stanza of the poem which unmasks the psychological reality behind the moral indignation with which the European is tempted to rationalize his attitude toward the luxurious and seemingly child-like East:

Roar once again, Roar morally!
Roar like a moral lion
Before the daughters of the desert!
For virtuous howling,
You dearest maidens,
Is loved best of all by
European ardor, European appetite!
And here I stand now,
As European,
I cannot do otherwise, so help me God!
Amen!
Deserts grow: woe to him who harbors deserts! (Z, 319; 4, 384–85)

The parodic references here are complex. There is first Luther's declaration of faith and principle, transformed into skeptical weakness. This is consistent with Nietzsche's general view of Protestantism and suggests his reading of modern subjectivism as a crucial stage in the development which culminates in passive nihilism. There is also an echo here of the *Symposium*, that great model, of a contest of discourses about desire. That dinner party also contains a great confession of unconsummated desire: the beautiful Alcibiades tells how Socrates, despite all his entreaties, spent an entire night with him in brotherly chastity. Yet the *Symposium* tells of an ascending hierarchy of desires, such that Socrates' refusal becomes intelligible on the basis of his stronger and more real desire (from the Platonic point of view) for beauty itself, as opposed to its lesser forms. The succession of songs at Zarathustra's party present a descending hierarchy of desire, in which it is suggested that it is just such desires for unworldly beauty which eventually lead to an inability to enjoy and take pleasure. Perhaps it was this passage that inspired Joyce's "also spuke zerothruster." Socrates suggests at the end of the *Symposium* that the true poet would be able to write both tragedy and comedy; the implication for the reader is that Plato has accomplished that in the very text in question. Similarly, Nietzsche has given us first a tragic and then a comic poem about desire. We suspect a private joke here. We wish that the sex at Zarathustra's party were better, and that he had affirmed sexuality in the way that *Finnegans Wake* does. Just as Socrates in his own person presents a paradigm of desire (or love) which stands in contrast to the lesser versions of desire expressed at the dinner party, so Zarathustra through his clowning and irony is suggesting a way in which desire can escape the traps of bad conscience (of the Enchanter's song) and impotent skepticism (of the Shadow's song). The choice that he offers is desert or carnival.

"Among the Daughters of the Desert" has become something of a fixture of the Nietzsche legend through the work of Thomas Mann. In a lecture of 1947, Mann attempted to tie the image of the Oriental dancing girls in their fluttering skirts to Nietzsche's shocking, involuntary visit to a brothel in Köln in 1865. As Nietzsche related the story in a letter to Paul Deussen, a porter who had been showing him the city took him there, although the young scholar had asked to be directed to a restaurant. Nietzsche reported being immobilized with shock in the midst of a number of girls in "flitter and gauze" until he saw a piano in the back of the room. He played a few chords, as if to free himself from a spell, and then left. What Mann adds to this account is his own theory that Nietzsche was haunted by the memory of the place and returned to a similar establishment twice, deliberately infecting himself with syphilis. The story is also given a fictional form in Mann's *Doctor Faustus* where the nihilistic composer, Adrian Leverkuhn, partially based on the figure of Nietzsche, does just that. The biographical data seem somewhat weaker than Mann supposed; in any case it is evident that his narrative is constructed in order to facilitate the theme of the inseparability of genius and disease that runs constantly through his writing. Given Mann's biographical interpretation, "Among the Daughters of the Desert" is "an orientalizing poem whose frightful jocosity with tortuously bad taste betrays a repressed sensualism and its needs whilst normal inhibitions are already crumbling."[18]

Now whatever Nietzsche may have done (or not done) in the 1860s, the poem is not so alien to the narrative of the book that it demands the exclusively symptomatic reading that Mann offers. The song completes an important movement in the articulation of the carnivalesque laughter which is the focus of the fourth part of *Zarathustra*. As a linguistic and poetic exercise (it is certainly not great poetry) the song shows a way of carrying further the enterprise of the *Büsser des Geistes* to which the Enchanter pretends. The "Song of Melancholy" is heavy with serious claims and anguished memories of loss. It renounces truth only to claim it again by rhetorical appeals for pity. While encapsulating some of Nietzsche's own skeptical critique of human knowledge, it would finally (and illegitimately) save itself from that critique. "Among the Daughters of the Desert" is much more consciously ironical and parodic than the Enchanter's false renunciation. It is presented as a mere memory or fancy, a song which just might be entertaining after dinner. Yet it goes further than the Enchanter in confessing a *real* incapacity, rather than making a show of such abnegation. And the confession itself is couched in a series of amusing, often amusingly grotesque, images and anecdotes, contrasting sharply with the contempt for the motley in the Enchanter's song. The European of the song is able to parody himself and the poetic tradition as he proceeds. The song parodies its own melancholy as well as the Enchanter's "Song of Melancholy." After describing his hesitations and confusions around the two tempting houris, Dudu and Suleika, he says neologistically that he felt "ensphinxed" ("*umsphinxt*") and follows this with a playful reflection on his own language:

> *Ensphinxed*, to crowd many
> Feelings into one word
> (May God forgive me
> This linguistic sin!) (Z, 317; 4, 382).

Similarly the lengthy and outrageous comparison of a swaying palm to a one-legged dancing girl ought to be seen not as a stylistic lapse on Nietzsche's part but as a deliberate exaggeration of the rhetorical excesses of European poetry of the exotic. The two songs juxtapose a true irony to a false one, with Zarathustra's Shadow (who is and is not Zarathustra) completing the carnivalesque dethronement of the Enchanter that was begun earlier. If anyone in *Zarathustra* is the *Büsser des Geistes* whose coming was anticipated, it is the Shadow.

From a structural point of view, "Among the Daughters of the Desert" confirms Derrida's attempt to demonstrate the undecidability of the figure of woman in Nietzsche. Each of the four parts of *Zarathustra* contains a distinctive attitude toward woman and the erotic. In part one there is the notorious motto "You are going to women? Do not forget the whip !" (Z, 93; 4, 86), which, it must be recalled, was said by Zarathustra only in reporting how it was told to him by a "little old woman." Woman, in part one, is a plaything, albeit "the most dangerous plaything" (Z, 91; 4, 85). She is that which insures that he will be continuously playful and childlike; she is the permanent possibility of metaphor. Part two varies this metaphorical dimension by introducing erotic rivalry and jealousy as Zarathustra is torn between Life, whom he loves, and Wisdom, whom he finds most seductive ("The Dancing Song"). This is in keeping with the focus on fragmentation and hostility that colors all existence in so far as it is merely will to power. The third part concludes with the image of marriage—a traditional representation of the integration and union of different elements. In the concluding part the Shadow introduces woman ironically and indirectly as the player in the paradigmatic erotic farce in which maximum opportunity is accompanied by minimum performance.

Zarathustra's guests are entertained by the song, for after it is over "the cave suddenly became full of noise and laughter" (Z, 319; 4, 387). Unlike Goethe who proceeded from the chaos of the Northern carnival to the emerging order of the *classical Walpurgisnacht*, Zarathustra's party moves toward the disorderly and the Dionysian. Even so, Zarathustra is still uncomfortable with the higher men, and leaves once more, noting that "if they have learned laughter from me it is not *my* laughter they have learned." Yet he has high hopes for these higher men, and his expectation that "before long they will be devising festivals and erecting memorials to their old joys" is soon realized when he returns to find them "kneeling like children and devout little old women and worshipping the ass" (Z, 321; 4, 388). Just as irony by itself can become an empty exercise of wit, so carnival laughter can become fixated on specific performances like the songs; it may be festive without being universal and ambivalent; that is, it may still hesitate to let one's self and one's highest ideals become objects of laughter. For this higher laughter, *parody* is necessary. It is the Ugliest Man, who could not bear God's seeing him, who makes a spectacle of himself by leading the litany in praise of the ass. The litany itself is a parody of the mass, the *sacra parodia* of carnival, and it is punctuated regularly by a refrain from the ass himself. The ass's "*I-A*" is both the German version of our "hee haw" and also sounds very much like the affirming "*Ja*" which Zarathustra urges the higher men to say to their lives and to eternity. So it is not only Christianity but the "religion" of Zarathustra that is mocked, as in this section of the litany: "He does not speak, except to say Yea [*Ja*] to the world he created: thus he praises his world. It is his subtlety that does not speak: thus he is seldom thought wrong. The ass, however, brayed 'Yea-Yuh' ['I-A']" (Z, 322; 4, 389).

Zarathustra interrupts the litany and challenges the higher men to justify what appears to be their backsliding to a degraded form of religion. Earlier he had explained that absolutely universal and indiscriminate affirmation—omnisatisfaction—is bad taste (Z, 212; 4, 244). It is not clear whether Zarathustra at first suspects that the ass festival is entirely sincere or whether he is testing the higher men to determine the quality of their laughter. But the Ugliest Man becomes the spokesman for the festival which he has been conducting and explains, in Zarathustra's own words, that "Whoever would kill most thoroughly, *laughs*" (Z, 324; 4, 392). This is one of the few places in the book—perhaps the only one—in which Zarathustra's words are quoted back to him in a meaningful way. In fact there is a double edge to this quotation which Zarathustra does not explicitly acknowledge. For the laughter of the ass festival has as its objects both Christianity *and* Zarathustra's teachings. The ass's "I-A" reminds us that affirmation is not exempt from being turned round by parody. This may happen in "ordinary language" as well as in the rather stagy spectacle that Nietzsche has invented here. Among Anglophone philosophers there is a story that J. L. Austin, while conducting one of his select Sunday discussions of linguistic nuances asked "Isn't it odd that while two negatives may be combined in English to make a positive statement, two positives will not make a negative?" To which Sidney Morgenbesser instantly replied "Yeah, yeah," in a mock-depressive tone that immediately effected the supposedly impossible equivalence.

That the guests are able to "roast" their own host, of whom they stood in awe just a few hours ago, suggests that the spirit of carnival and its ambivalent laughter has been well understood. This is what Zarathustra confirms when he pronounces this blessing upon the higher men and consecrates the ass–festival:

> "Truly, you all have blossomed forth; for such flowers as you, I think, *new festivals* are needed." A little brave nonsense, some divine service and ass festival. . . . And if you celebrate it again, this ass festival, do it for love of yourselves, do it also for love of me! And in remembrance of *me*".(Z, 325–26; *4*, 393–94)

The Ugliest Man is not only the spokesman for the ass festival; not coincidentally he is the one character in the book who comes to affirm eternal recurrence through Zarathustra's teaching. If Zarathustra is the teacher of recurrence, the Ugliest Man is perhaps his only successful student. At the ass festival Zarathustra says to him "You seem changed, your eyes are glowing, the mantle of the sublime covers your ugliness" (Z, 324; *4*, 392). The Ugliest Man, then, has found his own carnival mask which reverses his ordinary status and appearance. Having begun as the recluse who lived in the Valley of Snakes' Death he has now become the impresario of a public entertainment, a new festival. The Ugliest Man, it must be remembered, is God's killer; he murdered God because he could not bear to be seen and pitied. Zarathustra was not serious enough to murder, although he knew that God was dead. Rather he speaks of being able to believe only in a god who could dance; Zarathustra is closer to a playful polytheism than to an atheism based on revenge.

Just before midnight the Ugliest Man announces that "one day, one festival with Zarathustra, taught me to love the earth" and he quotes his host once more, like a diligent student " 'Was *that*—life?' I will say to death. 'Very well! Once more!' " (Z, 326; *4*, 396). Why does Nietzsche select the Ugliest Man to affirm Zarathustra's teaching of eternal recurrence and what is the significance of his affirmation? I suggested earlier that the Ugliest Man's reference to "one day, one festival with Zarathustra" can at least protect us against a misinterpretation of the thought of eternal recurrence. The Ugliest Man's ability to base his affirmation on a brief episode suggests that one need not see one's entire life as an aesthetic totality in order to make the requisite affirmation. Rather the thought of recurrence, when understood in circumstances that dramatize its sense, shows itself to be affirmable. In becoming another—by transforming himself from recluse to impresario and by the transfiguration of his inexpressible ugliness into sublimity—the Ugliest Man comes to understand the appeal of that thought which loosens the boundaries of the self and allows the delight of the moment.

As the murderer of God, the Ugliest Man was determined to rid the world of any spectator who would know him and pity him for his ugliness. At the beginning of his "one day" with Zarathustra, he is living in the Valley of Snakes' Death, which shows us one version of a world that lacks a divine witness or, for that matter, any form of universal spectator. It is a world that contains no life except for the snakes that come there to die. This is perhaps the desolate, twilight world of positivism in which not only is God dead but nature itself must be conceived as lifeless; such a positivistic consciousness is the death of wisdom, for the snake (the wisest animal, according to Zarathustra) dies here. Now as conceived through the thought of eternal recurrence the world also necessarily lacks any universal spectator. That is, if everything recurs and there is nothing that does not recur, there cannot be any consciousness, agent, or mechanism that would observe or count the various recurrences of events or cycles. In the world of recurrence there is no author of the world and no omniscient narrator. There is not a constant text to be read as an ideal reader might construe it but a text to be made and enjoyed in the making. In *Zarathustra* IV the festival, the carnival, and their freedom to parody any presumably fixed, monumental, or authorized text are the forms of existence that make vivid the possibility of writing and interpreting that can take place apart from any conception of a universal writer or interpreter. Surely this is the reason that the Ugliest Man's affirmation is followed immediately by a reflective passage that undermines any claim for the narrative authority of *Zarathustra* itself, in which after the uncertainties of the unnamed narrators (*Erzähler*) and story-tellers are mentioned, the quest for narrative authority is dismissed: "In brief, as Zarathustra's saying has it: 'What does it matter?'" (Z, 327; 4, 396). The story may be one thing or it may be another; the very uncertainties of the situation are conditions of the affirmation of recurrence.

Now Zarathustra sings and comments on "The Drunken Song" which celebrates not only his intoxication and that of the higher men but the drunkenness of the world itself. When next we hear of him he is waking refreshed while the higher men still sleep; now he is met by the flock of birds and the laughing lion which he takes as a sign that his children are near. He knows that he has been successful in his struggle with pity and so leaves his cave "glowing and strong, like a morning sun emerging from behind dark mountains" (Z, 333; 4, 405).

This end of the book heightens the air of allegory and myth which has been present throughout *Zarathustra* IV. The narrative is brought to a conclusion by certain signs being fulfilled, although Zarathustra (like Odysseus for whom signs are fulfilled at the end of the *Odyssey*) still has much to do. In a larger sense, all of part four is an interpretation and fulfillment of Zarathustra's prophetic dream of himself as the night watchman in the land of death (in "The Prophet"). There Zarathustra had been unable to interpret the "thousand masks of children, angels, owls, fools, and butterflies as big as children" which "laughed and mocked and roared" at him, shattering the monotonous sleep of death (Z, 157; 4, 174). Now it is disclosed that the true prophet is Zarathustra, not the one who had taught that "everything is empty, everything is one, everything is past." As Bakhtin notes, the parodic prophecy was a regular part of carnival festivity.[19] Its point is to deflate the gloomy official and nihilistic prophecies of the coming end of the world. Rather than looking for mysteries in Zarathustra's signs we should see them as parodically countering the prophecy of nihilism.

That which has happened is that which was to be fulfilled; as such the narrative achieves a mythical status which invites comparison with other philosophical myths. Of these, the most prominent are the Platonic stories in the *Symposium* and *Republic* which also revolve around the themes of the party, drunkenness, and the alternation of day and night. The aim of parody is to renew time; here that is done through a transformation or transvaluation of philosophy's sacred Platonic myths. The *Symposium* begins by a series of indirections as we learn that the story to be told is filtered through several narrators and many years; it ends, however by a reminder of the authority of Plato whose controlling authorship is evoked by the discussion of the true poet who can write both tragedy and comedy. *Zarathustra* IV, however, calls its own narrative into question at the end, leaving us without such a principle. Zarathustra's drunken song shows that he knows the proper uses of intoxication. Unlike Socrates, however, who used such an occasion to explain how desire leads us beyond the world, Zarathustra teaches that "so rich is joy that it thirsts for woe, for hell, for hatred, for shame, for the lame, for *world*—for it knows, oh it knows this world!" (Z, 332; 4, 403). Socrates, it will be remembered, stayed up all night discoursing until his companions dropped off to sleep one by one. Zarathustra honors the alternation of night and day, rather than the light alone, and so he pays the proper respect to night and the body by eventually going to sleep. In fact Zarathustra lives in a cave, an obviously dark place which recalls the Platonic myth about our emergence to genuine knowledge. But for Zarathustra both the darkness of the cave (and midnight) and the "great noon" have their own claims. The return to the cave is not, for him, a compromise with the limits of our condition, but an affirmation of the continuous play of all extremes that is opened up by eternal recurrence.

FIVE

The Text as Graffito: Historical Semiotics

(The Antichrist)

Even those writers who have good things to say about Nietzsche usually do not have good things to say about his penultimate book, *The Antichrist*. Like *Ecce Homo* it is often described as at least prefiguring Nietzsche's madness if not (as is sometimes the case) said to be part of that desperate glide itself. Those inclined to reject the book may be encouraged in this view by Nietzsche's statement to Brandes, in November 1888, that *The Antichrist* is the whole of *The Transvaluation of All Values* (originally announced as a series of four books) and that *Ecce Homo* is its necessary prelude. The reader will have already discerned my intention of retrieving this exorbitant text for the Nietzsche canon. Such operations of retrieval are standard enough moves within a certain kind of philological discourse which privileges the book as an expressive or cognitive totality. But Nietzsche, the arch-philologist, is today often regarded as undercutting the grounds of such moves not only by challenging their hermeneutic presuppositions but also by exemplifying in a paradigmatic fashion the discontinuous, fragmentary, or porous text. The second view of Nietzsche's writings is a very traditional one; it is a commonplace with Nietzsche's earlier readers to regard all of his writing as distressingly wanting in order and style, despite their admiration for his thought. Such has continued to be the assumption of Anglo-American readers such as Walter Kaufmann and Arthur Danto, who have aimed at articulating the internal order of Nietzsche's thought which the stylistic fireworks of the texts obscure. Recent French readers, most notably Jacques Derrida, have tried to show that fragmentation and undecidability are not merely secondary features of Nietzsche's writing but constitute its very element. Derrida outrageously suggests that the jotting "I forgot my umbrella" is typical of *all* Nietzsche's writing in its ambiguity and undecidability of meaning and in its systematic evasion of all contextual explication. One might wonder whether such a reading is indebted to Nietzsche's own hermeneutic strategy in *The Antichrist*. There Nietzsche anticipates Heidegger and Derrida by relying on the figure of *erasure* to designate his own relation to Christianity, its textual traditions, and its central figure, Jesus. Following the nineteenth-century philological and historical methods to their extreme and thereby overturning and transvaluing (*umkehren* and *umwerten*) both those methods and Christianity, Nietzsche tries to restore the blank page which is Jesus' life to its pristine purity of white paper, *tabula rasa*. We know that such a project of restoration can approach its goal only asymptotically. In this respect Nietzsche's project is very much like Robert Rauschenberg's erased De Kooning painting and like Derrida's attempt to shatter any determinate meaning in Nietzsche himself by revealing the irreducible plurality of woman in the apparently masculine ambitions of order and control in Nietzsche's style. All of these efforts nevertheless remain marked with the *signatures* of their authors; the negation of a negation cannot be negation itself. At the end there is Rauschenberg's art, Derrida's project of deconstruction, Nietzsche's graffito scrawled on the Christian text. This, however, is to anticipate the results of my project of retrieval.

Just as erasure is always an act that leaves its own mark, so retrieval is possible but need not produce that totalizing organic unity that has been the constant phantom of aesthetic thought. If retrieval is always partial it is also easier because the excesses of Nietzsche's readers here have been egregious. Consider, for example, Eugen Fink's Heideggerean book on Nietzsche which discounts any philosophical value the book might have by means of a brief analysis of *The Antichrist*:

> In the text *The Antichrist (Attempt at a Critique of Christianity)* Nietzsche battles against the Christian religion with an unparalleled fervor of hatred, and with a flood of invectives and accusations. Here the virtuosity of his attack, leaving no stone unturned, reverses itself. The lack of measure destroys the intended effect; one can't convince while foaming at the mouth. Essentially the text offers nothing new; Nietzsche collects what he has already said about the morality of pity and the psychology of the priest—but now he gives his thoughts an exorbitant, violent edge and wants to insult, to strike the tradition in the face, to "transvalue" by valuing in an anti-Christian way.[1]

Fink's comment suggests that his reasons for thinking that "the text offers nothing new" may be just the stylistic excesses and rhetorical failures of which he accuses it. Certainly his judgment on the book follows well-established opinion about its place in the Nietzsche canon. Even when the book is regarded as a culminating work (applying a dubious schema of linear development), it is usually employed to demonstrate the tragedy of Nietzsche's career as author and thinker. Karl Löwith calls it the "logical conclusion" of the critique of Christianity begun in the untimely meditation on D. F. Strauss, author of the nineteenth century's first great life of Jesus. Yet according to Löwith even this late work shows that Nietzsche has not escaped his obsession with Christianity. From this perspective we would have to say that Nietzsche the philosopher is not free of the bad blood of German theology which he denounces so vehemently: "Among Germans one will understand immediately when I say that philosophy has been corrupted by theologian blood. The Protestant pastor is the grandfather of German philosophy, Protestantism itself is *peccatum originale*" (A 10; 6, 176). It could then be argued that the growth and intensity of the obsession is part of the madness that prevented Nietzsche from seeing the book through to publication and which led him to consider it alternatively as the first part of the *Transvaluation*, as the entire *Transvaluation*, and then as the *Curse on Christendom* which required *Ecce Homo* as a balance.[2] Yet even the last self-interpretation permits another construction: *Ecce Homo* balances *The Antichrist* by showing that the great curser and destroyer is one who lives in the halcyon element of the "perfect day when everything is ripening and not only the grape turns brown" and asks *"How could I fail to be grateful to my whole life?"*[3]

What Arthur Danto calls the "unrelievedly vituperative" tone of the book is everywhere evident. At the conclusion of the book Nietzsche says of the Christian church that "to me, it is the extremest thinkable form of corruption, it has had the will to the ultimate corruption conceivably possible. The Christian church has left nothing untouched by its depravity" (*A* 62; 6, 252). And Nietzsche pushes the rhetorical contrast to the extreme by defending the Roman Empire against Christianity, inverting the usual belief in the civilizing virtue or necessity of the latter's conversion of the former:

> Christianity was the vampire of the *Imperium Romanum* . . . this most admirable of all works of art in the grand style was a beginning, its structure was calculated to prove itself by millennia. . . . But it was not firm enough to endure the *corruptest* form of corruption, to endure the *Christian*. . . . These stealthy vermin which, shrouded in night, fog and ambiguity crept up to every individual and sucked seriousness for *real* things, the instinct for *realities* of any kind, out of him, this cowardly, womanish and honeyed crew gradually alienated the "souls" of this tremendous structure. (*A* 58; 6, 245–46)

It is this tone which might be taken to justify the reduction of Nietzsche's thought to be the first-liner of a graffito sometimes found in certain modern tiled cells and catacombs:

God is dead—Nietzsche
Nietzsche is dead—God

This reduction could appear to be the creative interpretation of a masterful will to power—if Nietzsche's thought and style are as uncontrolled as the critics suggest. Yet there are some signs at the beginning and end of the book that might lead us to hesitate. Nietzsche himself anticipates the strife of revengeful graffiti at the conclusion of his text: "Wherever there are walls I shall inscribe this eternal accusation against Christianity upon them—I can write in letters which make even the blind see" (*A* 62; 6, 253). At the same time Nietzsche says in his preface that his readers must have a "predestination for the labyrinth" and "new ears for new music" if they are to understand this difficult writing. So like all of Nietzsche's books, *The Antichrist* is self-referential. It is concerned with those very questions of how it is to be read and how it exists as a piece of writing which we are supposed to think of as derivative and external interests of the critic and historian. The words which can be written on the wall are also directed by a powerful thought and a complex rhetorical strategy.

In *Ecce Homo* Nietzsche imagines "a perfect reader" who would be "a monster of courage and curiosity; moreover, supple, cunning, cautious; a born adventurer and discoverer" (*EH*, 264; 6, 303). *The Antichrist* is in search of such readers and its need is compounded and complicated by the fact that it offers a Nietzschean account of what might variously be called interpretation, hermeneutics, or semiotics. To see this point it is necessary to contest an expressivist or emotivist reading of the text. That is, we must question the assumption that because of the emotional intensity of its utterance we must read the book primarily as an outburst of rage or hostility. The rage and hostility are there in abundance; but we should not assume that their very presence excludes a significant structure of thought or that a writing with such a tone could not possibly contain any new thoughts of its own.

As both the inscription and the quotation from Nietzsche suggest, a graffito, whatever its peculiarly individual and private aspects, is inscribed in a public space, often in reply to others and inviting its own challenges and defacements. Like other texts, but in a self-conscious way, *The Antichrist* makes sense only in relation to other texts. It is a book that recalls a number of similar genres (lives of Christ, polemical histories of religion) which were an important part of nineteenth-century thought. Even its title is one which had been used (for somewhat different purposes) by Ernest Renan in 1873, in a book which Nietzsche read a year before writing his own *Antichrist*. It is worth pointing out that Renan is a frequent antagonist both in *The Antichrist* and in other texts of the same period. In Renan's *Antichrist*, the Antichrist is Nero; not Nero merely as a savage persecutor but as the anxious parodic artist whose terrible and genuine aesthetic accomplishment is the theater of cruelty. Renan credits Nero with the discovery of a new form of beauty in which the defenseless virgin torn by the wild beast replaces the classic beauty of the integral and well-formed sculpture. Did Nietzsche, whose juxtaposition of Rome and Christianity is a constant theme of *The Antichrist* and *The Genealogy of Morals*, identify himself wih Nero? Perhaps only later when, mad, he entertains fantasies of imperial or divine power and writes "I am all the names of history": Renan notes that Nero's histrionic ambitions led him to imitate or parody all of the great poetry of the classical world.[4]

These resonances are meant to suggest that *The Antichrist* is not simply immediate expression but a book which refers us back to other books and that the processes of writing, interpreting, reading, censoring, and defacing are so far from being taken for granted that they form the chief means of elucidating Nietzsche's attack on Christianity. Nietzsche's *Antichrist* is full of references to the texts of the Old and New Testaments, to their textual histories, to the priestly fraudulence which produced them, to the texts of the liberal apologists for religion of the nineteenth century, to the textual sophistication of philologists and to the possible text, better and more accurate than all the others, which Dostoyevsky or his like would have written if alive at the time of Jesus. Within this context *The Antichrist* offers, at its heart, one more narrative of the life of Jesus and one of the choicest examples of what Paul Ricoeur has called the hermeneutics of suspicion.

All of the book either leads up to or proceeds from Nietzsche's concern with the textual politics of Judaism and Christianity. That Nietzsche should focus so much of his attention on the way in which the Bible was successively produced, edited, re-edited, interpreted, and criticized could be justified simply in terms of the Jewish and Christian claims to be religions of the book. But Nietzsche has more specific reasons for this concern. All morality is a semiotic interpretation of the body and society; if there is to be a transvaluation of values it must proceed by offering a new reading of that which has been misread. So we find, as in *The Genealogy of Morals*, that the great hermeneutical conflict in *The Antichrist* is between the priest and the philologist. Nietzsche's great enemy is Paul, whom he credits with a genius for lying which was immediately taken up by the church; in doing so they declare war on the philologists:

> Paul *wants* to confound the "wisdom of the world": his enemies are the *good* philologists and physicians of the Alexandrian School—upon them he makes war. In fact, one is not philologist and physician without also being at the same time *Anti-Christian*. For as philologist one sees *behind* the "sacred books," as physician *behind* the physiological depravity of the typical Christian. The physician says "incurable," the philologist "fraud." (*A* 47; *6*, 226)

The paradigm of priestly misreading and fraud is to be found in the editing of the Old Testament. Nietzsche accepts the general results of the higher criticism here, although his tone is completely different from the scholarly objectivity at which the professional philologists aimed. Just ten years before the writing of *The Antichrist*, Julius Wellhausen had written his *Prolegomena to the History of Ancient Israel* in which he argued that the Law could not be the basis of the histories and prophetic writings but must have been composed at a later date.[5] More specifically he attempted to show that it was only during the exile, following the Assyrian victory in the sixth century, that the shift occurred from Israel—a land of warriors, kings, and prophets—to Judaism, a religion of extensive law and ritual reserving a special place of power for the priests. It was the priests who attempted to preserve the life of their people even at the cost of exchanging a vital life for ritualistic constraint; and part of the price to be paid for this change would be a tremendous enhancement of the power of the priests within Judaism. In order to consolidate their power they edited the sacred writings which already existed and added new ones of their own which radically displaced priestly law and the political supremacy of the priest much further back into the past, providing them with divine and traditional sanction. The work of Wellhausen and others like him is not at all Nietzschean in tone; it is not only firmly grounded in contemporary philology but offers a brilliant example of how that philology could be employed with methodical precision in order to produce works of the greatest scope.

Nietzsche alludes to this scholarly tradition although he never explicitly mentions

Wellhausen. Certainly the five-stage history which Nietzsche offers of Judaism and which he declares to be "invaluable as a typical history of the *denaturalizing* of natural values" is a radicalization of Wellhausen's method of distinguishing exilic and pre-exilic Judaism; here it is filtered through the opposition of "good and bad," "good and evil," and the psychology of the priest. This capsule history may bear some comparison with that which Nietzsche had written concerning ontological inversion in his previous book, *The Twilight of the Idols*: "How the 'True World' Finally Became an Error." According to Nietzsche the strata of Jewish History are: (1) "In the period of the Kingdom, Israel too stood in a *correct*, that is to say natural relationship to all things. Their Yahweh was the expression of their consciousness of power, of their delight in the expression of their consciousness of power, of their delight in themselves, their hopes of themselves"; (2) after internal anarchy and external oppression have destroyed this natural state, it remains as an ideal—expressed by the prophets; (3) when the ideal fails as an ideal, Yahweh becomes *only* a god of justice "in the hands of priestly agitators" who establish that most mendacious mode of interpretation of a supposed "moral world-order"; (4) the priests, who have seized power within Judaism, rewrite history in order to disparage the earlier great age in which the priest counted for almost nothing; (5) the rise of Christianity extends priestly *ressentiment* to all hierarchy and rank by attacking the conception of the Jewish people (the chosen poeople) as such. For Nietzsche this is not a new narrative analysis except insofar as it extends and intensifies his philological conception of history as a forceful reading and rereading of texts. When Nietzsche says that there are only interpretations he must be understood not as licensing all logically possible interpretations whatsoever but as indicating that each and every meaning or change of meaning is an exercise of power. To the extent that we accept this principle we are being prepared both for the content of Nietzsche's erasure of Jesus and for an understanding of how such an operation is possible. What Nietzsche objects to in priestly reading is hardly forceful interpretation as such but that specific interpretation, "the moral world-order," which is incapable of recognizing itself as interpretation.

Consider the following observation on priestly reading from Nietzsche's history of the five stages:

> The "will of God" (that is to say the conditions for preserving the power of the priest) has to be *known*—to this end a "revelation" is required. In plain words a great literary forgery becomes necessary, a "sacred book" is discovered—it is made public with all hieratic pomp, with days of repentance and with lamentation over the long years of "sinfulness" . . . the whole evil lay in the nation's having become estranged from the "sacred book". (*A* 26; *6*, 196)

The passage is noteworthy for several reasons, and not the least of them is a typographical one. The extensive use of quotation marks is a philosophical device for quite literally *bracketing* the ideas and expressions with which Nietzsche is dealing. Unlike Husserlian bracketing, Nietzschean quotation is not so much designed to put the ontological status of its objects into doubt as to suggest that we are dealing here with what has been said by specific people on specific occasions, perhaps gathering force through being repeated or reprinted. As opposed to conceptual analysis, it refuses to grant that its objects are part of an impersonal world of ideas to be assessed on their own merits. Instead they are texts which issue from and are signs of power; to put them into quotation marks is to show that the method employed here is that of textual politics. In analyzing the Bible and the culture of the Bible this synthesis of philology and the hermeneutics of power finds its most important and most inexhaustible subject. That which is quoted is often provided with a translation: "sacrifice" as food for the priests, and " 'God forgives him who repents'—in German: *who subjects himself to the priest*" (A 26; 6, 197). Transvaluation is accomplished by translation. What gives the book its fevered pitch and shrill tone is this *duality*, its constant sense of turning one extreme into another. The duality is introduced by Nietzsche's own catechism of values defining good and bad in terms of power and weakness (A 2; 6, 170), is continued through a declaration of war on theology (A 9; 6, 175–6), and concludes with the antithetical translations of Biblical language and anti-narrative of the life of Jesus. Within the Christian tradition itself the church has been constructed "out of the antithesis to the Gospel" (A 36; 6, 208) and Paul "embodied the antithetical type to the 'bringer of glad tidings' " (A 42; 6, 215). What seems at first like stylistic excess is simply a consistent carrying through of the polarity announced by the book's title. In a letter to Georg Brandes, Nietzsche himself indicates that such an analysis is appropriate when he calls the *Umwertung* a trope.[6] It is not just a deflection from the imagined normal path of thought but a movement of inversion and upending.

In this sharp play of oppositions there are also some surprising continuities. Christianity is simply a continuation of Judaism and the New Testament employs a falsification similar to that of the Old. At the same time things which seemed to belong together turn out to be opposed: the real contrast is not Judaism and Christianity but early Israel, with its heroism and passion, and the late development of both religions; Jesus is not the origin of the church but its opposite. More radically Jesus is the antithesis of Christianity because the real " 'glad tidings' are precisely that there are no more opposites" (A 32; 6, 203), while Christianity is committed to the antithetical "good and evil" mode of value which Nietzsche analyzed in *The Genealogy of Morals*.

Jesus is the center of *The Antichrist*, but it is possible to reach him only by decoding and restoring the false oppositions of the gospels and the church. The church led by Paul is said to have practiced the same falsification on the life of Jesus as the priests of Judaism did on the early history of Israel. The more modern and more secular quest for the historical Jesus (Nietzsche refers explicitly to the work of D. F. Strauss and Renan, and shows a familiarity with other toilers in this philological vineyard) does not arrive at its object for it is vitiated by the same assumption that structured the earliest accounts. That assumption is that the truth about Jesus must take the form of a story or narrative. Whether the principles are the miraculous history which begins with a remarkable birth and is punctuated by incursions of the supernatural or whether we are presented with a demythologized Jesus, there is a common presupposition that there is a significant temporal sequence of events which will illuminate Jesus' life.

Nietzsche proposes an ahistorical and non-narrative psychology of the redeemer, according to which Jesus was, in our everyday language, "blissed out." Nietzsche's Jesus does not develop from a theological perspective because he is not a supernatural figure; no divine interventions mark off the different stages of his career. But neither does he develop in the secular and biographical sense because his whole life and teachings consist in the notion that the kingdom of heaven is a present condition of the heart to which we can all have instant access by becoming as children. All that seems to be fixed is melted down into its experiential import. "If I understand anything of this great symbolist," Nietzsche says, "it is that he took for realities, for 'truths,' only *inner* realities—that he understood the rest, everything pertaining to nature, time, space, history, only as signs, as occasion for metaphor" (*A* 39). In calling Jesus "a symbolist *par excellence*" Nietzsche suggests that Jesus is both the origin of the many interpretations which have accrued to him (or, more accurately, which have been *imposed* on him) and also the refutation of all these interpretations. Jesus is a symbolist in the late-nineteenth-century sense of an artist seeking to reveal a single great timeless insight through a variety of devices; like Jesus' parables, none of these will be perfectly adequate to its subject matter, yet taken collectively they will all point to the ineffable experience that generates them. Symbolism is a non-narrative and nonrepresentational style; if it uses narrative or representational elements, as Jesus sometimes does, they are employed metaphorically in order to point beyond themselves. A true symbolist such as the one under analysis

> stands outside of all religion, all conceptions of divine worship, all history, all natural science, all experience of the world, all acquirements, all psychology, all books, all art—his 'knowledge' is precisely the *pure folly* of the fact *that* anything of this kind exists. (*A* 32; *6*, 204)

The history of Christianity is that of a complex series of signs and interpretations in which each sign points back to an earlier one and is susceptible to interpretation by later ones. Now Christian hermeneutics, from its beginnings in Paul to its sophisticated secular forms, supposes that this sign chain, if followed backwards, is not an infinite regress but terminates in an ultimate meaning which is the life of Jesus. Nietzsche perceives the chain of signs but sees them finally leading back to an absence rather than a fullness of meaning. Bruno Bauer, a young Hegelian whom Nietzsche referred to as one of his few genuine readers, had suggested the same view in a somewhat crude and material fashion by arguing that Jesus never lived and that the literature of the early church was all fabrication or delusion.[7] Nietzsche accepts a historical Jesus who is historically relevant only because his actual presence was that of a radically ambiguous sign capable of indefinite interpretation. As a philologist Nietzsche seems to have asked himself the Kantian question, "How is a Christian semiotics possible?'' and to have answered it by the transcendental deduction of a man who stands so far outside the usual processes of signification that everything is metaphor and symbol for him. Whereas later Christian semiotics assumes that there is some proper relationship between signs and their referents (or between signified and signifier), the semiotics of Jesus consists in a radical refusal of any such relationship. For Nietzsche, Jesus is an anti-sign or "floating signifier" who, if he was the incarnation of anything, embodied the absence of meaning. The signs that Jesus uses are always *mere* signs or *only* signs: "Blessedness is not promised, it is not tied to any conditions: it is the only reality—the rest is signs for speaking of it" (*A* 33; *6*, 205). In the beginning, then, there is not the word, but the enigmatic indication of the insufficiency of the word. The difference between Jesus and the church is that Jesus' signs are used with a consciousness of their inadequacy to their subject while the church believes that the gospels are divinely inspired and hence adequate signs. The growth of allegorical methods of interpretation within Christianity should not be cited as a counter-instance because its practitioners still tend to believe in a literal level along with the non-literal modes and because they suppose that the non-literal methods of interpretation are capable of elucidating their subject matter. Nietzsche's Jesus could be thought of as the metaphorical or symbolic principle itself; for him there is always such a large discrepancy between experience and its representation that he fails to establish any determinacy of meanings. It is just this indeterminate condition which allows Paul and the church to impose their own meanings on Jesus.

The same result follows from Jesus' lack of a history. If Jesus had a history then the tradition of text and commentary would have been under some constraint, such that even falsifications of Jesus' career would have contained internal evidence pointing back to their original. This is the case in the Old Testament, "that miracle of falsification the documentation of which lies before us in a good part of the Bible" (*A* 26; *6*, 194). It is because there are historical narratives of a sort, based on the history of Israel, in the Old Testament, that scholars like Wellhausen are able to detect internal inconsistencies in the whole and reconstruct a *critical* history of Israel in which the formation of different historical accounts itself plays a role. In dealing with the Christian records, philology has no such role to play because of the radical indeterminacy of its beginnings. Nietzsche throws up his arms in distress at the prospect of a philological study of the gospels. Here D. F. Strauss and others had expended enormous energy. But what was the point of it?

I confess there are few books which present me with so many difficulties as the Gospels do. These difficulties are quite other than those which the learned curiosity of the German mind celebrated one of its most unforgettable triumphs in pointing out. The time is far distant when I too, like every young scholar and with the clever dullness of a refined philologist, savored the work of the incomparable Strauss. I was then twenty years old: now I am too serious for that. What do I care for the contradictions of "tradition?" How can legends of saints be called "tradition" at all! The stories of saints are the most ambiguous literature in existence: to apply to them scientific procedures *when no other records are extant* seems to me wrong in principle—mere learned idling. (A 28; 6, 199)

The same holds for the more imaginative attempts to reconstruct the life of Jesus, such as the immensely popular and influential *Life of Jesus* by Ernest Renan; that book serves as a foil for Nietzsche to exhibit the more radical accomplishment of his own anti-biography. Renan was himself a philologist specializing in the Semitic languages. His *Life of Jesus* walks a thin line between the philological concerns of Strauss and the Germans and a tendency toward imaginative biography (incipient psychobiography) with a heavy dose of religious liberalism. Aware of the discrepancies in the sources, Renan explains the gospel narratives as the result of confusion, wishful thinking, and the tendency of the disciples and others to read their own idiosyncracies into Jesus' life. The gospels are neither biographies nor legends but "legendary biographies."[8] Renan's basic hermeneutic principle is borrowed, more or less consciously, from the well-formed nineteenth-century novel with its omniscient narrator:

> The essential condition of the creations of art is, that they shall form a living system of which all the parts are mutually dependent and related. In histories such as this, the great test that we have got the truth is, to have succeeded in combining the texts in such a manner that they shall constitute a logical, probable narrative, harmonious through-out. . . . Each trait which departs from the rules of classic narrative ought to warn us to be careful.[9]

The disordered paratactic form of the gospels is to be overcome for the sake of both art and history.[10] Accordingly Renan constructs a biography of Jesus as a child of nature who lived blissfully but briefly ("for some months, perhaps a year") with the consciousness that the Kingdom of God was within. Soon he becomes involved with John the Baptist and begins to preach a moral revolution to be produced by men. Meeting with opposition Jesus proclaims himself the son of God, alienates himself from nature, and preaches that the kingdom of heaven is at hand, although it will be brought about through a divine rather than human agency. Yet this extreme tone, involving as it did a confrontation with established society and religion, could be maintained only briefly; at this point Jesus' death was a necessity, and Renan seems to mean that it was an aesthetic and narrative necessity.

It is worth noting that Renan ascribes to Jesus' life that same distinction between a blissful inwardness and the spirit of opposition and revenge which is, from Nietzsche's perspective, the difference between Jesus and the early church. By this move Renan makes Jesus' more or less unconscious barbarization of his own message the pattern and the basis for the rancorous element within the whole Christian tradition. A continuous life serves as the model of an intelligible history. In this respect, Renan, despite the church's opposition to his book, is a reformer rather than a revolutionary; he just wants to purge the intelligible history of Jesus and the church of legendary and supernatural elements. This motive of Renan's work appears even more clearly when it is realized that the *Life* is only one of seven parts of his comprehensive series, *The Origins of Christianity*. Nietzsche was acquainted with this ambitious historical project. A year before writing *The Antichrist* he wrote in a letter to Overbeck, himself a church historian,

> This winter I have also read Renan's *Origines*, with much spite and—little profit. . . . At root, my distrust goes so far as to question whether history is really *possible*. What is it that people want to establish—something which was not itself established at the moment it occurred?[11]

For Nietzsche, Renan represents the modern attempt to salvage the values of religion by means of history and science. He must have been particularly angered by Renan's use of his philological credentials to interpolate a continuity into discontinuous materials. In *The Antichrist*, Renan is mentioned repeatedly, and always as another example of one who has constructed a false narrative. There is too great a

> contradiction between the mountain, lake and field preacher, whose appearance strikes one as that of a Buddha on a soil very little like that of India, and the aggressive fanatic, the mortal enemy of theologian and priest, which Renan has wickedly glorified as '*le grand maître en ironie*.' (A 31; 6, 202)

Given this discontinuity, Nietzsche argues that it is more plausible to see it as the radical break between Jesus and those who invoke his name. This is also a critique of Renan in his own terms; for the attempt to impose a narrative form on his materials causes him to violate his own canons of organic unity.

Renan also errs in importing the narrative and character types of the hero and the genius into his story. But "to speak with the precision of the physiologist a quite different word would rather be in place here: the word 'idiot' " (A 29; 6, 200). Such a character ought not to be portrayed as if he were the hero of a narrative; rather "one has to regret that no Dostoyevsky lived in the neighborhood of this most interesting *décadent*; I mean someone who could feel the thrilling fascination of such a combination of the sublime, the sick and the childish" (A 31). Nietzsche may very well have had *The Idiot* in mind as literary model for his own analysis of Jesus.[12] That book exemplifies and solves the narrative problem that is essential to Nietzsche's account. It has long been thought that the portrayal of a thoroughly good main character in the novel must be problematic, for one who is thoroughly good will not exhibit the tensions and contradictions which lend themselves to action and development. The problem goes back to Plato who objected to the traditional stories of the gods on the grounds that they represented that which was perfect as changing; such change was, strictly speaking, impossible, but to imagine it as occurring is to imagine the perfect becoming worse, or as having a defect which must be repaired through growth. Now Dostoyevsky's Prince Myshkin is the still point of a narrative which is constituted by the feverishly spiralling reactions of those around him to such a mixture of "the sublime, the sick and the childish." Just because he does not act and does not desire, he exists as a kind of empty space upon which the other characters can impose their own acts, desires, and fantasies. In citing these parallels and contrasts with the work of Renan and Dostoyevsky I mean to indicate more than influences and thematic correspondences. Nietzsche's polemic against Christianity is concerned with the falsifications of Christian narrative. Only by considering a variety of literary models can we begin to work our way back to the event at the heart of Christian semiotics. There is a kind of Platonic correspondence for Nietzsche between the large texts, which are the body and the instincts, and the smaller ones, which are actual written documents; unlike Plato, however, he will use the smaller in order to read the larger. An even more striking difference, however, is that both texts stand in need of extensive emendation; like graffiti they do not have the permanent existence of the forms, but are always in danger of corruption and effacement by any who are powerful enough to wield an actual or a metaphorical pen.

To understand Christianity is to understand the blank wall which must be presupposed as the support of all of the inscriptions of history. In this respect Nietzsche's view of semiotic history, or at least of this portion of it, more closely resembles that of C. S. Peirce than it does that of Jacques Derrida. Derrida frequently cites Nietzsche in behalf of his idea that all writing refers back to an earlier writing and so on *ad infinitum*; he believes that an infinite regress of writings implies that in flowing back the chain of texts and interpretations we will never reach a point prior to the writing process itself.[13] Peirce on the other hand makes a crucial distinction between the continuity of the sign-process and its indefinite or infinite extension. According to him the sign-process is continuous in that it has no absolute first or last term. But there are many cases of continuous series which are not indefinitely or infinitely extended—such as a line segment. We can consistently conceive of a sign-process beginning (or ending) at some point in time, even though it makes no sense to talk of the absolutely first (or last) sign in the series.[14]

The difference between Peirce and Derrida here is like that between Aristotle and Zeno on the possiblity of motion. Aristotle showed that the infinite density and intensive continuity of the interval, however short, between Achilles and the tortoise ought not to be mistaken for an infinitely extended line. Motion is impossible, argues Zeno, because movement across any given interval requires an infinite number of steps, each taking a finite bit of time. Therefore, not even the first step is possible. But (as Peirce points out) motion is a continuous process in which there is no unique first step or movement. Yet motion has a beginning despite its lack of a unique first or final term. Derrida is a skeptic about meaning who thinks that if there were to be any meaning at all it would require the inclusion of an infinite number of moments at the "beginning" and the "end" of the process of meaning. But all intervals here are too dense to be traversed, and all presumed ends or beginnings dissolve into endless ranges or prior and posterior nodes of meaning. Anything with such indeterminate boundaries can hardly be that full, present, and defined thing which we are wont to think of as meaning. Therefore there is no meaning, although in its place there is an ultimately plural and diffuse web of *écriture*. From a Peircean point of view this is to confuse intensive and extensive infinity. It is to suppose that that which has an internal complexity of the highest degree must necessarily lack all definition and boundary. What Nietzsche adds to this account is an explanation of the setting and dissolution of boundaries by acts of force. What is variously designated as will to power by Nietzsche, as secondness by Peirce, and simply as power by Foucault is what gives a contour and integrity to meaning. Such power is exercized variously in the different modes of writing, interpreting, rewriting, censoring, defacing, and erasing. Both Peirce and Derrida see the impossibility of a Cartesian account which would found all meaning on the intuitive presence of clear and distinct ideas, a first sign. Every sign is also an interpretation, as Nietzsche and Peirce would agree. But it does not follow that the process is without beginnings, ends, or limits.[15]

For Nietzsche, Jesus is not the first sign in the series (corresponding to a Cartesian intuition), as he is for Christian tradition, but neither is he caught up, as he would be on Derrida's reading, in a chain of signs which extends back indefinitely behind him. He is rather a break or rupture in semiotic history which is the ground of a new branch of that history; like the *tabula rasa* he is the empty presupposition of a history of signs, or like the wall on which the graffiti are inscribed he is the now invisible background of all that is visible. The significant difference between Nietzsche and Peirce here is that Nietzsche rejects the Peircean eschatology of the last sign as well as the first sign of Christianity. Peirce's vision of the "ultimate interpretant" has posed a major problem for his commentators, who should have noted earlier than they did that the "ultimate interpretant" can only be attained by the Christian virtues of faith, hope, and charity.[16]

At this point there may appear to be a tension between Nietzsche's psychological reconstruction of Jesus and his semiotic use of him. According to the latter the entire quest for the historical Jesus is misguided, whether carried out along orthodox, philological, or Hegelian-aesthetic lines (the last being Renan's case). Yet Nietzsche does seem at times in *The Antichrist* to be writing one more life of Jesus to add to the pile he is simultaneously rejecting in principle. If Jesus is properly a blank page in semiotic history then why does Nietzsche provide us with his vivid sketch of a blissful naïf? The case may appear even more difficult when it is noticed that despite Nietzsche's polemic against Renan, the two, read from a certain modern perspective and juxtaposed either with orthodox Christian predecessors, thorough philologists (such as Strauss and Wellhausen) or with the form criticism of the last fifty years, appear to share a number of distinctive theses concerning Jesus' life. Yet this would be a truncated reading of Nietzsche's argument. It is the semiotic rather than the biographical thematic which takes priority in *The Antichrist*. The blankness of the semiotic account, the project of erasure, is not one which can be accomplished by a simple pronouncement that "Jesus had no meaning, no life, no history"; the biographical obsession, the urge to find intelligible development and character, is not so easily suppressed. In order to approximate a sense of semiotic blankness, erasure is an activity to be ever renewed. So to write of the blissed-out Palestinian is to approximate such blankness within the framework of the biographial project. Like Socrates attempting to give his young men a sense of that which is "beyond Being" by a series of analogies, Nietzsche suggests the series formed by accounts of the orthodox, the philologists, the historical aesthetes, his own reconstruction— all suggesting the erasure, the break, the motivated but powerfully instituted boundary.[17] When Nietzsche talks of Jesus he is careful to suggest the many *different* narratives which might be written to replace the standard ones. The wish to have a Dostoyevskian novel of Jesus must not be understood on the assumption that *The Idiot* (or any narrative, in Nietzsche's view) is to be seen as mimetic or referential. This becomes clear when Nietzsche invokes the Amphitryon story, the philologists, and the aestheticians. Such methodological reflexivity distinguishes Nietzsche's approach from Renan's: Renan shows no awareness of the possible divergence of the demands of the *Bildungsroman* and those of historical truth.

Nietzsche undertakes to tell "the real history of Christianity" (*A* 39; 6, 211), by showing how the church's narrative distortions of Jesus are intertwined with the untold narrative of its own depredations of culture. Even where Jesus may plausibly be believed to have used narrative expressions himself, they must be construed in terms of his timeless experience; yet the church has not only misconstrued them as narratives but has written a poor and hackneyed story. Jesus speaks of himself as the Son in relation to the Father. What is the semiotic analysis of these expressions?

> It is patently obvious what is alluded to in the signs [*Zeichen*], "Father" and "Son"— not patently obvious to everyone, I grant: in the word "Son" is expressed the *entry* into the collective feeling of the transfiguration of all things (blessedness), in the word "Father" *this feeling itself*, the feeling of perfection and eternity. I am ashamed to recall what the church has made of this symbolism: has it not set an Amphitryon story at the threshold of Christian faith? (*A* 34)

As Giraudoux's title for his modern version of that story (*Amphitryon 38*) indicates, the story has been told many times of a god (Zeus), having impregnated a mortal woman (Alcmene) who then gives birth to an extraordinary son (Herakles). Surely one could have discovered a better model than this, a model that is more suitable for comedy than sacred narrative; this is the sort of thing that Nietzsche may have intended in the remark that it was very strange of God to learn Greek when he wanted to become a writer and then to learn it so badly (*BGE* 121; 5, 94). "Dionysus vs. the crucified" (the last words of *Ecce Homo*) can refer to the opposition between the true and false gods of tragedy and comedy—among other things. Yet what is most appalling is the generation of such stories, whose early believers, if not their fabricators, may be presumed to have been naive ("I take care not to make mankind responsible for its insanities"), but the modern man and the modern church who *know* the falsity of the tradition while continuing to reaffirm it. Now these signs are used and "recognized for what they are: the most malicious false-coinage there is for the purpose of disvaluing nature and natural values" (*A* 38; 6, 210). Like Hegel, Nietzsche believes that history has produced a self-consciousness about the irrelevance of the narrative and mythological forms in which religious doctrines are presented; but this self-consciousness has the effect of keeping the spirit entangled in ever more hypocritical deceptions rather than liberating it. To tell the "real history of Christianity" then is to tell it *critically* (in the sense of critical history developed in *The Use and Abuse of History*) in order to explode the ruling falsities of the day.

The plan of Nietzsche's critical history of Christianity has three stages. He begins *The Antichrist* by reiterating those theses about power and the distinction between a morality of self-affirmation and one of *ressentiment* which are familiar from his earlier writings. He proceeds to show how, in the case of Judaism, the priest's distortion of texts is both the product of *ressentiment* and a philological clue to its reconstruction. Given this general understanding of the politics of misreading and miswriting, Nietzsche analyzes the central case of Jesus himself, a man so opposed to the narrative mode that he had no defenses against those who would inscribe their own messages on his body. The final part of the book traces the history of these wicked writers whose imaginary narratives mask the real story of their own envy of the healthy and their subterranean pursuit of power.

To reconstruct what they have done we need to know not only their own motives, instincts, and bodily condition, but something of the more or less instinctive hermeneutics and semiotics which such people will employ in constructing their narratives. Now an intelligible narrative will have as its skeleton a sequence of causes and effects. Because of its hostility to the healthy body, however, Christianity refuses to recognize the natural, physiological causes of human experience. Therefore it constructs a world of imaginary causes and effects (such as the soul and redemption) which is also populated by imaginary beings; consequently "this entire fictional world has its roots in hatred of the natural" (*A* 15; *6*, 181). Much of Nietzsche's semiotics, as I argued in chapter one, is, like Freud's, based on the dream; it is a natural part of the dream-work to construct an imaginary narrative to explain some experience after the fact, as when being on the verge of awaking because of a loud noise we invent some dream story which culminates in a cannonshot. We do the same thing in waking life, however, in seeking reasons for feeling well or poorly; never satisfied with experiences by themselves we feel compelled to produce some narrative account of them. Ordinary narrative thus tends to be confused enough, but this confusion will be heightened immeasurably when the typical terms of the narrative are Christianity's sin and repentance, the flesh and the spirit, and so on.

Nietzsche's account of the history of the church after Jesus can be encapsulated rather briefly. Jesus' followers were in revolt against the Jewish establishment and so naturally sought even greater revenge upon that order; thus the early church shows itself to be a continuation of Judaism by other means, extending the Jewish attack on the "world" to institutional Judaism itself. Yet God permitted Jesus' death, so that must be interpreted as a sacrifice for the sake of sins. Paul, who sought power above all things, employed the instincts of *ressentiment* to shift attention away from this life by the fiction of the resurrected Christ. Only then are the gospels written with their willful distortions and their "seduction by means of morality" (*A* 44; *6*, 220). The text itself is dirty: "one does well to put gloves on when reading the New Testament" (*A* 46; *6*, 223). These dirty graffiti are also symptoms of the defacing or rewriting of some of mankind's cleaner texts, the ancient world, Islam, and the Renaissance (*A* 59–61; *6*, 247–252). Nietzsche's account of these naughtiest writings on the cultural wall is always bound up with his analysis of the book which justifies them and reveals their psychological principles. The New Testament is a bad dream constructed on the principle of *ressentiment*. After giving an extensive account of its alleged falsifications of Jesus' sayings (*A* 45; *6*, 221–23), Nietzsche says that "every book becomes clean if one has just read the New Testament: to give an example . . . Petronius" (*A* 46; *6*, 224). This *Umwertung* of the idea of the dirty book is a characteristic strategy in *The Antichrist*. I suggest that we read the admittedly feverish imagery of dirt and cleanliness, body, blood and poison, which becomes more and more pronounced as one reaches the end of the book, as intrinsic to the strategies and economy of the text rather than as symptoms of a loss of control. Nietzsche's transvaluation is meant to be an affirmation of the body in opposition to its denial in Christianity. Therefore it must openly be a text of the body and must describe its pretext as a desecration of the body.

It is striking that Nietzsche invokes Zarathustra in the midst of his narrative (*A* 53–54; *6*, 234–36), for what unites Zarathustra and Nietzsche's Jesus is a break with that metanarrativist style of thought that requires a notion of first and last things. For both, the totality of experience is sufficient unto itself and stands in no need of external explanations. Jesus' opposition to narrative is instinctive and naive while Zarathustra's living of the eternal return is post-narrative and achieved only with great difficulty. The eternal recurrence is opposed to traditional narrative thought because it knows no isolated agents in the sequence of all events, but only the interconnection of events; it knows no beginning, middle and end of the narrative but simply the continuous fabric of becoming; and it tends to dissolve the mainstay of conventional narrative, the individual agent, into the ring of becoming. Carefully distinguishing himself from Zarathustra, Nietzsche indicates that he has not attained such a radically anti-narrative stance himself, or if he did experience the eternal recurrence he also forgot it from time to time. In constructing his own narratives such as *The Genealogy of Morals* and *The Antichrist*, Nietzsche attempts to incorporate an awareness of the fallibility and perspectival character of conventional narrative which is rejected by the dogmatic, priestly variety. We might think of the distinction between these two narrative modalities as somewhat like the distinction which Marx would make between ideology and science. Ideological accounts of history are dogmatic and uncritical of their own principles of interpretation while scientific accounts are distinguished not only by knowing where to look for causes (in the relations of production or in the condition of the body) but by their knowledge that they too are products of these causes and therefore subject to explanation and correction from a more comprehensive standpoint. So it would be in the spirit of Marxism to regard Marxist science as itself tied to the material conditions of capitalism and subject to revision when capitalism is overcome. Of course Marx does not envision a non-historical science; Nietzsche's pluralizing narratives are even more provisional in that they anticipate the erosion of the narrative principle itself. Or one might point out that just as the eternal recurrence will bring back the last man, so it will, even though opposed to the narrative principle, bring back that principle as well.

Nietzsche recalls Zarathustra in *The Antichrist* both for his opposition to priestly writing in blood and for his skepticism. As in the passage chosen for *Auslegung* in *The Genealogy of Morals*, Nietzsche chooses a section explicitly touching on the activities of reading and writing. Zarathustra speaks twice of the connection between blood and writing, once to announce "I love only that which is written in blood" (Z, 67) and then, in the passage quoted in *The Antichrist* to criticize the priests for writing in blood:

> They wrote letters of blood on the path they followed, and their folly taught that truth is proved by blood.
> But blood is the worst witness of truth. (Z, 116; 4, 119)

Both passages seem to apply to the *Antichrist* but only one of them is quoted. In part their difference has to do with the polyphonic or polytropic character of *Zarathustra*. But beyond that there is still the problem of the bloody tone of *The Antichrist* in addition to its bloody subject matter. In fact the conclusion of the passage makes a distinction between two sorts of bloody writing: "And if someone goes through fire for his teaching—what does that prove? Truly, it is more when one's own teaching comes out of one's burning." One kind of writing in blood is that of the ascetic who deliberately spills his blood and then imagines that whatever he writes with it must be true. He has too much of an investment, through self-sacrifice, to allow him to question his own writing. The other sort is that which flows out of powerful and healthy impulses which cannot be suppressed; it is thus that Nietzsche describes his own composition of *Zarathustra*. *The Antichrist* would like to be bloody, presumably in the second sense, not the first. Only this second kind of bloodiness is compatible with the skepticism which Nietzsche here attributes to Zarathustra and to Pilate, whose "What is truth?" makes him the "*one* solitary figure one is obliged to respect" in the New Testament (A 46; 6, 225). Writing in blood, like that in *The Antichrist* or *Zarathustra*, can be skeptical if it combines intensity with an awareness of the perspectival character of all discourse emanating from the body. The antithesis to the Christian set of sacred writings, beliefs, and values is not a new sacred text and alternative beliefs to be held with the same force; it is the *Umwertung* of all those things, not simply a change in their content. *The Antichrist* aims at being the antithesis of Christian graffiti by opening up a space for playful writings like Nietzsche's own; it is meant to clear the walls for an exuberant profusion of inscriptions which will break out of the narrow circle of revenge in which writing under the sway of Christianity and morality has moved.

At the same time, however, this text becomes caught up in a larger Nietzschean project which renders questionable some of these very ambitions. In particular, *The Antichrist* becomes involved in a dizzying series of inclusions, exclusions, and reversals with Nietzsche's parodic narrative of his own life in *Ecce Homo*, the text to which we now turn.

How One Becomes What One Is Not

(Ecce Homo)

Ecce Homo has always been the most contested and controversial of Nietzsche's writings. Tendentiously edited and censored by his sister and Peter Gast, it has been the subject of sharp polemics among scholars who have attempted to establish an authentic text.[1] Förster-Nietzsche withheld its publication until 1905, seventeen years after its composition. As soon as it appeared there were critics who were quick to classify it as a product of Nietzsche's madness while others, in a slightly more moderate vein, saw it as a sign of a madness about to overtake him. Alternating between lyrical passages that dwell on his experiences of ripe perfection and the sharpest invectives against his German contemporaries, the text may appear to be a melange of the most diverse elements. But whatever else it may be, *Ecce Homo* is a narrative account of his own life by a writer who has already tried his hand at a number of other narrative genres and has modified them significantly in the process. While this book is Nietzsche's fullest account of his own life, it is hardly his only venture in self-description.

As a student at Schulpforta he had already composed several vitae; the imposing bulk of his correspondence contains many letters embodying rather detailed and complex autobiographical reflections that go far beyond the demands of their superficial occasions.[2] What is distinctive about *Ecce Homo* in this context is that Nietzsche is now going public; as the book's title suggests, he is not simply making himself available but demanding attention, an attention that he claims is justified by his unique fate in which the personal intersects with historical exigencies. This theme is announced in the first sentence of the preface: "Seeing that before long I must confront humanity with the most difficult demand ever made of it, it seems indispensable to me to say *who I am*" *(EH*, 217; *6*, 257). This "most difficult demand" is involved with Nietzsche's expectation that his thought will produce unprecedented transformations:

> I know my fate. One day my name will be associated with the memory of something tremendous—a crisis without equal on earth, the most profound collision of conscience,

a decision that was conjured up *against* everything that had been believed, demanded, hallowed so far. I am no man, I am dynamite. *(EH*, 326; *6*, 365)

Two related but distinct trains of thought can be distinguished in such pronouncements. The first is one which finds some support in Nietzsche's earlier publications and notes. It is his idea of himself as the teacher of a Dionysian philosophy, centered around the doctrine of eternal recurrence; he expects that this philosophy will gradually attain a cultural ascendancy or hegemony. In *Ecce Homo* Nietzsche refers to such a project in his section on *Daybreak*. This is worth noting because *Daybreak* is, on the surface at least, one of Nietzsche's least apocalyptic books; and even in this later account he describes it as lying "in the sun, round, happy, like some sea animal basking among rocks." But Nietzsche goes on to explain that the book seeks *its* daybreak and "a whole world of new days" in the transvaluation of values and this gives rise to an account of his project:

My task of preparing a moment of the highest self-examination for humanity, a *great noon* when it looks back and far forward, when it emerges from the domain of accidents and priests and for the first time poses, *as a whole*, the question of Why? and For What?—this task follows of necessity from the insight that humanity is *not* all by itself on the right way, that it is by no means governed divinely, that, on the contrary, it has been precisely among its holiest value concepts that the instinct of denial, corruption, and decadence has ruled seductively. *(EH*, 291; *6*, 330)

What is the "great noon" to which Nietzsche refers here? The expression "great noon," along with literary projects with titles like *Noon and Eternity*, begins to appear in Nietzsche's notebooks at about the time of his first notes on eternal recurrence in 1881. As described in the text above, the "great noon" is a kind of apocalyptic moment; that is, a moment of clarity and revelation; the scales fall from the eyes so that a question of the first importance can be asked for the first time. From the beginning of the appearances of this theme, however, it is doubly determined as both a general metaphor for human enlightenment and also as a specific moment *(Augenblick)* in which that enlightenment occurs. Both are, of course, traditional themes that can be associated with philosophical and religious conceptions of emerging from error into truth.

The metaphorics of the "great noon" are affiliated with Plato's myth of the cave and the sun, and the European Enlightenment. Plato's notion of what it is to be freed from the veils of illusion is relatively timeless and ahistorical; seeing the sun is the result, for him, of a philosophical discipline and training which does not seem to be intrinsically tied to one's historical position. At Platonic high noon, we might say, one does not look "back and far forward" at human history, but gazes at the sun itself. Beginning roughly with Bacon and Descartes, however, the figure takes on a collective, historical meaning and implies that there will be a general moment of illumination that depends on an entire society (at least its leading figures or illuminati) liberating itself from what Kant called its "self-imposed tutelage."

Nietzsche suggests an even greater degree of temporal specificity to the great noon by calling it an *Augenblick*. The *Augenblick* is the time founded from a phenomenological point of view by the blinking of one's eyes; this sense of concrete content with sharp boundaries is not conveyed by "moment," the usual English equivalent. What recurs in eternal recurrence are *Augenblicke*. And in the vision of Zarathustra where he confronts the spirit of gravity, the two stand before a gate that is inscribed *Augenblick* at the conjunction of two paths that stretch indefinitely into the past and the future. While the dwarf who is the spirit of gravity sees the two roads and even approximates one aspect of eternal recurrence by saying "all that is straight lies . . . all truth is crooked; time itself is a circle" he apparently does not see the *Augenblick*, even though it is inscribed on the gateway in front of him.

In the notes of 1881–82, the emphasis is mainly on the long process of criticism, education, and political transformation that is necessary in order to lay the groundwork for the "great noon." In Nietzsche's first notation concerning eternal recurrence, for example, he asks:

> What should we do with the *rest* of our lives—we who have spent the greater part of our lives in essential ignorance? We *teach the teaching* [*Lehren die lehre*]—it is the strongest means of *incorporating* it in ourselves. Our kind of blessedness, as teachers of the greatest teaching. (*9*, 494)

Here blessedness consists only in teaching eternal recurrence; the task is not obviously associated with "great events" of any immediate sort.

Ecce Homo, however, is pervaded by the apocalyptic tone in which Nietzsche calls forth "upheavals, a convulsion of earthquakes, a moving of mountains and valleys, the like of which has never been dreamed of." The process is already underway, Nietzsche's rhetoric suggests; whatever has to be done has already been done. The tenses of his language are the prophetic ones of the future and the future perfect: "The conquest of politics *will have merged* entirely with a war of spirits; all power structures of the old society *will have been exploded*—all of them are based on lies." *(EH*, 327; 6, 366).

In *Ecce Homo* and in the burst of self-aggrandizing and self-promoting correspondence accompanying its composition, Nietzsche makes it clear that the event which "breaks the history of mankind in two" (*EH*, 333; 6, 373) is the transvaluation of all values. But that is an insufficiently precise way of putting it. What Nietzsche's writings of 1888 show is an increasing *condensation* and *concretization* of the notion of a transvaluation, and along with this condensation there is an increased attention to the thematics of the great noon as a specific historical *Augenblick*. Initially "transvaluation" is a term for the general activity of criticism and teaching in which Nietzsche is engaged. Then it becomes the title, *The Transvaluation of All Values*, of the definitive philosophical work that he is about to write; Nietzsche expects that it will produce a much greater and more immediate impact than his earlier writings have (*13*, 545).

The plan was for a work in four parts, of which *The Antichrist* would be the first. But at some point during the last months of 1888 Nietzsche comes to think of the just completed *Antichrist* as being identical with the *whole* of the *Transvaluation*. At the same time his expectations for an immediate and explosive effect become much more specific; he wants to arrange for the book's translation and simultaneous appearance in seven languages. In the account of *Twilight of the Idols* in *Ecce Homo*, Nietzsche says with some bravado that he proceeded immediately from the completion of that work "to the tremendous task of the *Transvaluation*, with a sovereign feeling of pride that was incomparable, certain at every moment of my immortality, engraving sign upon sign on bronze tablets with the sureness of a destiny" (*EH*, 315; 6, 355). Nietzsche's latest and most judicious editors, Giorgio Colli and Mazzino Montinari, have decided to include the following lines in this section of the text, despite some uncertainties:

Am 30 September grosser Sieg; Beendigung der Umwertung;
Mussigang eines Gottes am Po entlang (6, 356).[3]

On September 30th a great victory; completion of the
Transvaluation; the leisure of a god along the Po.

That there is some uncertainty about the phrase *Beendigung der Umwertung* is significant. Assuming that Montinari is right in arguing that Nietzsche did want to include it in *Ecce Homo*, the uncertainty evidenced by the erasures and reinscriptions which he documents contrasts interestingly with Nietzsche's talk of writing *The Antichrist* by "engraving sign upon sign on bronze tablets." Because *Ecce Homo* itself is ambivalent about the project of transvaluation and the appropriate text of that project, the text must appear ambivalent in respect to its general purpose. If the *Transvaluation* has been completed, then *Ecce Homo* can be read, as Nietzsche wanted us to read it, as a prelude to that work (although it could not have been read that way between 1895, when *The Antichrist* was published, and 1908 when *Ecce Homo* finally appeared). Another way of understanding the relation between *Ecce Homo* and the *Transvaluation* suggests itself, however. For a long time Nietzsche planned to write a comprehensive work, *The Transvaluation of All Values*, from which he expected great things. At one time he projected *The Antichrist* as the first of the work's four parts. But rather than complete the work he turned to the composition of *Ecce Homo* which became, in effect, a substitution for a work that was never written. So the real rhythm of Nietzsche's activities would be the opposite of that given in his bravura picture of himself as proceeding boldly and without pause from one work to the next, completing the *Transvaluation* and enjoying the well-deserved leisure of a god strolling alongside the Po. This actual rhythm would be one of postponement and displacement in which *Ecce Homo* is substituted for a book that is not written. The text which was to serve as a kind of personal appendix to the event and text of transvaluation becomes a means of not completing either. In effect, Nietzsche writes "Why I Write Such Good Books," rather than writing his great book.

What is it about *The Antichrist* that might lead Nietzsche to identify it as the whole of the *Transvaluation*? His earlier plans are for a four-part work with a relatively systematic structure; some outlines for the parts that could have succeeded *The Antichrist* are preserved in his notes. Around the same time that Nietzsche came to see *The Antichrist* as identical to the *Transvaluation* he added the "Decree [*Gesetz*] Against Christianity" (now published in the Colli-Montinari edition, 6, 254). The "Decree" is a remarkable document, translated here in full (since it is not otherwise available in English):

Decree Against Christianity

Proclaimed on the first day of the year one (—on
September 30, 1888 of the false time scheme)

War to the death against depravity:
depravity is Christianity

First Proposition:—Every form of anti-nature is depraved. The most depraved type of man is the priest: he *teaches* anti-nature. Don't use arguments against the priest, but prison.

Second proposition:—Every participation in a religious service is an attack on public morality. Be more severe toward Protestants than toward Catholics and more severe toward liberal Protestants than toward those of strict belief. The criminality of being a Christian increases in so far as the Christian approaches science. The criminal of criminals is consequently the *philosopher*.

Third proposition:—The accursed places in which Christianity has hatched its basilisk eggs should be flattened to the ground and regarded as the *vile* places of the earth, to the terror of all posterity. Poisonous snakes should be bred there.

Fourth proposition:—The preaching of chastity is a public incitement to anti-nature. Every condemnation of sexual love, and every dirtying of it through the concept "dirty" [*unrein*] is original sin against the holy spirit of life.

Fifth proposition:—Eating at a table with a priest is forbidden: in doing so one excommunicates oneself from honest society. The priest is *our* chandala—he should be condemned, starved, and driven into every kind of desert.

Sixth proposition:—The "holy" story [*Geschichte*] should be called by the name it has earned, the *accursed* story; the words "God," "Savior," "redeemer," "saint" should be used as terms of abuse and as criminal insignia.

Seventh proposition:—The rest follows from the above.

The Antichrist

One can see why Nietzsche's friends and later editors did not publish this "Decree" which eventually was classified along with the materials for *Ecce Homo*. The date, the signature, and the movement from a philosophical to a political mode of attack all confirm and intensify Nietzsche's announced intention of "writing in letters so large that even the blind can see" or of "writing on the wall, wherever there are walls" (*A*, 62; *6*, 253). The "Decree" itself could well be printed as a poster in large letters and pasted up on many walls. This is indeed a typical mode of communication employed by military authorities during a condition of martial law. One could imagine it being pasted up by the occupying armies of its signatory, the Antichrist. Such a use would be consistent with Nietzsche's plan that the *Transvaluation* be presented as a broadside attack on Christianity; he wanted it to appear simultaneously in seven languages, in editions of one million copies each.

The last words of *The Antichrist* before the "Decree" are:

> And one reckons *time* from the *dies nefastus* [unlucky day] with which this fatality began—according to the *first* day of Christianity!—*Why not rather according to its last?—According to today?—Transvaluation of All Values*! (*A*, 62, *6*, 253)

The theme of changing the way in which time is reckoned appears frequently in Nietzsche's letters at this time and, of course, in *Ecce Homo*. The "Decree Against Christianity" shows Nietzsche struggling to employ this concept as more than a trope. He no longer limits himself to producing narratives that call the philosophical and Christian traditions into question or that offer alternative stories about human possibilities. He sees himself as "splitting the history of mankind into two" by means of the *Transvaluation*.

It might be noted that the idea of redating history and beginning anew has a history and tradition of its own. All of the main religions of the West have their own schemes of reckoning time. It has been typical of revolutions since the eighteenth century to adopt novel calendrical systems, demarcating a new era from the old and hated regime that has been overthrown. The French revolution, for example, introduced a new calendar in which the years and months were renamed. Nietzsche's revision of history draws upon such precedents and upon his argument that it is Christianity, or more generally the nihilism in which it culminates, that is the most significant tendency of past history.

From this perspective it becomes clearer what the task of *Ecce Homo* is. *The Antichrist* is an attack on Christianity in the name of this-worldliness and the life of the body. But while the attack is very specific and its strategies have to do with the history of Christianity's misinterpretations, there may still seem to be some idealism in Nietzsche's conception of the body and this-worldly life in behalf of which he announces a "war to the death." They must be made more concrete by being seen as particular moments *(Augenblicke)* of existence. More specifically, if some parallel is intended between the moment from which Christianity dates time and the moment (the fall of 1888, "by the false time scheme") from which time is now to be reckoned, then we ought to know something about the significance of that moment. What *Ecce Homo* does, then, is to tell us precisely about that unusual moment. ("On this perfect day, when everything is ripening and not only the grape turns brown, the eye of the sun just fell upon my life: I looked back, I looked forward, and never saw so many such good things at once.") The last words of the "interleaf" text, "and so I tell my life to myself," suggest that it is this perfect moment that is the appropriate time for telling one's own story. It is appropriate because Nietzsche's life, as told from the perspective of this moment, exhibits those affirmative feelings—in regard to the bodily matters of climate and food and also with respect to his works and his destiny—that enable him to issue the "Decree Against Christianity." If time is to be split into two, then the moment of the transition, at which one looks both backward and forward, must be an especially rich one. It is also the antithesis of that blank moment that Nietzche reconstructs in *The Antichrist* as having given rise to Christianity.

It might seem as if Nietzsche's strategy here could be collapsed into a kind of solipsistic fetishism of the moment, such that an excess of good spirits would be sufficient to qualify him to rearrange the structure of historical time. This would be the case in an unqualified sense only if he also believed in a solipsism of the *Augenblick*, that is, in the total self-sufficiency and self-reference of the specific moment of experience. But in stressing the delight of the moment here Nietzsche explains that it is a vantage point *from which* he looks forward and backward and on the basis of which he can narrate his life to himself. Historical time is not to be eliminated but to be reconstrued, renamed, and given a new turning point. Such an enterprise requires not simply a profession of well-being but some new narratives. These have now been narrowed to two: Nietzsche's metahistory of philosophy and religion and the account of his own life that he provides in *Ecce Homo*. "How is transvaluation possible?" would be the Kantian form of the question to which these two narratives would be the parallel replies.

So we could read Nietzsche's *Ecce Homo* as offering an account of himself which demonstrates that transvaluation is possible in general because it is possible in his case; the explanation of why it is possible in his case will necessarily involve understanding the historical juncture that makes it possible at all. Such a reading supposes an intense degree of self-knowledge on Nietzsche's part. It supposes that his gesture "Ecce homo!" depends on his knowing well of whom he speaks. But this text also suggests that Nietzsche cannot (and should not) have that degree of self-knowledge. The subtitle of Nietzsche's book about himself, let us remember, is "How One Becomes What One Is." One obvious stratum of the text assumes that the author has both become what he is and knows what he is. But in the course of explaining "Why I am so clever," Nietzsche suggests that knowledge is not helpful in becoming what one is:

> To become what one is, one must not have the faintest notion *what* one is. From this point of view even the *blunders* of life have their own meaning and value—where *nosce te ipsum* would be the recipe for ruin, forgetting oneself, *misunderstanding* oneself, making oneself smaller, narrower, mediocre, becoming reason itself. *(EH*, 254; 6, 293)

The contradiction between knowledge and becoming what one is could perhaps be softened in a certain way by suggesting that *while* becoming what one is, one knows oneself. Nietzsche engages in a rather constant polemic against such Hegelian views because they presuppose an impossible coincidence between knowledge and existence. In order to present themselves plausibly such conceptions must in any case allow for a *becoming* of knowledge; otherwise the final self-knowledge would be completely adventitious and gratuitous. We must also ask whether, according to Nietzsche, one ever ceases to become what one is (short of death) and whether one ever becomes what one finally is. For if becoming what one is is a process that proceeds indefinitely, then it is clear that, according to the text above, one ought not to have self-knowledge at any point in the process; one should rather constantly practice the art of forgetting oneself.

So we might look at *Ecce Homo* as containing several distinct strands of thought. According to one of them Nietzsche has come to understand what he is and can truthfully announce that he is the author of the completed *Transvaluation*, with the right to take his leisure like a god, strolling along the Po. But among the things that he knows is that one is *always* becoming what one is and that one is never really in a position to say what one is. Or, perhaps more precisely, he knows that if self-knowledge were possible it would have a deadening effect on the process whereby one becomes what one is. That is, even if a Hegelian coincidence between knowledge and being is possible, it is not to be desired; for its price is what Hegel announced in speaking of the end or completion of philosophy and what Nietzsche glossed in his untimely meditation on history: a form of nihilistic passivity in regard to the present and the future. Moreover, Nietzsche draws some practical maxims from the nescience necessary to becoming what one is that seem flatly incompatible with his implicit claim to know himself as a fatality and a destiny. For example: "The whole surface consciousness—consciousness is a surface—must be kept clear of all great imperatives. Beware even of every great word, every great pose! (*EH*, 254; 6, 294)." Nietzsche follows this maxim with an account of self-becoming as the slow, unconscious working of an "organizing 'idea' " that operates without the knowledge of the subject. And he relates this to his own case:

> Its *higher protection* manifested itself to such a high degree that I never even suspected what was growing in me—and one day all my capacities, suddenly ripe, *leaped forth* in their ultimate perfection. (*EH*, 245–55; 6, 294)

But Nietzsche does not tell us when that day was, or how he knew that *this* newly attained level of life was the ultimate stage in the process of becoming. If we suppose that having attained this stage of "ultimate perfection" includes, among other things, being the writer who will split the history of mankind into two halves by means of the *Transvaluation*, then the ambivalence that we have already noted in Nietzsche's position in regard to these roles makes his account of himself suspect in the same degree.

The intrepid hermeneut (with whom I acknowledge a limited sympathy) may at this point object that the account given so far ignores both the texture of *Ecce Homo* and its narrative voice. He will point out that the use of an apparently contradictory or unreliable narrator is a condition of several kinds of narrative, and that it will be a mistake to see every instance of such ambiguity as naive. And he will then proceed to show that Nietzsche does, in fact, use a whole language of duplicity or doubleness about himself. The first main section of *Ecce Homo*, "Why I Am So Wise," explains that his wisdom is just to be so fortunately doubled as he is: alive as his father and dead as his mother, a decadent and beginning, sick and healthy *(EH*, 222–224; *6*, 264–67). Yet Nietzsche does not tell us that he both knows himself and has forgotten himself, although the teaching of eternal recurrence and the frequent praise of active forgetfulness would lead us toward such a view of the Nietzschean *Doppelgänger*. Instead his rhetoric in the long discussion of his doubleness emphasizes that he *knows* his doubleness; the knowing subject then stands outside the system of doubles, rather than being opposed within the system to the ignorant or forgetful subject. Nietzsche claims not only to have an unusual system of multiple perspectives available to him but to be in a position (to have a metaperspective) that allows to him to play upon the system. For example:

> Looking from the perspective of the sick toward *healthier* concepts and values and, conversely, looking again from the fullness and self-assurance of a *rich* life down into the secret work of the instinct of decadence—in this I have had the longest training, my truest experience; if in anything, I became master in *this*. Now I know how, have the know-how, [*ich habe es jetzt in der Hand, ich habe die Hand dafür*] to *reverse perspectives*: the first reason why a *Transvaluation of Values* is perhaps possible for me alone. *(EH*, 223; *6*, 266)

Ought we, then, to read *Ecce Homo* as the sign of a Nietzsche who knows exactly what he is about? Derrida warns us against such a hermeneutic approach which believes that

> Nietzsche's mastery is infinite, his power impregnable, or his manipulation of the snare impeccable. One cannot conclude, in order to outmaneuver the hermeneutic hold, that his is an infinite calculus which, but that it would calculate the undecidable, is similar to that of Leibniz's God. Such a conclusion, in its very attempt to elude the snare, succumbs all the more surely to it. To use parody or the simulacrum as a weapon in the service of truth or castration would be in fact to reconstitute religion, as a Nietzsche cult for example, in the interest of a priesthood of parody interpreters.[4]

Derrida reminds us of the oddness of seeking a definitive interpretation of those texts that display the maxim, "Facts are just what there are not, only interpretations" *(WP*, 481). What then is Nietzsche announcing in the text from *Ecce Homo*, quoted above, where he speaks of his unique capacity for a *Transvaluation of Values*? Both Walter Kaufmann and R. J. Hollingdale here make an interpretive decision with some consequences. Nietzsche uses the term *Umwertung alle Werte* in the last sentence. German orthography and Nietzsche's practice suggest that, so written, the phrase can be a book title as well as a term for a process or event. But Kaufmann's italicizing the words, without capital letters, and Hollingdale's use of quotation marks, again without capitals, prejudges the issue. This hermeneutic decision is repeated several times by both translators. For example, on the "interleaf" page of *Ecce Homo*, Nietzsche lists *The Transvaluation of All Values* as one of several books he has completed during the year; the English translators gratuitously translate this as "the first book" of the *Transvaluation*. By such decisions the tension between Nietzsche's deferral of his grand project and his perhaps desperate claim that the project is indeed complete is softened and obscured.

Nietzsche's systematic oscillation between knowledge and its opposite is a fundamental feature of the text. We will understand this pervading theme of doubleness or binary opposition only if we hold in parentheses, or "bracket" (to speak phenomenologically), Nietzsche's tendency to portray himself as a *master* of doubleness and reversed perspectives. I am suggesting then that we might effect a doubled reading of Nietzsche's doubleness. In addition to the untenable claims of mastery with which he presents the series of binary oppositions, Nietzsche may also be a *function* of a play of doubles that he cannot control. One bit of evidence that suggests such lack of control is to be found in the now notorious passage on his mother and sister that has only recently been restored to the text of *Ecce Homo*:

> If I were to seek the deepest contradiction to me, an incalculable commonness of instinct, I would always find my mother and sister,—to believe myself related to such *canaille* would be blasphemy against my divinity. The treatment that I have experienced from the side of my mother and sister, up until this moment, fills me with an unspeakable horror: here a perfect infernal machine [*Höllenmaschine*] is at work, with an unfailing certainty as to the moment [*Augenblick*] in which I can be bloodily wounded—in my highest moments . . . then one lacks all strength to protect oneself against the poisonous worm. . . . The physiological contiguity makes possible such a *disharmonia praestabilita* [pre-established disharmony]. . . . But I recognize that the deepest objection to "eternal recurrence," my own most abysmal thought, is always mother and sister. (*6*, 268)[5]

This part of the text was erased, we may plausibly infer, within a few months after the onset of Nietzsche's madness. It is presumably one of those passages that Peter Gast eliminated from his own copy because they gave the impression of "a too great self-intoxication or of a much too wide-ranging contempt and injustice."[6] The variation on the family romance that surfaces here and elsewhere in *Ecce Homo* will concern us soon more directly, but it should be noted that this passage could be read not as (or not merely as) an instance of Nietzsche's loss of control, but as an acknowledgment on his part that such control was not, for him, an attainable ideal. The image of the machine and of the pre-established disharmony (an inversion of the Leibnizian world-order) suggest that he is not a masterful commanding subject who can either transcend the opposition of father/mother and sister or identify only with the "good father."

He is, rather, caught in the machine, constantly susceptible to bloody wounds, and tempted to disavow his deepest thought. Here Nietzsche has explained that in his case there is a machine or structure at work that forces him to "forget himself." We might say that the machine of mother and sister are the Nietzschean equivalent of Christianity's "fortunate fall": because it distracts himself from himself, makes him forget himself, the machine saves him from knowing what he is. This is another sense in which even the parts of *Ecce Homo* that seem to betray the most *ressentiment* can be springboards for the affirmation called for by the thought of eternal recurrence. So it is that Nietzsche can describe his life as free of accidents and ask *"How could I fail to be grateful to my whole life?"* (*EH* 221; 6, 263).

In *Ecce Homo*, then, Nietzsche faces the task of being the narrator of his own life. Just after expressing his gratitude (as above) he says "and so I tell my life to myself [*Und so erzähle ich mir mein Leben*]." Such a narrative will be told by an imperfect narrator and its content, Nietzsche's life, can not be a complete, well-rounded totality, but is a structure (perhaps a "machine") that will generate indefinitely many variations on the basis of certain fundamental oppositions. The principles of such a narrative will be radically distinct from the Aristotelian conception of development as the actualization of a given potential and they will also differ from the Hegelian spiritualization of Aristotle in which, through dialectical reversals, every increase in actualization is accompanied by an increase in self-consciousness. I will shortly be sketching a more detailed analysis of the structure or machine that both generates *Ecce Homo* and is its theme. At this point I want to suggest the need for such an approach by considering a recent plausible construal of Nietzsche's "How One Becomes What One Is" which emphasizes unity and coherence.

In a chapter of his book with the same title as the subtitle of *Ecce Homo*, Alexander Nehamas offers such a construction of Nietzsche.[7] His interpretation draws upon many of Nietzsche's writings and concentrates on *Ecce Homo* only as the final exemplification of a principle of self-creation that is attributed to Nietzsche on the basis of his other works. Nehamas proposes that we begin by noting the apparent conflict between Nietzsche's motto: "Become who you are," and two principles to which he is said to subscribe: (1) that the self is something which is created, rather than discovered, and (2) that there is no soul or substance that anchors self-identity, but, rather, the personality is to be construed as simply the sum of its various activities of feeling, willing, thinking, perceiving, and so forth. Nehamas thinks that the spirit of "Become who you are" can be reconstructed along the lines of a maxim from *The Gay Science*: "*One thing is needful*—To 'give style' to one's character" (*GS*, 290; 3, 530). The twist which Nehamas proposes is to abandon any Aristotelian or Hegelian conception of a final state of style, and to concentrate on the process itself:

Nietzsche does not think of unity as a state of being that follows and replaces an earlier process of becoming. Rather, he seems to think of it as a continual process of integrating one's character traits, habits and patterns of action with one another. This process can also, in a sense, reach backwards and integrate even a discarded characteristic into the personality by showing that it was necessary for one's subsequent development.[8]

According to Nehamas, Nietzsche's conception of becoming oneself then involves not a substantial but only a formal or aesthetic conception of unity. It is not a question of identifying the individual who successfully completes such a process in terms of an enumeration of specific instances or kinds of thought, desires, and actions, but "self-creation . . . appears to be the creation, or imposition, of a higher-order accord among our lower-level thoughts, desires, and actions."[9] In the place of a final or achieved substantive state we have instead the intention that one's future development of self-creation be in accordance with certain very general expectations:

> To desire to remain who I am in this context is not so much to want any specific character traits to remain constant . . . it is to desire to appropriate and to organize as my own all that I have done, or at least that I know I have done, into a coherent whole . . . it is to become flexible enough to use whatever I have done, do, or will do as elements in a constantly changing, never finally completed whole.[10]

Nehamas recognizes that such a whole-in-process ought, from a Nietzschean perspective, to be such that it can be affirmed wholeheartedly by the creator-in-process. The highest degree and test of affirmation is the willing of eternal recurrence: the desire that one's life, should it recur, be precisely as it has been. Where, asks Nehamas, can we find a concrete model of such a personality whose desirability is based not on moral virtue but on the more formal or aesthetic characteristics connected with total integration? The answer is to be found, he suggests, in the fact that Nietzsche models his conceptions of self and character on the basis of literature. A great literary character, on this view, is one who is all of a piece; a narrative will show such a character as ultimately including and comprehending that which might have initially seemed to be accidental or inconsistent. "Become who you are" requires that we not only become such characters but that we be their *authors* as well.

Nehamas's understanding of how Nietzsche saw that process is worth quoting because it includes an interpretation of *Ecce Homo* that appears to contrast strongly with the one developed here:

> How, then, can one achieve the perfect unity and freedom that are primarily possessed by perfect literary characters? How does one become both a literary character who, unlike either the base Charlus or the noble Brutus, really exists, and also that character's very author?
>
> One way of achieving this perhaps impossible goal might be to write a great number of very good books that exhibit great apparent inconsistencies but that can be seen to be deeply continuous with one another when they are read carefully and well. Toward the

end of this enterprise one can even write a book about those books that shows how they fit together, how a single figure emerges through them, how even the most damaging contradictions may have been necessary for the figure or character or author or person (the word hardly matters here) to emerge fully from them.[11]

Nehamas's way of putting Nietzsche together again is attractive, for it manages to preserve some of the traditional values of coherence and integration while acknowledging Nietzsche's critique of substance and identity. Yet the structural (or machine) model of the self that governs *Ecce Homo* is, I believe, more radical and not subsumable under even such a generously expanded conception of the unity of the "figure or character or author or person." But Nehamas's approach is specially interesting because it employs a narrativist model to make sense of becoming what one is; this helps to make it clear both that such models are internal to Nietzsche's philosophical and literary practice, and that our perspective on that practice must be interrelated at many levels with our understanding of those narrative models.

Nehamas is surely right in supposing that *if* the view which he ascribes to Nietzsche is indeed his understanding of "how one becomes what one is," then *Ecce Homo* should exemplify that conception. But does *Ecce Homo* sustain such a reading? Nehamas does not offer a more detailed reading of the text (on whose subtitle he comments) than the one just cited. Even the specific meaning of that motto is, however, in question. A close reading of the text would begin by asking why Nietzsche speaks of becoming *what* one is rather than of becoming *who* one is. In fact, he uses the more personal form in several earlier books; Nehamas assumes that the various formulations are equivalent and goes on to read them all as if they were in the personal mode. If we attend to Nietzsche's language, however, we see that what one becomes is a "*what*," a something, rather than a "who." If we were to look for literary models of what it is like to become *what* one is rather than *who* one is we would look to examples of figures who become uncanny, monstrous, or *Doppelgängers* rather than to those who become complete characters. We would think not only of modernist and postmodernist dissolving figures such as those in James Joyce, Samuel Beckett, or Thomas Pynchon but of more classical examples of the contradictory, the multiple, and the grotesque such as Gargantua and Don Quixote. Here too one might wonder how it is that Nietzsche has helped to inspire writers like Roland Barthes, who offer powerful readings of texts that we might take to exemplify classical conceptions of character (such as Balzac's) in which character is not after all a unity but at most a shifting function of codes or figures of speech.[12]

If Nietzsche employed literary models, which ones did he appropriate? And what understanding of literature governed his appropriation of them? Certainly Nietzsche's most extended treatment of "literature" is in *The Birth of Tragedy*. There he is as explicit as possible in depicting the individual within tragic drama as an Apollonian illusion. Because of the interest in the "family romance" theme in *Ecce Homo*, this approach to the Oedipal theme could be an indication of what literary models are relevant to that text and how they are understood. After Nietzsche has explained the primacy of the chorus and the Dionysian experience of the loss of self, he goes on to comment on that which is apparently clear and well-formed:

> The language of Sophocles' heroes amazes us by its Apollonian precision and lucidity, so we immediately have the feeling that we are looking into the innermost ground of their being, with some astonishment that the way to this ground would be so short. But suppose we disregard the character of the hero as it comes to the surface, visibly—after all, it is in the last analysis nothing but a bright image projected on a dark wall, which means appearance through and through; suppose we penetrate into the myth that projects itself in those lucid projections; then we suddenly experience a phenomenon that is just the opposite of a familiar optical phenomenon. When after a forceful attempt to gaze on the sun we turn away blinded, we see dark-colored spots before our eyes, as a cure, as it were. Conversely, the bright image projections of the Sophoclean hero—in short, the Apollonian aspect of the mask—are necessary effects of a glance into the inside and terrors of nature; as it were, luminous spots to cure eyes damaged by gruesome night. (*BT.* 9; *1*, 64–65)

Here Nietzsche describes the Sophoclean hero as luminously intelligible, and so we might take his analysis as supporting Nehamas's conception of character. But to the extent that he is analyzing *literature* Nietzsche is radically dislocating and de-emphasizing the role of character in drama.

If becoming what one is is something like the way in which a literary text becomes what it is, why not consider the entire dynamics of the text? Indeed, as Nietzsche goes on to describe the uncanniness of the Oedipus figure, it is difficult not to be reminded of his use of the Oedipal motif in *The Genealogy of Morals* as well as in the themes of *Ecce Homo* itself. Nietzsche's account of Oedipus the character does not suggest any special interest in him as a unified or integrated figure; rather the accent is on the uncanniness of the man whose existence challenges our tendency to see humans (and other things in the world) as individuals; the legend of Oedipus suggests that "where prophetic and magical powers have broken the spell of present and future, the rigid law of individuation, and the real magic of nature, some enormously unnatural event—such as incest—must have occurred earlier as a cause." Nietzsche's comments on the aged Oedipus of *Oedipus at Colonus* again emphasize a paradoxical duality with no hint that it is *aufgehoben* in a higher unity: "the hero attains his highest activity, extending far beyond his life, through his purely passive posture, while his conscious deeds and desires, earlier in his life, merely led him to passivity" *(BT,* sec. 9; *BW,* p. 68). Nietzsche also claims that until Euripides "all the celebrated figures [*Figuren*] of the Greek state—Prometheus, Oedipus, etc.—are mere masks of this original hero, Dionysus" *(BT,* sec. 10, *BW,* p. 73). Dionysus, the god of many forms, constantly torn apart but reappearing in new guises, seems to be at the opposite pole from the organically unified character or the uncanniness of an Oedipus. The question has a special poignancy because Nietzsche may be credited, along with Freud, for having effected a transformation in the relative weight which our culture ascribes to Oedipus and other figures of Greek myth. George Steiner has convincingly displayed that the eighteenth and nineteenth centuries were more attracted to Antigone (and her conflict with Creon) than to father Oedipus.[13] Steiner credits Freud with having produced the displacement. But *The Birth of Tragedy* should probably be seen as the first radical revaluation of the Antigone and Oedipus myths. Antigone is referred to only once, and there is no analysis of her character or destiny; Oedipus, on the other hand, is the constant paradigm of the tragic hero and Nietzsche introduces his discussion of others such as Hamlet by noting their resemblance to Oedipus or their exemplification of an Oedipal uncanny knowledge *(BT*, 4, 7; *1*, 38, 52). Nietzsche takes Oedipus to be the emblematic figure for philosophy in his sketches for an uncompleted book, "Oedipus: Soliloquies of the Last Philosopher." That sketch begins with an expression of total solitude anticipating both some of the self-descriptions in *Ecce Homo* and Zarathustra's complex form of internal conversation:

"I call myself the last philosopher, because I am the last man. No one speaks with me except I myself and my voice comes to me like the voice of one who is dying. Let me change places with you for just an hour, beloved voice, with you, the last breath of a memory of all human happiness; through you I can deceive myself that loneliness is gone and I can lie to myself about multiplicity and love, for my heart refuses to believe that love is dead, it cannot bear the terror of the loneliness and it forces me to speak as if I were two." (7, 46)

Freud is quoted as having said that Nietzsche had more self-knowledge than any man that ever lived.[14] This remark could be interpreted in two senses. It might be construed on what was earlier called a Hegelian model in which it is supposed that a kind of absolute self-knowledge is possible in principle and that we can evaluate people in order to discover to what extent they approximate this ideal. Or one might interpret it in a radically Socratic sense, according to which genuine self-knowledge must confess that it is in some respects blind, partial, forgetful, poetic, and constructive. Moreover, it cannot claim to know precisely in what respects it does not know itself or what the limits of its self-knowledge are. This last proviso would make Freud's conception of self-knowledge distinct from both the Hegelian and radical Socratic versions. Jacques Lacan has shown it is possible to articulate a powerful understanding of Freud and psychoanalysis that acknowledges the intrinsic limits of self-knowledge and self-consciousness. On this view the unconscious is the "language of the other"; that is, my thoughts and intentions always escape me because they are always already embedded in a language that exists prior to me and which I cannot deliberately control. From this perspective both the Hegelian conception and some slightly weaker versions of the principle of self-knowledge are forms of the *imaginary*, that illusion of self-sufficiency and wholeness which the child first constructs in his or her desperate struggle with the chaos of raging instincts, sensations, and demands. According to Lacan every person exemplifies some intersection of such an imaginary conception of the self with two other levels or dimensions of physical interaction with the world. These are the *symbolic* and the *real*. The real is that which imposes itself on the subject regardless of the subject's desires and independently of any mediation. For example, my bodily constitution and my place in history are aspects of the real which I can neither choose nor avoid. It would be a terrible fate to live in such a way as to oscillate between the grandiose fantasies of the imaginary and the harsh lessons and perpetual shocks administered by the real. In fact our world is also constituted by a linguistic, symbolic dimension.

Lacan finds the paradigm of our entrance into the symbolic in Freud's account of the child who, anguished by the periodic disappearance of his mother, comes to play the game of *fort /da*. He no longer wails for the mother but symbolizes the alternation of her presence and absence by his feigned loss and retrieval of some toy. Submitting himself to the linguistic world that surrounds him, the child has subordinated his original desire to the generalized system of socialized desires that is implied in language. What he desires is simultaneously altered and made expressible by his coming to play his first language-game. As Lacan describes this epochal transformation,

> the moment in which desire becomes human is also that in which the child is born into language . . . *fort*! /da! It is precisely in his solitude that the desire of the little child has already become the desire of another, of an *alter ego* who dominates him and whose object of desire is henceforth his own affliction.[15]

Lacan's adaptation of Freud's narrative should itself be taken as emblematic of the category of the symbolic rather than as the discovery of a specific ontogenetic pattern which each human being must traverse in a rigorous order. The symbolic is at least potentially public; for each subject (or speaker) it embodies what Lacan calls "the desire of the other."

Let us consider the text of *Ecce Homo* as a constellation of the dimensions of the real, the symbolic, and the imaginary. We will be struck immediately by the blatant role of the imaginary. The usual forces that tend to soften or obscure the expression of a grandiose, exalted conception of the writer's self are absent and we have an author who openly glories in telling us "Why I Am So Wise," "Why I Write Such Good Books," and "Why I Am a Destiny." At the same time Nietzsche is concerned with the question of the commensurability of this conception of himself with his linguistic, symbolic persona, that is, with the body of thought and discourse constituted by the books he has written (or has still to write). He acknowledges that "I am one thing, my writings are another matter" (*EH*, 259; 6, 298). Nietzsche is not content to retreat behind his writings; it is in fact his writing, as an historical event, that requires the self-revelation of the author. But he also fears that neither he nor his writings nor, consequently, the connection between them can be understood by his contemporaries. Both points are made in the first sentences of *Ecce Homo*:

> Seeing that before long I must confront humanity with the most difficult demand ever made of it, it seems indispensable to me to say *who I am*. Really, one should know it, for I have not left myself "without testimony." But the disproportion between the greatness of my task and the *smallness* of my contemporaries has found expression in the fact that one has neither heard nor even seen me. I live on my own credit; it is perhaps a mere prejudice that I live. (EH, 217; 6, 257)

As we have seen, Nietzsche thinks of himself as posing the most difficult demand by means of a book, *The Transvaluation of All Values*. Ordinarily, one might suppose, a text can be accepted or rejected, understood or misunderstood, without a necessary reference to the person of the author. But since the projected aim of the *Transvaluation* is to "break the history of mankind into two" by teaching a radical form of this-worldliness and self-affirmation, it is important to show Nietzsche's affirmative relation to his own texts, since it is he who occupies the juncture at which this historical break occurs.

Nietzsche's strategy in disclosing himself is a double one of deferral and seduction. Deferral, because Nietzsche explains himself as the author of the *Transvaluation* before that work has been written; it may be his discomfort with this strategy that finally leads him to identify the *Transvaluation* with the (already written) *Antichrist*. Seduction, because Nietzsche appeals to us, his future readers, to demonstrate our superiority to his shallow contemporaries by understanding him. If we have understood him, and if there is an essential connection between what he is and the event or operation of transvaluation, then we may suppose that we have also understood the latter, even if there is no *Transvaluation*—which was the pre-text of the seductive strategy. Moreover, Nietzsche continues to up the ante in *Ecce Homo*, explaining the difficulty of understanding his work in terms that should delight the reader who comes to feel that he has indeed attained some understanding:

> Ultimately, nobody can get more out of things, including books, than he already knows. For what one lacks access to from experience one will have no ear. Now let us imagine an extreme case: that a book speaks of nothing but events that lie altogether beyond the possibility of any frequent or even rare experience—that it is the first language for a new series of experiences. In that case, simply nothing will be heard, but there will be the acoustic illusion that where nothing is heard, nothing is there. That is, in the end, my average experience and, if you will, the originality of my experience. (*EH*, 261; 6, 299–300

We might say that Nietzsche uses the symbolic order with the purpose of seducing the reader into an imaginary conception of him or herself. That is, if the seduction is successful the reader will agree with Nietzsche that "having understood six sentences from *Zarathustra* would raise one to a higher level of existence than 'modern' men could attain'' (*EH*, 259; 6, 299).

Yet Nietzsche's strategy is patently disrupted by the effects of the real. Because of his breakdown in January 1889, *Ecce Homo* was not published until 1905, and then in a version bowdlerized by Peter Gast and Elizabeth Förster-Nietzsche. The *Transvaluation* as originally projected was never written but some of Nietzsche's notes were published as *The Will to Power* in a context suggesting some of the grandiose claims that their author had made for the other project. The text we have of *Ecce Homo* is questionable; Nietzsche's most thorough and conscientious editor, Mazzino Montinari, concludes that ''It is certain that Nietzsche left behind a completed *Ecce Homo*, but we do not have it.''[16] Not only did the event that was to consist in the appearance and effect of the *Transvaluation* never occur, but the small book which was to accompany it was defaced by the very ''infernal machine'' that Nietzsche had described in the manuscript that he sent to the printer.

Aiming at a world-historical event of his own devising, Nietzsche was overcome by the real in the form of history. His sister had learned the techniques of imperialist profiteering and the big lie of the publicist while working with her husband in a scheme to create a German colony in Paraguay. With the husband's suicide and the collapse of the colony, she returned to Germany and applied some of the same methods to building an institution around her brother's work. Since that was a more genuine capital investment than the first and because the market had been primed, the second venture met with much greater success.[17]

This is the aspect of the real that impinges most obviously on Nietzsche. But as an analyst of himself, as a teller of his own tale, Nietzsche also undertook to explain the nuanced ways in which climate, surroundings, and cuisine provided the conditions of his moods and his work. In the long-suppressed passage dealing with his mother and sister he begins by saying that he will touch on the question of race, and claims Polish descent through his father. The Germans, he suggests, cannot understand him because they are genealogically disposed against all *Witz* and high spirits. In this approach to the real, however, Nietzsche embeds it in a symbolic structure of binary oppositions, to which we may now turn our attention. These positions can be understood both synchronically as the different sides of Nietzsche the *Doppelgänger* and diachronically as the alternating phases of his career. In every case, however, it seems to be a matter of something analogous to the child's *fort! /da!* game. Nietzsche plays a game with his own life by telling his life to himself. He is not simply doubled, but the observer of the doubles. He knows, as part of this game, that should the ''good'' side be eclipsed it will not be so forever. And he claims to gain strength from the very alteration. In recounting his miraculous recovery in 1880 at the age of thirty-six (the same age at which his father died— ''I am already dead as my father''), Nietzsche sketches the typical dynamics:

The following winter, my first one in Genoa, that sweetening and spiritualization which is almost inseparably connected with an extreme poverty of blood and muscle, produced *Daybreak*. The perfect brightness and cheerfulness, even exuberance of the spirit, re-

flected in this work, is compatible in my case not only with the most profound physiological weakness, but even with an excess of pain. (*EH*, 222; 6, 265)

We should not misconstrue this movement of exchange and oscillation as a dialectical process, however. For while claiming that the illness of 1880 sharpened
his dialectical skills, he adds that ''my readers know perhaps in what way I consider
dialectic as a symptom of decadence; for example in the most famous case, the case
of Socrates'' (*EH*, 223; 6, 265). Dialectic would create synthesis and totalities, it
would exploit contradictions in order to press on toward a full and integrated account
of things. One becomes what one is non-dialectically, by the play and intensification
of one's various (here doubled) propensities.[18]
    Consider a partial list of these pairs of inclinations, heritages, circumstances,
and surroundings that weave their way through *Ecce Homo*:

    affirmative/negative
    health/illness
    live as mother/dead as father
    being a beginning/being a decadent
    Dionysus/the crucified
    good food/German food
    good climate/poor climate
    Polish ancestry/German ancestry
    work/recreation

In Nietzsche's need to construct a narrative around these various polarities we may
find an instance of the procedure that, according to Claude Lévi-Strauss, is typical
of all mythical thinking. On Lévi-Strauss's view *la pensée sauvage* or ''untamed
thinking'' is constantly faced with the task of reconciling, compromising, or coming
to terms with such opposed elements, aspects, or tendencies. He suggests that
thought when left to itself (unconstricted, for example, by science or dialectic) will
deal with these oppositions by creating a narrative myth.[19] In a celebrated account
of the Oedipus myth, for example, Lévi-Strauss detects a structure of oppositions
beneath the narrative sequence of events as they follow one another in the story.
One set of incidents exemplifies the overvaluation of family ties (e.g., Oedipus'
incest with Jocasta) while anther exhibits their undervaluation (e.g., Oedipus' par-
ricide of Laius); similarly, one set of incidents involves the view that man is born
of the earth and another set supposes that he has a higher origin. A story like the
Oedipus myth enables its audience to *think* these oppositions or contradictions in
a way that they could not do without the story.
    In *Ecce Homo* Nietzsche tells the story of his life, then, as a structured play of
these binary oppositions. That is, he not only tells us the story, as a Bororo native
might relate a myth to a Lévi-Straussian anthropologist, but like Lévi-Strauss
Nietzsche simultaneously offers a structural analysis of the story that is told. Alex-

ander Nehamas concludes his account of "How One Becomes What One Is" by finding an analogous, yet significantly distinct, concentration of functions:

> One way then to become one thing, one's own character, or what one is, is, after having written all these other books, to write *Ecce Homo* and even to give it the subtitle "How One Becomes What One Is." It is to write this self-referential work, in which Nietzsche can be said with equal justice to invent or to discover himself, and in which the character who speaks to us is the author who has created him and who is in turn a character created by or implicit in all the books that were written by the author who is writing this one.[20]

Nehamas's claim should be revised by representing Nietzsche not as a self-created character but as a text, and not as an omniscient and omnipotent author but as a structuralist critic who aims at revealing the laws of the text's transformations.

We do not know exactly what was contained in the manuscript of *Ecce Homo* which Nietzsche sent to the printer. In addition to the manuscript which Nietzsche's sister prepared for the first publication in 1908, there is also a copy made by Peter Gast in February 1889, just after Nietzsche's collapse. This copy is almost identical with the one used in 1908. But, as Gast reported to Franz Overbeck when he sent the manuscript to him, that copy had already been edited:

> I only wanted you, respected Professor, to become acquainted with this text through my copy, and so *without* the passages which give even me the impression of a too great self-intoxication or of a much too far ranging condemnation and injustice. (*14*, 459)

There is no way of knowing just what these passages were, except for the section on Nietzsche's mother and sister that was eventually retrieved from Peter Gast's *Nachlass*. Elizabeth also acknowledges that a number of passages, supposedly characteristic of delirium, were destroyed shortly after the collapse because she feared that on Nietzsche's recovery (which she claimed to have expected) he would be terribly hurt by seeing what he had written. As Montinari observes, there are some final entries preserved in Nietzsche's notebooks that might be indicative of the kinds of materials deleted from *Ecce Homo* by Gast and Elizabeth; but any effort to reconstruct a "complete" *Ecce Homo* must be a very speculative endeavor. These last notes deal with such social and political topics as the psychology of Jews and antisemites; the possible receptivity of the "officer class" to Nietzsche's thought; a hope to enlist the financial support of Jewish bankers in an anti-Christian campaign; and attacks on Bismarck, the Hohenzollerns, and the German Reich; they announce Nietzsche's readiness for war and his willingness to rule the world.

Montinari remarks that "despite all of the omissions, additions and other changes, the printer's manuscript of *Ecce Homo* can be read effortlessly as a continuous text" (*14*, 458). But what a strange text this must be if it can appear complete when it is actually fragmentary. One wonders, if the text were actually "complete," whether it would appear even more fragmentary. This is the undecidable question around which editorial (and consequently hermeneutical) controversies have revolved in recent Nietzsche scholarship. Erich Podach articulated one of the options in his edition of *Nietzsches Werke des Zusammenbruchs*: "One thing is certain: Nietzsche left behind no completed *Ecce Homo*, but we have one." Podach means to suggest that the various editorial efforts have produced a relatively unified text from an incomplete and disordered one. Montinari's reply is: "One thing is certain: Nietzsche left behind a completed *Ecce Homo* but we do not have it."

One might propose a common-sensical way out of the dilemma. Let us suppose that Nietzsche has recovered from his "breakdown" (to translate Podach's *Zusammenbruch*) and that he had decided to revise the manuscript of *Ecce Homo* a final time. Might he not have produced a version close to the one that we have now which has been mediated to us by Nietzsche's sister and Peter Gast? After all, one might say, Nietzsche was like other authors in so far as he frequently revised his works in order to produce a total effect, avoid unnecessary digressions, and so on. But the hypothesis of a recovered Nietzsche is radically unclear. Would part of such a recovery have been the abandonment of the conviction that he was on the verge of presenting humanity with its greatest challenge ever? Would he, upon recovering, have continued to identify the whole of the *Transvaluation* with *The Antichrist* or would he have realized that there was more work to be done? Would he have maintained the radicalism of the "Decree Against Christianity" (newly restored by Montinari) which concludes *The Antichrist*? That declaration is issued as "promulgated on the day of salvation, on the first day of the year one (September 30, 1888 of the false mode of reckoning time)" and it is signed by "the Antichrist." Would Nietzsche also have recovered from his own view of himself as constituted by the alternation of illness and recovery? Questions such as these are unanswerable because they require us to operate with reduced and oversimplified conceptions of the very opposition between health and illness which Nietzsche calls into question in *Ecce Homo*.

We may simply need to recognize that conventional editorial ideas of completeness and incompleteness are inapplicable to *Ecce Homo*. Montinari's tendency is to defend the coherence of the "complete" text, which he thinks is the background for the one that we have, by appealing to Nietzsche's changing but knowable authorial intentions. He makes a number of editorial decisions, for example, that are based upon Nietzsche's late identification of *The Antichrist* as the whole of the *Transvaluation*. This allows for a certain coherence and simplification, but it also depends upon not attending to Nietzsche's thesis in *Ecce Homo* that one becomes what one is only by not knowing what one is. Surely this principle applies to authorship as well as to other modes of activity or becoming oneself. To become an author requires that one not know oneself, or forget oneself, as an author. Of course an editor might simply reject the principle, treating it as just one linguistic expression within a more complex text. But then one wonders whether something has gone wrong with a reading that would so compartmentalize Nietzsche's concern with doubleness. Perhaps we should say that the text of *Ecce Homo* that Nietzsche prepared is both complete and incomplete, as is the one that we have.

So it is not self-evident that Nietzsche has been successful in producing a total structural analysis of his own story and of the multiple myths which it intersects. He is too much given over to the imaginary for such a task, which may be impossible in any case. Let us consider Nietzsche's constantly repeated assurances that his life has reached a point of perfection and peacefulness. Knowing what was to happen just two months after such assurances, we may wonder at their force and at Nietzsche's need for repetition. The opening of the short "interleaf" may, however, stand for a number of such claims:

> On this perfect day, when everything is ripening and not only the grape turns brown, the eye of the sun just fell upon my life: I looked back, I looked forward, and never saw so many and such good things at once. It was not for nothing that I buried my forty-fourth year today; I had the *right* to bury it; whatever was life in it has been saved is immortal. (*EH*, 221, 6, 263)

The typical elements in these many expressions of well-being could perhaps be sketched in the following way, and can be seen in the paradigmatic text above: a feeling of ripeness or pregnancy; a sense of extended horizons, expressed through metaphors of large, open spaces; and a framework having to do with privileged but recurring temporal events or phases (here the autumn and his birthday). One of Nietzsche's key words for such moods, experiences, and moments is "halcyon." In *Ecce Homo* Nietzsche praises *Zarathustra* as not only the best of his books but as the highest and deepest book that there is and as the greatest gift ever given to mankind (*EH*, 219; 6, 259). In describing the great good spirit of that book Nietzsche refers to it three times as "halcyon."

Since Nietzsche takes *Zarathustra* to be his emblematic book and since he employs this term in his most intimate accounts of this prized, inspired creation, we may hope that it will help illuminate the structure of the narrative that he constructs about himself. The concept—actually a myth or mytheme—is worth exploring because it contains, amplifies, and connects the typical elements in Nietzsche's claims to peacefulness. It is the symbolic form (or one symbolic form) that allows him to escape from the solipsism of the imaginary and the horrors of the real. In order to articulate the myth it will be necessary to examine the set of meanings both philologically and in terms of Nietzsche's imaginary (in the Lacanian sense) picture of himself. But first we should read the three references to the halcyon in *Ecce Homo*. In the Preface Nietzsche explains that "Among my writings my *Zarathustra* stands to my mind by itself" and suggests how important it is that we not misconstrue it as a prophetic book. Instead, "Above all one must *hear* aright the tone that comes from the mouth, the halcyon tone, lest one should do wretched injustice to the meaning of its wisdom" (*EH*, 219; 6, 259). In the long commentary on *Zarathustra* that comes later Nietzsche recounts his experience of inspiration in composing its first three parts in separate periods of ten days each. After the first two parts were finished, he relates: "The next winter, under the halcyon sky of Nizza, which then shone into my life for the first time, I found *Zarathustra* III— and was finished" (*EH*, 302; 6, 341). Here the reference seems to be to an accidental accompaniment of writing (Nizza's climate); as we will see, however, dates, places, and Nietzsche's feeling of deep intimacy with his natural surroundings are essential to his conception of himself as halcyon. The last use of the term in *Ecce Homo* comes in Nietzsche's attempt to explain how, in *Zarathustra*, man is overcome at every moment and the *Übermensch* has become real:

> The halcyon, the light feet, the omnipresence of malice and exuberance, and whatever else is typical of the type of Zarathustra—none of this has even before been dreamed as essential to greatness. Precisely in this width of space and this accessibility for what is contradictory, Zarathustra experiences himself as the *supreme type of all beings*; and once one hears how he defines this, one will refrain from seeking any metaphor for it. (*EH*, 305, 6, 344)

It is also worth mentioning that a draft of the chapter "Why I Am a Destiny" makes explicit the self-identification as a "halcyon figure" (*Halkyonier*) that is latent in the passages above:

> Have I been understood? He who enlightens about morality is a *force majeure*, a destiny— this shouldn't prevent me from being the most cheerful man, from being a halcyon figure, and I even have a right to that; for who has even done a greater service to humanity?— I bring it the very happiest message. (*14*, 512)

As a classicist who inscribes the riddle of Ariadne and Dionysus in *Ecce Homo*, Nietzsche must be supposed to have been aware of the story of Alcyone (from whose name "halcyon" is derived) and of the notion of the halcyon days associated with that myth. The fullest version is perhaps to be found in Ovid. Alcyone was the daughter of Aeolus, the king of the winds. Her husband, Ceyx, was drowned on a sea voyage undertaken despite Alcyone's warning. From the shore she saw his body floating on the waves and, as she leapt into the water to join him, the gods transformed her into a sea-bird. Ovid explains the results of the transformation:

> The gods changed both to birds, and both were one,
> Though love had given them a strange mutation.
> Today they live and breed upon those waters
> And for a week in winter, Alcyone
> Keeps her brood warm within a floating nest,
> Aeolus stills the winds that shake the waters
> To guard his grandsons on a peaceful sea.[21]

The original halcyon days were that period of a week or two after the winter solstice when the halcyon bird (or kingfisher) was believed to lay its eggs in a floating nest. The winds were stilled and this peaceful interlude between the storms of the winter was a boon for sailors. The image of vast calm seas suggests "the width of space" and "accessibility for what is contradictory" that Nietzsche invokes in his account of *Zarathustra*'s halcyon tone. The time of year also coincides with the composition of *Zarathustra* III "under the halcyon sky of Nizza" and with Nietzsche's frequent praise of January as a time of fresh life. And it suggests a possible connection between Nietzsche's mania of late December 1888 to early January 1889, and the recurrence of the halcyon days. The traditional "halcyon days" would have ended around January 3, the day that Nietzsche collapsed in the street in Turin.

For Nietzsche, then, the halcyon is not only the time of perfect weather or, more generally, a time of great peace, calm, and good cheer. It is also a time within a cycle that includes both an emergence from a period of storms and an expectation that the wild forces will be set loose once more. As a cyclical myth, Alcyone's story is appropriate for the philosopher of eternal recurrence in several ways. It is a form of periodicity which, like the cycles of the day revolving around the poles of noon and midnight in *Zarathustra,* can offer an image of recurrence itself. It also suggests a way in which Friedrich Nietzsche can "tell the story of his life" in such a way as to affirm a career regularly bedeviled by illness and renewed by convalescence. Eternal recurrence, Zarathustra says, involves the idea that every moment of joy is so necessarily connected with every moment of suffering that to affirm any joyous moment is to affirm all moments of the cycle.

What the halcyon myth enables Nietzsche to do is to effect a connection between his own cycle of health and illness and the cosmic, this-worldly cycle of eternal recurrence. Many of the high and low points that Nietzsche records are indeed clustered around the winter solstice, December 21, and the ensuing halcyon days. In verses from the *Gay Science* included in *Ecce Homo* Nietzsche blesses the "Sanctus Januarius" of 1881 and alludes to the legend of Saint January (a Christian halcyon?) whose blood is believed to liquify and revive each January. Nietzsche's greatest moments of exaltation, toward which *Ecce Homo* seems to build, occur in December 1888; the final storm, we might say, breaks out savagely at the close of the halcyon days on January 3 or 4, 1889. *Ecce Homo* has been thought by some to foreshadow that collapse with its megalomaniacal tone; but to the extent that Nietzsche thinks the halcyon myth he evades the traps of the purely imaginary.

In the play of doubles which the text of *Ecce Homo* presents, the halcyon theme is, we might say, its own double. Taken superficially, Nietzsche's pride in the "calm seas" of his life would seem to be a perfected form of self-assurance (cf. *EH*, 255; 6, 294). Yet if these calm seas are the seas of the halcyon days then they are opposed or doubled by death and turbulence. The myth, then, is another form of *fort*! /*da*! play and another way that Nietzsche has of being a *Doppelgänger*. In this instance, however, we seem to be dealing not with Nietzsche as the structuralist critic of his own text but with a Nietzsche caught between the seductive sense of wholeness and power characteristic of the imaginary, on the one hand, and, on the other, the play of language in which preverbal desire has been recast and is available only as a trace or residue. Perhaps Nietzsche's anticipation of the great noon when there will be a general acceptance of eternal recurrence should be seen in turn as a mapping of the halcyon days onto history's *longue durée;* and the age of great wars which he believes that he is ushering in would be a corresponding extension of the storm following the sea-bird's peaceful brooding time.

What should we make of this mythic narrative? Clearly it is only one strand that might be read in Nietzsche's last texts. Perhaps I have invented it, succumbing to the seductive temptation always hovering around Nietzsche's writings to believe one has found a clue to the structure of the labyrinth. Surely it would be a mistake to suppose, as so many writers have done, that because we find a myth in Nietzsche we can characterize his entire works as a modern restoration of the mythical. Nietzsche tells too many stories to allow us to do that; there is always a plurality of stories in different modes: myth is only one form of Nietzschean narrative. To the extent that it is there, it functions as part of a set of myths (Zarathustra, Sanctus Januarius, Dionysus and Ariadne, the halcyon) that are not to be integrated into any comprehensive metanarrative. Nor should we suppose that such a mythical level must be the deep, intended meaning of Nietzsche's writing. It is more like a dream that is neither fully remembered nor analytically understood, but which coexists more or less easily with other strata of the texts. In the case of *Ecce Homo* such dreams demonstrate the inability of Nietzsche, and perhaps of any writer, to establish a comprehensive mastery over the language, rhetoric and narrative with which he works.

That such dreams should surface in *Ecce Homo,* designed as it is to prepare the way for a *Transvaluation of All Values*, may, however, have a more specific significance. The thought of the transvaluation, I have suggested, is increasingly condensed into the appearance of the book, *The Transvaluation,* and the attached ''Decree.'' The great noon is increasingly concretized as a moment *(Augenblick).* In *The Advantage and Disadvantage of History for Life*, Nietzsche had defined strength as the ability to maintain, simultaneously, a sense of the historical and of the unhistorical.

> The stronger the innermost roots of a man's nature, the more readily will he be able to assimilate and appropriate the things of the past; and the most powerful and tremendous nature would be characterized by the fact that it would know no boundary at all at which the historical sense began to overwhelm it . . . *the unhistorical and the historical are necessary in equal degree for the health of an individual, of a people and of a culture.* (UM, 62–63; *1*, 251–52)

To return to Zarathustra's visionary confrontation with the spirit of gravity, we might say that health is defined as the ability simultaneously to live in the *Augenblick* (the inscription unread by the dwarf) and to project oneself as far as possible along the two paths of past and future that seem to run endlessly away from the gate of the *Augenblick* in opposite directions. But it is not clear how such health is to be achieved, maintained, and preserved. Nietzsche's last writings suggest not an ultimate strength that holds both in a simultaneous balance, but rather an oscillation between one and the other. At one moment all is to be condensed, radically, into a single moment or great noon that will split history into two; at the next moment

Nietzsche is "all the names of history." But the reasons for Nietzsche's failure to maintain a balance are obscure and they do not necessarily lead to the conclusion of the general impossibility of the project. We might ask what would happen to Nietzsche's version of the project, for example, if he had been able to decouple the conceptions of eternal recurrence and of the great noon. One side of the thought of eternal recurrence, clearly present in Nietzsche's texts, is that it is a thought addressed to the individual in his "loneliest loneliness, (*GS*, 341; *3*, 570). We need not attribute a conception of an ultimate, integral individual to Nietzsche in order to see that the rhetoric of that demon's challenge to think the eternal recurrence focusses the question of the abysmal thought on a set of particular experiences rather than on history as a whole. And certainly no suggestion is made that there must be a general, collective experience or understanding of eternal recurrence at any time. It is not clear why eternal recurrence, as a counter-thought to the historically oriented metanarratives of the West, should require either a cadre of teachers of the recurrence or an expectation of a great noon consisting either in the general acceptance of the thought or in some world-shaking announcement (such as the appearance of the *Transvaluation*) that would provoke such an acceptance. Yet there are signs of a kind of hallucinatory fusion of the thought of eternal recurrence with a new metanarrative of the great noon in Nietzsche's notebooks, in entries that are roughly simultaneous with the first appearance of the thought of recurrence itself. This may suggest some reflections on just how deeply the metanarrative impulse is rooted in the Western mind; it may be that, as Derrida has suggested, such conceptions are not to be rooted out all at once, but to be attacked obliquely with a complex strategy that is constantly vigilant in seeking out new disguises of the idea under attack. That Nietzsche was not altogether successful in his own struggle with metanarrative ought not to distract one either from the serious nature of the challenge or from the exemplary character of his own battles and skirmishes with the worldview that is structured by first and last things.

Notes

1. HOW PHILOSOPHICAL TRUTH FINALLY BECAME A FABLE

1. Jürgen Habermas, "Nachwort," in Nietzsche, *Erkentnisstheoretische Schriften* (Frankfurt, 1968), p. 237.

2. Jürgen Habermas, "Critical Theory and Modernity," *New German Critique* 26 (Spring/Summer 1982):22.

3. Ibid., p. 25.

4. Ibid., p. 27.

5. See Jacques Derrida, *Spurs: Nietzsche's Styles*, tr. Barbara Harlow (Chicago, 1979) and Gilles Deleuze, *Nietzsche and Philosophy* (New York, 1983); essays by a number of recent French and German writers on Nietzsche are included in *The New Nietzsche*, ed. David Allison (New York, 1977).

6. Jean-François Lyotard, *The Postmodern Condition*, trans. Geoff Bennington and Brian Massumi (Minneapolis, 1984), p. 31.

7. Vincent Descombes analyzes the French revolt against Hegel in *Modern French Philosophy*, trans. L. Scott-Fox and J. M. Harding (Cambridge, 1980).

8. On Nietzsche and Schiller see Benjamin Bennett, "Nietzsche's Idea of Myth: The Birth of Tragedy out of the Spirit of Eighteenth Century Aesthetics," Publications of the Modern Language Association 94 (1979).

9. Such periodization is a commonplace in the literature on Nietzsche. A recent example is in Alan Megill's *Prophets of Extremity* (Berkeley, 1985); despite the fact that Megill's study is concerned with Nietzsche, Heidegger, Foucault, and Derrida, all of whom are antagonists of Hegelian history, he continues to employ developmental and synthesizing patterns in attempting to articulate their thought.

10. Letter to Jacob Burckhardt, dated January 6, 1889 (postmarked January 5), in *Selected Letters of Friedrich Nietzsche*, ed. and trans. Christopher Middleton (Chicago, 1969), p. 346.

11. Werner Kaegi, *Jacob Burckhardt: Eine Biographie* (Basel, 1967).

12. Nietzsche, *Werke* (Kroner edition, 1912), XVIII, p. 248 (my translation). Cf. also Paul de Man, "Nietzsche's Theory of Rhetoric," in *Symposium*, Spring 1974: 33–51.

13. Hubert Dreyfus and Paul Rabinow, *Michel Foucault: Beyond Structuralism and Hermeneutics*, 2nd ed. (Chicago, 1983), p. 187.

14. Jacques Derrida, *The Ear of the Other*, ed. Christie McDonald (New York, 1985), pp. 29–32.

15. Cf. my paper "Nietzschean Aphorism as Art and Act," in *Phenomenology and the Human Sciences*, ed. J. N. Mohanty (The Hague, 1985), pp. 159–190.

16. Alexander Nehamas, *Nietzsche: Life as Literature* (Cambridge, Mass., 1985).

17. Cf. Kenneth Burke, "Four Master Tropes," in his *A Grammar of Motives* (Berkeley, 1969), pp. 503–517, and Hayden White, *Metahistory* (Baltimore, 1973), pp. 31–39.

18. Georg Lukacs, "Nietzsche as Founder of Irrationalism in the Imperialist Period," in his *The Destruction of Reason*, trans. Peter Palmer (London, 1980).

19. Derrida, *Spurs*, p. 87.

20. Martin Heidegger, *Nietzsche I: The Will to Power as Art*, trans. David Farrell Krell (New York, 1979), p. 208.

21. Derrida, *Spurs*, p. 99.

2. METAPHORICAL OVERCOMING / METONYMICAL STRIFE (*ZARATHUSTRA* I AND II)

1. References are first to the *pages* of R. J. Hollingdale's translation (which I have used with some modifications), *Thus Spoke Zarathustra* (Baltimore, 1969), and second to the pages of the *Kritische Studienausgabe*.

2. Harold Alderman, *Nietzsche's Gift* (Athens, Ohio, 1977), pp. 18–19. See my review in *Philosophy and Literature*, Fall 1978: 272–274.

3. Alderman, *Nietzsche's Gift*, p. 173.

4. This is the general argument of Hegel's *Aesthetics*, in which poetry is the highest (most philosophical) of the arts, and drama the highest (most philosophical) form of poetry.

5. Such works are Sarah Kofman, *Nietzsche et la métaphore* (Paris, 1972); Bernard Pautrat, *Versions du soleil* (Paris, 1971); and Jacques Derrida, *Spurs*. There are a number of important essays in *The New Nietzsche*, ed. David Allison. There is a useful review of recent French studies of Nietzsche by Rudolf Kuenzli, "Nietzsche und die Semiologie," in *Nietzsche-Studien* 1976: 263–288.

6. "The Intentional Structure of the Romantic Image," in *Romanticism and Consciousness*, ed. Harold Bloom (New York, 1970), p. 69).

7. For a good example of such doubts about the fourth part of *Zarathustra*, see Eugen Fink's Heideggerian study, *Nietzsches Philosophie* (Stuttgart, 1960), pp. 114–118.

8. See Paul Ricoeur, *The Rule of Metaphor* (Toronto, 1977), for a philosophical view of the rise and fall of tropology, the attempt to distinguish and define a variety of figures of speech. For a contemporary attempt to define metaphor using the techniques of transformational grammar, see Samuel Levin, *The Semantics of Metaphor* (Baltimore, 1977).

9. Aristotle, in considering the linguistic powers of the poet or rhetorician, says that the greatest thing is to be metaphorical. This cannot be learnt; it is a sign of genius, for it implies an intuitive perception of similarities in dissimilars. See *Poetics* 1459a 3–8 and *Rhetoric* 1412a 10.

10. *Rhetoric* 1407a 10; see also 1411a-b.

11. For example, see Hegel's analysis of the transfer of bodily qualities to spiritual things (and the reverse), in *Hegel's Aesthetics*, trans. T. M. Knox (London, 1975), pp. 405–406.

12. Jacques Derrida, "White Mythology," trans. F. C. T. Moore, *New Literary History* 6 (Autumn 1974): 5–74.

3. HOMECOMING, PRIVATE LANGUAGE, AND THE FATE OF THE SELF (*ZARATHUSTRA* III)

1. Martin Heidegger, "Hölderlin's 'Homecoming,' " in *Existence and Being*, trans. Werner Brock (London, 1949).

2. For suggestive accounts of a distinction between identity and "being own" or belonging, see Heidegger's *Identity and Difference* (New York, 1969) and Albert Hofstadter's essay "Being: The Act of Belonging" in *Agony and Epitaph* (New York, 1970).

3. Heidegger discusses some of the complexity involved in accepting the animals' account of Zarathustra as the teacher of eternal recurrence; cf. Martin Heidegger, "Who is Nietzsche's Zarathustra?" in David Allison, ed., *The New Nietzsche*, pp. 65–66.

4. For a concise statement and some references to the literature, cf. Bernd Magnus, *Nietzsche's Existential Imperative* (Bloomington, 1978), ch. 4, pp. 89–110.

5. Ibid., pp. 98–110.

6. Hegel, "Sense-Certainty: or the 'This' and 'Meaning' " in *The Phenomenology of Spirit*, trans. A. V. Miller (New York, 1977).

7. Alexander Nehamas, *Nietzsche: Life as Literature*, p. 164.

8. Ibid., p. 165.
9. Ibid., p. 166.
10. Ibid., p. 163.
11. Ibid., p. 168.
12. Cf. Gerard Genette, *Narrative Discourse* (Ithaca, 1980). Paul de Man's suggestion that there is a substantial but largely neglected Nietzschean thematic in Proust is relevant here; cf. his *Allegories of Reading* (New Haven, 1979), p. 15.
13. Cf. Pierre Klossowski, "Nietzsche's Experience of the Eternal Recurrence," in David Allison, ed., *The New Nietzsche*, pp. 107–120.
14. *Republic*, 586a.
15. Jacques Derrida, *Spurs*; cf. also my review of this book in *Man and World*, 1981: 428–437.
16. Eugen Fink, *Nietzsches Philosophie*, p. 114.
17. Martin Heidegger, "What are Poets For?" in *Poetry, Language, Thought*, trans. Albert Hofstadter (New York, 1971), pp. 91–142.

4. FESTIVAL, CARNIVAL, AND PARODY (*ZARATHUSTRA* IV)

1. Eugen Fink, *Nietzsches Philosophie*, pp. 114–115 and 118. Two significant exceptions to judgments such as Fink's are Harold Alderman's *Nietzsche's Gift* and James Ogilvy, *Many-Dimensional Man* (New York, 1977). Both offer penetrating interpretations of the characters of some of the higher men in part four and of the development of its story.
2. Cf. Alderman:

"Both Zarathustra and his disciples have grown in their sense of play and so there is often in their encounters much deliberate comic dissembling. Part IV often seems a Shakespearean comedy requiring not only its own brilliance of language, but also the backdrops, the masks and the movement of a performed play. Part IV is, at bottom, a *Midsummer Night's Dream*."

Nietzsche's Gift, p. 115. While recognizing these dramatic aspects of part four, the reading in this chapter suggests that they are qualified by the diegetic (narrative) context; a genuine drama, as Plato noted, must be performed (it must be mimetic).
3. I am in disagreement, then, with Harold Alderman who although he points out that the Nietzschean self ought not to be conceived as a constant and substantial ego, still claims that "Part IV emphasizes the egocentric character of experience and understanding. Zarathustra teaches only himself: his rightful children are his own future self-creations," *Nietzsche's Gift*, p. 134. On the other hand James Ogilvy in *Many-Dimensional Man* has shown that part four can be read as a decentering, pluralistic allegory on both the psychological and political levels.
4. Thomas Hobbes, *Human Nature* IX.13; quoted in Walter Kaufmann's note to his translation of *Beyond Good and Evil*, paragraph 294. In representing *Zarathustra* IV as simply a satiric comparison of Zarathustra with the many higher men, none of whom can measure up to him, Fink seems to have read this part through the Hobbesian form of laughter and to have missed the other comic carnivalesque dimensions of the text. This is ironic,.given Fink's interest in play as an ontological category; cf. Eugen Fink, *Spiel als Weltsymbol* (Stuttgart, 1960).
5. Hans-Georg Gadamer, *Truth and Method*, translation edited by Garret Barden and John Cumming (New York, 1975), pp. 110. Cf. also my essay "Gadamer, Habermas, and the Death of Art," *The British Journal of Aesthetics*, Winter 1986: 39–47.
6. Mikhail Bakhtin, *Rabelais and His World*, trans. Helene Iswolsky (Cambridge, Mass., 1968), p. 203.

7. See Jacques Derrida's commentary on Nietzsche's note "I have forgotten my umbrella" in *Spurs*, esp. pp. 123–42.

8. Cf. also *The Gay Science*, 89:

> *Now and Formerly.*—What good is all the art of our works of art if we lose that higher art, the art of festivals? Formerly, all works of art adorned the great festival road of humanity, to commemorate high and happy moments. Now one uses works of art to lure aside from the great *via dolorosa* of humanity those who are wretched, exhausted, and sick, and to offer them a brief lustful moment—a little intoxication and madness.

The *Gay Science*, as its title suggests, is a carnivalesque work containing Nietzsche's headiest mixture of prose and poetry; the latter is usually satiric or parodic. Cf. the many discussions of the transition from tragedy to comedy (e.g., 1, 153, 382–383).

9. Cf. Hans-Georg Gadamer's exploration of this theme (and its background in Hegel's *Phenomenology of Spirit*) in his book *Hegel's Dialectic*.

10. See Bakhtin, *Rabelais and His World*, especially ch. 6. Consider Bakhtin's description of the carnivalesque banquet and its discourse:

> Free play with the sacred—this is the basic content of the symposium of the Middle Ages. This does not represent nihilism, nor the primitive enjoyment of debasing the higher level. We will not understand the spirit of grotesque feasting if we do not take into account the deeply positive element, the victorious truimph inherent in every banquet image of folklore origin. The awareness of a purely human material bodily power fills this genre. Man is not afraid of the world, he has defeated it and eats of it. In the atmosphere of this victorious meal the world acquires a different aspect; it becomes an abundant harvest, a superabundant increase. All mystical fears are dissipated. . . . The banquet speech is universal and materialistic at the same time. This is why the grotesque symposium travesties and debases the purely idealistic, mystic and ascetic victory over the world (that is, the victory of the abstract spirit). In the comic banquet there are nearly always elements parodying and travestying the Last Supper. (*Rabelais and His World*, p. 296)

If this account seems couched in surprisingly Nietzschean language ("nihilism," "abstract spirit," etc.), it may be because Bakhtin, who was originally a student of German philosophy, knew both Nietzsche and the tradition of German thought on which he so often draws.

11. Quoted in Bakhtin, *Rabelais and His World*, p. 69.

12. Jacques Derrida, *Writing and Difference*, trans. Alan Bass (Chicago, 1978), pp. 256–257.

13. Nietzsche, "On Truth and Lie in an Extra-Moral Sense," in *Philosophy and Truth*, trans. Daniel Brezeale (Atlantic Highlands, N.J., 1979), p. 84.

14. The figure in motley is a *Possenreiser*, a jester or tomfool, and is thus distinguished from Zarathustra who plays the *Hanswurst*; he refers with some affection to his animals as *Schalks-Narren*, scamps or rogues, when he ridicules their response to his wrestling with the thought of eternal recurrence.

15. Cf. Alderman, *Nietzsche's Gift*, ch. VI, "The Comedy of Affirmation."

16. See Karl-Heinz Volkmann-Schluck, *Nietzsches Gedicht "Die Wüste wächst, weh dem, der Wüsten birgt . . . ,"* (Frankfurt am Main, 1958) and Walter Kaufmann's brief discussion in *Nietzsche*, 4th ed. (Princeton, 1974), p. 429.

17. For a persuasive and detailed account of Nietzsche's lyric parodies, see Sander Gilman, *Nietzschean Parody* (Bonn: Bouvier Verlag, 1976). On the background of the song, see C. A. Miller, "Nietzsche's 'Daughters of the Desert': A Reconsideration" in *Nietzsche-Studien* 2(1973): 157–195.

18. Thomas Mann, *Nietzsche's Philosophy in the Light of Contemporary Events* (Washington, D.C., 1947), p. 7.

19. Bakhtin, *Rabelais and His World*, pp. 233–234.

The basic artistic purpose of the parodic and travestied prophecies and riddles is to uncrown gloomy eschatological time, that is, the medieval concept of the world. The parodies renew time on the material bodily level, transforming it into a propitious and merry notion. (p. 238)

5. THE TEXT AS GRAFFITO: HISTORICAL SEMIOTICS (*THE ANTICHRIST*)

1. Eugen Fink, *Nietzsches Philosophie*, p. 34.

2. *The Antichrist* and *Ecce Homo* are often treated together in this respect. According to Kaufmann "The ending of *The Antichrist* and much of *Ecce Homo* show so strange a lack of inhibition and contain such extraordinary claims concerning Nietzsche's own importance that, knowing of his later insanity, one cannot help finding here the first signs of it." Walter Kaufmann, *Nietzsche*, 4th ed., p. 66. Arthur Danto's judgment is a measured one: "The *Antichrist* is unrelievedly vituperative and would indeed sound insane were it not informed in its polemic by a structure of analysis and a theory of morality and religion worked out elsewhere and accessible even here to the informed reader." Arthur Danto, *Nietzsche as Philosopher* (New York, 1965), p. 182. Even in Danto's view the structure of thought which saves the *Antichrist* is one worked out elsewhere; he would apparently agree with Fink that the book offers nothing new.

3. *Ecce Homo*, page following preface; 5, 263.

4. Nietzsche calls Renan his "antipodes" (*Beyond Good and Evil*, sec. 48); the sense of opposition was made more precise a year later in a polemic on modern historiography in *The Genealogy of Morals* (III, 26):

> I know of nothing that excites such a disgust as this kind of 'objective' armchair scholar, this kind of scented voluptuary of history, half person, half satyr, perfume by Renan, who betrays immediately with the high falsetto of his applause what he lacks, *where* he lacks it, *where* in this case the Fates have applied their cruel shears with, also, such surgical skill!

Renan, then, is Nietzsche's anti-historian; it is notable that both *The Genealogy of Morals* and Renan's *Origins of Christianity* are philosophical histories which focus on the transition from Greek and Roman culture to Christianity. Nietzsche not only narrates the events differently but does so, to speak more precisely, in a genealogical rather than a historical manner. For an anarcho-marxist assessment by a writer sometimes considered a Nietzschean, see Georges Sorel, *Le Système Historique de Renan* (Paris, 1905). Cf. also my essay "Nietzsche contra Renan," *History and Theory* 1982: 193–222.

5. Julius Wellhausen, *Prolegomena to the History of Ancient Israel* (New York, 1957).

6. Georg Brandes, *Friedrich Nietzsche* (New York, n.d.), p. 85.

7. Nietzsche's admiring references to Bauer (e.g., *Ecce Homo*, V 2) indicate that he may have known Bauer's works on the history of Christianity. Albert Schweitzer's The Quest of the Historical Jesus, tr. W. Montgomery (New York, 1961) is the most accessible account of Bauer's writing and of other nineteenth-century works of this character.

8. Ernest Renan, *The Life of Jesus* (New York, 1927), p. 45–54.

9. Ibid., pp. 62–63.

10. Ibid., p. 64.

11. Letter to Overbeck, February 23, 1887; *Selected Letters*, p. 261.

12. For a scholarly account of Nietzsche's knowledge of Dostoyevsky, see the articles by C. A. Miller in *Nietzsche-Studien* 1973, 1975, and 1978.

13. Jacques Derrida, *Of Grammatology*, trans. G. Spivak (Baltimore, 1974), and other writings. In saying that for Derrida all writing refers back to an earlier writing, the notion of "referring back" must not be understood as implying a linear temporal sequence but as suggesting that writing always occurs within an infinitely dense texture of writing. Derrida

associates his view of writing with the Nietzschean and Heideggerian critique of the linear conception of time (*Of Grammatology*, pp. 86–87).

14. In his classical exposition of the theory of signs in 1868 Peirce argues for the impossibility of a "first sign." See *Collected Papers* (Cambridge, Mass.), vol. 5, paragraphs 213–317, and especially 259–263. Cf. also my paper "Peirce and Derrida on First and Last Things," *University of Dayton Review* 17 (1984) 1: 33–38.

15. For Derrida's celebration of undecidability see *Spurs*; for the understanding of such celebrations as sacrificial religious rites see "From Restricted to General Economy: A Hegelianism without Reserve," in *Writing and Difference*. There are discussions of *Spurs* by David Allison and David Hoy in *boundary 2*. For Peirce on Zeno in a semiotic context, see *Collected Papers*, vol. 5, pars. 333–334.

16. For Peirce's claim that logic requires faith, hope, and charity, see *Collected Papers*, vol. 2, pars. 264–265, and Josiah Royce's Hegelian extension of Peirce in *The Problem of Christianity*, vol. 2 (New York, 1913).

17. Derrida explains the asymptotic conception of the deconstructive process in "Structure, Science, and Play in the Discourse of the Human Sciences," in *Writing and Difference*, pp. 278–293.

6. HOW ONE BECOMES WHAT ONE IS NOT (*ECCE HOMO*)

1. The best account of the history of *Ecce Homo* is to be found in the Colli and Montinari, eds., *Kritische-Studienausgabe* (14, 454–470); see also Mazzino Montinari, "Ein neuer Abschnitt in Nietzsches *Ecce Homo*," *Nietzsche Lesen* (Berlin, 1982), pp. 120–168.

2. For Nietzsche's early autobiographical writings see Friedrich Nietzsche, *Werke in Drie Bänden*, ed. Karl Schlechta (Munchen, 1956), pp. 7–154. The best collection of letters in English is *Selected Letters of Friedrich Nietzsche*, trans. Christopher Middleton.

3. See Montinari, "Ein neuer Abschnitt in Nietzsches *Ecce Homo*, pp. 145–147.

4. Jacques Derrida, *Spurs*, p. 99.

5. I have used Tracy Strong's translation from his article "Oedipus as Hero: Family and Family Metaphors in Nietzsche," *boundary 2*, spring/fall 1981: 327.

6. Montinari, "Ein neuer Abschnitt in Nietzsches *Ecce Homo*," pp. 148–149.

7. Alexander Nehamas, *Nietzsche: Life as Literature*, pp. 170–199.

8. Ibid., p. 188.

9. Ibid.

10. Ibid., pp. 189–190.

11. Ibid., p. 195. Nehamas quotes a passage from Nietzsche (*WS*, 198) in which biographers are admonished to look for unsuspected continuities at the places where there are the greatest apparent breaks in their subjects' careers. But looking for such continuities, one at a time, does not suggest that the emerging product is a continually more integrated one, for it is compatible with there being a series of transitions such that each one exhibits some kind of immediate before and after continuity, based on certain themes, but that each transition exhibits such continuities by developing themes not prominent in the other transitions.

12. Cf. Roland Barthes, *S/Z*, trans. Richard Miller (New York, 1974).

13. Cf. George Steiner, *Antigones* (New York, 1984).

14. Ernest Jones, reporting on the discussion at the Vienna Psychoanalytic Society on October 28, 1908, says that Freud "several times said of Nietzsche that he had a more penetrating knowledge of himself than any other man who ever lived or was likely to live." *Sigmund Freud: Life and Work* (London, 1955), vol. 2, p. 385.

15. Jacques Lacan, *Ecrits: A Selection*, trans. Alan Sheridan (New York, 1977), pp. 103–104.

16. Montinari, "Ein neuer Abschnitt in Nietzsche *Ecce Homo*," p. 149.

17. For an account of Elizabeth Förster-Nietzsche's career see H. F. Peters, *Zarathustra's Sister* (New York, 1977).

18. In *Nietzsche and Philosophy*, Gilles Deleuze gives a full analysis of Nietzsche as an anti-dialectical thinker.

19. Cf. Claude Lévi-Strauss, "The Structural Study of Myth" in *The Structuralists*, ed. Richard and Fernande De George (New York, 1972), pp. 169–194.

20. Nehamas, *Nietzsche: Life as Literature*, p. 196.

21. Ovid, *Metamorphoses*, XI, 11. 741–748 (trans. Horace Gregory).

Index